Maude

by

Donna Mabry

Acknowledgements

I owe a debt of gratitude to many people for their help with this book:

I thank my sister-friend Shelby Turnbull MacFarlane, who is the witness to my life. She knows things about me that even my children don't. She helped me with some of the research to call up details in places where my memory was fuzzy and retrieved documents to verify the story of my aunt's death.

My editors: Lawrence Montaigne, Elaine Stubbs, Scotty Curran, Maryann Unger, and Phil Schlaeger from Anthem Authors. The story is much better with their assistance.

Barbara Winters, Jeane Harvey, Judy Kuncewicki and Lawrence Montaigne, my proofreaders, who not only make corrections, but who encourage me constantly by reading my work.

Sandy Novarro, who now has a shelf full of things she told me to write.

And my daughter, Melanie Mabry, who wanted to hear this story in the first place. Boy, is she in for a few surprises.

FOREWARD

My parents divorced when I was three, and my mother left me to be raised by my maternal grandparents. For the next nine years, whenever he wasn't working overtime, my daddy came to get me almost every Friday night and every school vacation. He returned me to my grandmother's custody the last possible day.

My earliest memory is a winter morning when he carried me to her house, my cheek resting against the chilly smoothness of his brown leather jacket. I was his almost every weekend, in summers from June to September, and over spring and Christmas vacations.

At my father's house, I shared my grandmother's room. She would read me to sleep each night, not with stories out of books, but with the spoken stories of her life. As we lay there in the darkened room, I struggled to stay awake to hear the amazing things she had to tell. At the same time, her soft voice was a lullaby inviting me to sleep. I wonder now if she found it her personal therapy to murmur her burdens in the darkness to a very interested listener.

As I grew older, and she felt I could understand them, she revealed more of the intimate details, until finally, when I was sixteen or so, she even talked about what part sex played in her life.

She didn't go in chronological order, but spoke of whatever came to her mind. One night she would talk of her childhood, another of the wars or the depression.

Sometimes she talked about losing four of her five children.

It wasn't until many years later when I repeated some of these things to my daughter that I fully realized how epic a tale my grandmother's life had actually been.

My daughter said to me, "Why don't you write it down for me?"

So this book is dedicated to my Melanie and to the great-grandmother that she knew only as an infant.

A small part of what I have written here is fictionalized, and some of it falls back on my own memories of later events, which may be biased. I have included some of my grandfather's comments, but he mostly joked about things and wasn't a serious person like my grandmother.

Evelyn, my mother would tell you a different story, but I am representing my grandmother's point of view.

The greater substance of this, and many of the direct quotes, are written in my grandmother's words, and are what I heard from her during those long-ago nights we shared a bed.

Maude

Prologue

I was barely over fourteen years old, and it was my wedding day. My older sister, Helen, came to my room, took me by the hand, and sat me down on the bed. She opened her mouth to say something, but then her face flushed, and she turned her head to look out the window. After a second, she squeezed my hand and looked back in my eyes. She stopped, dropped her gaze to the floor, and then said, "You've always been a good girl, Maude, and done what I told you. Now, you're going to be a married woman, and he will be the head of the house. When you go home tonight after your party, no matter what he wants to do to you, you have to let him do it. Do you understand?"

I didn't understand, but I nodded my head anyway. It sounded strange to me, the way so many things did. I would do what she told me. I didn't have a choice, any more than I had a choice in being born.

Chapter 1

I came into this world as Nola Maude Clayborn in 1892, in Perkinsville, in the northwest corner of Tennessee, a few miles west of Dyersburg. Pinned to the ground by a church spire at each end of the road that cut the town in half, Perkinsville was barely a wide space in the road. The houses were so far apart it was almost country. It was made up mostly of farmers and the businesses that served them.

Most of the houses had a barn in the back for one or two horses, and a buggy to ride in or a wagon for farm work. We all had chickens, and a cow for milk. Every house had a vegetable garden, and most of them had some sort of orchard with apple, cherry, and pear trees.

There was one general store and one doctor. A widow in town sometimes rented out sleeping rooms to travelers, but there was no hotel, no restaurant, no bank, and certainly, no saloon. Almost everyone still raised their own chickens, hogs, fruit and vegetables.

I remember it partly by its smells. Walking through town in the winter, I could smell the smoke from the wood burning fireplaces and stoves, the farm animals, and if the wind was right, the stink of the chicken coops. In spring, the air was heavy with the sweetness of fruit blossoms and freshly turned soil.

There was a Baptist church to the east end and a Holiness church to the west. My family was Holiness, and our lives revolved around our church. We went to meeting Sunday morning, Sunday night, and Wednesday night. Once a year, there would be a visiting preacher, and a revival that would go on every evening for a week.

The steeples of the two churches served as a sort of city limits. You could walk from one church to the other in less than a half-hour. There were no Catholics and no Jews, and most of us didn't even know that there was any such thing as an atheist. Not one person there would even have understood what an atheist was, except maybe the doctor. He had more education than most, and had lived in other places until he was in his sixties, when his wife died, and he gave up his practice in the city to come back to live where he grew up.

Most folks in my town were born there and died there and maybe took one trip to Memphis on their honeymoon.

There were some colored folk too, but they lived down the road, a short distance from the larger part of town.

In looks, I took after my father, Charles Eugene Clayborn, with straight brown hair, and brown eyes. I was big for my age and built sturdy, like my daddy.

My sister, Helen, was eleven years older, and took after our mother, Faith. They were both small and trim. Daddy used to say they weren't as big as a minute. They were fair, with sparkling blue eyes and hair of a pale blonde shade.

Helen's hair hung in waves over her shoulders, but Momma wore hers pinned up in a bun at the back of her neck, the way all the married women did. I loved the way little wisps of curls would escape the pins. When Momma was outside, they would flutter in the breeze, like butterflies dancing on her neck.

Helen had an hourglass figure, and the neighbors used to say that she had a waist a man could clasp his hands around. Those ladies would smile kindly at me and pat me on the head as if to comfort me. I hated that. I knew early on that I was plain. I got used to it. My mother fussed over Helen all the time, making her pretty dresses, tying ribbons in her hair. Other than telling me what to do, she didn't pay me any mind.

It really didn't bother me all that much. I was a daddy's girl. He ran the livery stable directly across the street from our little house. He trained a few horses to sell, rented out horses and buggies, and boarded traveler's mounts. He was up and gone to tend the stock before I got out of bed in the morning.

When he came home for dinner he would give Momma a kiss and then scoop me up in his strong arms and give me a big hug. Then he'd sit me on his knee and talk to me, just me, until dinner was on the table. He'd look down at me and smile, and ask me about school and my friends. He'd tease me about liking James Connor, who lived down the road from us.

Daddy was a big man, his chest and arms thick with muscles from lifting bales of hay. I'd lean my head against his chest and smell the horses and the feed on him. I found the only comfort there was for myself in his attention. He was my world.

After dinner, he would go back to the barn to settle the animals for the night. I was usually asleep when he got back. It was precious little time he was able to give me, but it was enough.

As 1899 came to an end, everyone was excited about the New Year, 1900, and a new century. I found the number interesting, but didn't see what all the fuss was about. Wouldn't things be just the same the day after as they had been the day before? It was all people talked about for weeks. I listened to them at school and at church and at the store. I didn't really feel it had anything to do with me. I didn't think the coming century would change my life much, but it did. That year turned my life upside down.

I was seven, and Helen eighteen, in April of 1900, when Helen married Tommy Spencer. He was one of the nicest young men. His parents owned the general store, and they were about the richest family in town. Helen packed up her things and moved to the pretty little house Tommy had built just for her. It had a porch all the way across the front, like ours, with another one across the back so you could sit in the sun or the shade at any time of day. Tommy had a water pump right there in the kitchen so Helen wouldn't have to go outside to get water. There was a washroom in the back, a bedroom on each side, and a parlor in the front.

People kept trying to make me feel better about being alone after Helen married, but I didn't miss her all that much. I visited her from time to time and saw her at church every meeting. Her moving out meant that I had a room of my own, and my life was quieter without the young people that hung around my sister. Before she left, it seemed to me that they were always at the house. Helen's girlfriends were there almost every day after school. They sat on the front porch, drinking iced tea and giggling and whispering into one another's ear about some boy or the other, mostly things that they didn't want me to hear.

The boys made up excuses to stop by, asking about school or church, falling quiet if I came in earshot. My sister's friends either looked at me like I wasn't welcome, or looked right past me, as if it weren't my porch, too, or my house, as if I didn't have any right to be there.

With Helen married and gone I got real attention from my mother for the first time that I could remember. She set about the job of making me a fit wife for some man, someday. We planted the spring garden together, rows of lettuce, greens, tomatoes, and corn. She talked to me all the while in a way she never had before, like I was a grown-up. We hoed the ground, and she showed me how to poke my finger into the soft soil to make a little hole to drop the seeds in one at a time. With Helen out of the house, Momma and I became a team.

We cooked together in the kitchen on the big wood-burning stove, with me standing on a little step-stool my Daddy made for me. I got to mix the sugar and spices for the apple pies, and watched how Mom rolled out the piecrust, talking all the while about how to use the coldest water to mix the dough.

She taught me how to listen for the sound of the chicken frying in the pan, how when the sound of the cooking changed from a murmur to a crackle, it was time to turn it over, how to salt the potatoes before I cooked them and the chicken after. She showed me how to make light dumplings and good biscuits.

In the fall, I learned how to can fruits and vegetables from the big garden my mother kept. I wore an apron, folded up in a pleat at the waist to make it fit, and sat at the table stringing the green beans, popping off the top end the way she showed me, and pulling the strings down to the bottom, then snapping the bean into four sections. Mom put them in the big pot on the stove with some fatback bacon, where they would cook all day before they went into the Mason jars.

In the afternoons, we would sit on the porch where the sun shone bright and sew. Mom showed me how she cut the fabric so there wasn't much waste. When she finished cutting out a dress, she could hold the scraps in the palm of her hand. She taught me how to make tiny, even stitches that wouldn't pull apart, and how to pull the thread over a candle before I started sewing so it wouldn't tangle. I learned how to knit, crochet, and embroider a chain stitch, and to make flowers and an alphabet with the needle.

Even though I was usually fidgety when I had to sit still, like in church, I loved needlework. There's a peacefulness that comes over you when you sew. I guess that it's because you don't think about any of your worries, you just let your mind work on the fabric and the thread. When you concentrate on one small section at a time, it's almost a surprise when it's finished and you see it as completed work. When I sewed other things, long after my mother was gone, I could almost hear her voice at times, telling me to knot the end tightly, or to twirl the needle just so to untangle the thread. As long as I lived, I remembered everything my mother taught me, and not just about sewing.

One Saturday night, not long after Helen left, my mother curled my hair for the first time. She stood me up on a chair and ran a wet comb through my hair, rolling up the strands in white cotton strips she had torn from a flour sack. It wasn't easy to fall asleep that night, with the knots pulling at my scalp, but when my mother untied the strips the next morning and combed it out, my stiff, straight hair lay in soft waves, just like Helen's.

I ran to the kitchen to show my daddy. He swooped me up off the floor and gave me a big hug. "Look how pretty you are this morning," he said.

It was something that no one had ever said to me in my life. He held me close to his chest and swung me back and forth before he set me down.

I expected that everyone in the church would o-o-oh and a-a-ah over how I looked, but Helen was the only one who noticed. She treated me nicer, now that she was out of the house.

I asked Momma to roll up my hair again that night, but she said it was too much trouble to do every day. I tried to do it myself, but it came out all crooked, wavy in parts but with the ends still straight. I decided I would be satisfied with having it curled for Sunday service. Being pretty, even just once a week, would make me happy.

The first year of the new century ran right by me without notice, but one day the next summer, when I was eight years old, I was spending the afternoon at Helen's house. Helen was seven months into carrying her first baby, and not having an easy time of it. She still threw up about ten times a day, and lifting anything made her feel lightheaded. For the last few months, I'd been sent over on weekends to help with the cleaning.

I loved doing it. While I did the chores I pretended it was my own home and that my own husband would come home from work and greet me with a kiss just the way Helen's husband did.

I was in the back yard hanging a load of clothes on the line when I heard a short scream, like a hurt animal, come from the house. I dropped the towel I was holding back in the basket and ran to the house. Helen's husband Tommy and the town doctor, who had delivered all three of us, were there and Tommy was holding Helen in his arms. She leaned against him and looked like she was about to fall. I grabbed Helen's skirt.

"What's wrong? What happened?"

Tommy looked panicked. He pulled my hands away from her. "Go wait in the bedroom."

I obeyed, just as I always did, going into the bedroom and sitting on the bed. Someone closed the door after me, and I strained to hear the voices from the living room, but couldn't make out any of what they were saying. After what seemed to me to be forever, the door opened and Tommy carried Helen in the room. She was passed out. Doctor Wilson folded down the covers and Tommy laid Helen on the bed and pulled the blankets up over her. Then, the doctor motioned to me and Tommy to go to the living room, and we followed him out, closing the door after us.

I clutched Tommy's hand. "Is she going to be all right? What's the matter with her?"

He looked at me with sad eyes, and then looked over at the doctor. Tommy dropped his head and went to the kitchen. Doctor Wilson sighed loudly, took my hand in his and told me the most horrible thing I ever heard. "There was an accident, Maude," he stopped, like he was searching for the right words." Something caught fire in the kitchen of your house. When your dad heard the neighbors yelling, he ran in the house looking for your mother."

I felt the panic run through my entire body. It shot from my head to my toes. All of a sudden, I was freezing cold. My body shivered, and I clutched my arms around myself. "Is my Daddy all right? Is he burnt up?"

Doctor Wilson patted me on the shoulder, "I'm sorry, Maude, it was an old house, all wood frame. They didn't make it out in time."

For a split-second, I couldn't understand what he was saying. The sound of my heart pounding roared in my ears and made me almost deaf. Then it dawned on me that both my momma and daddy were gone.

I searched for words, but couldn't find any. I dropped both hands to my sides and just stood there, staring at the floor and shaking. The doctor patted me on the back again, turned, and went to the kitchen. He and Tommy were talking quietly, I was still standing where they left me when I heard a strange, weak cry come from Helen in the bedroom.

I ran in the room. The smell of the blood and something else I didn't recognize filled the room. I let out a screech, and Tommy came bursting through the door with Dr. Wilson right behind him. They pushed me out of their way and I pressed myself against the wall. The doctor jerked the covers off Helen.

"Her water's broke," he said, "get my bag."

Tommy went running to the living room, where Dr. Wilson had left his bag on the floor next to the chair, brought it, and put it in the doctor's hands.

The doctor looked at me. "Get me all your towels and some water."

That made me come to myself, and both Tommy and I ran for the kitchen. While Tommy pumped a big bowl full of water from the kitchen pump, I grabbed a stack of towels from the pantry and ran back in the bedroom.

The doctor had pulled all the covers off Helen and pushed her feet back toward her hips. Her skirt was up around her waist, and she wasn't wearing any step-ins. I stopped dead in my tracks. I couldn't move. I had never even seen my sister naked and now this was awful.

"Give me the towels," the doctor said.

I dropped the pile onto the bed next to Helen. Tommy, his face white as a ghost, brought the water. He put it down on the floor and then dragged a small table over so it was at the doctor's hands.

"Get some more water and heat it up," the doctor said to Tommy, who looked relieved to have a task and ran back out of the room. Helen moaned loudly, but never opened her eyes. I couldn't tell if she was even conscious.

The blood flow seemed to have let up. Doctor Wilson straightened out Helen's legs and pulled the covers over her. He pressed his hands against the sides of her stomach and held them there for a long time.

"She's not having pains yet. Maude, get me a clock or a watch."

I ran to the living room and found Tommy's watch from the little pedestal that it rested on. It was the one that his father had given him that he carried only on Sundays. The doctor stood and pulled the chair up next to the bed. He motioned for me to sit. He took my hand and pressed my palm against Helen's side.

"First babies take a long time coming. I can't stay

here all afternoon and night. I'll be in my office when you need me. It's right down the street." He pushed my hand firmly against Helen's side. "Feel her stomach?"

I nodded.

"Watch her face, and you'll be able to tell when a pain is coming, even if she doesn't wake up. When the pain starts, her stomach will get real hard for a few minutes and then it will let up for a while. At first it will be a long time from one pain to the next, but they'll get closer together all the time. Do you understand?"

I nodded again.

"Good, now, when those pains start coming about five minutes apart you have Tommy come and get me."

Again, I just nodded that I understood. The doctor stood and left the room. I could hear him talking to Tommy in the kitchen, then the slamming of the screen door.

All afternoon and into the evening, I sat staring at Helen's face and watching for it to change. I kept one hand or the other pressed against my sister's side, changing hands when one got tired, but her stomach never changed. Tommy came in and out of the room every half-hour with a puzzled expression on his face. He would look at me and ask if anything was happening, and I would shake my head in silence. Finally he threw his hands up in the air in surrender. "I have to get another woman to help us. It isn't right for only a little girl and a man to be in here with this going on. I'm going to get my Aunt Deborah."

Tommy's mother had passed away the year before, and Deborah was the only female relative he had left. She lived on the other end of town.

I knew it would take more than a few minutes for him to get back, and I was afraid to be left alone with such a big responsibility, but the thought of having someone else come to take over the job eased my mind. My eyes locked onto Tommy's. He seemed to be asking for my approval. I forgot I was only seven years old.

"That'll be good," I said. "Hurry up."

He raced out of the house. He hadn't been gone two minutes before Helen let out a loud moan and stiffened her body. Under my palm, I could feel Helen's stomach become as hard as rock. I looked at the watch standing on the table. It was seven thirty-five.

"Seven thirty-five." I said it out loud so I would remember the time. After a few minutes Helen relaxed and her stomach softened. It was happening like the doctor said it would, and it made me feel better. It was going to be all right. Tommy would bring Aunt Deborah, and when the pains got close enough, they would have the doctor there.

Only, it wasn't a half-hour before the next pain came. I stared at the watch as Helen's stomach hardened under my hand. It was only five minutes. I wanted to call out for help, but there wasn't anyone else within the reach of my voice. I was afraid to leave Helen alone to go run for the doctor, and afraid not to run for the doctor.

After a few minutes the pain let up. I bolted from my chair and ran out to the front porch, down the steps and over to the Thompson's house next door. I pounded on the door with the side of my fist as hard as I could. One of the older boys opened the door and looked at me in surprise.

I shouted, "The baby's coming! I need Doctor Wilson at Tommy's right now, please go get him." Then I turned on my heel and ran back to Helen's bedside. Helen was relaxed again and looked like she was sleeping. I sat back down on the chair and pressed my hand against Helen's now-familiar stomach. In a few minutes another pain came, only this time Helen's eyes popped open for the first time since that afternoon, and she screamed loudly. She turned her head and saw me. She gave me an accusing look, as if I was what was hurting her. I caught Helen's hand in both of mine and squeezed it a little. "It's going to be all right, the baby's coming. Tommy went to get his Aunt Deborah and the doctor is on his way."

Helen pinched her eyes shut, threw back her head and screamed again. I was terrified. I didn't know what to do. Helen pulled her knees up, pressed her chin down, and gasped for air.

"Oh, no, oh, no, here it comes now," Helen hissed from between her clenched teeth.

I pulled down the covers and looked. The baby's head was sticking out of her. It was covered in blood and ooze. My stomach churned. I held onto Helen's hand. It was all I could think of, I didn't have the slightest idea what I should do. Then I heard the screen door slam again and the doctor came in the room carrying his bag.

I looked up at him, and I know I must have looked scared to death. "It's coming out already," I said.

Doctor Wilson pushed me aside. He laid his bag on the bed next to Helen and flipped the top of it open. He spread out one of the towels I'd brought in earlier over the table next to the bed and began pulling strange looking tools out of the bag, lining them up on the towel.

"Get one of those other towels and hold it open," the doctor said to me. I shook out a towel and held it out to the doctor with one hand.

"No, I'm going to put the baby into it, drape it over your arms so you can take the baby and wrap it up."

I did what he said with the towel and stood there holding out my hands. I watched, scared to death, as the baby's shoulders and arms came out. It was horrible and terrifying and like I was in some sort of spell. I couldn't turn away. The doctor held onto the baby's sides and pulled gently until the rest of its body came sliding out. It had a long, rope-like thing on its stomach, with the other end still fastened inside Helen. The baby looked very small to me, but I had no idea what it was supposed to look like. I saw the private parts and realized it was a boy. I had never seen a human boy's parts before. The only babies I'd ever seen were already dressed, and much larger, but they were at least a few weeks old and born after nine months and not just seven.

I waited for a cry, but it didn't come. The doctor held the baby upside down and shook it a little. There was still no cry. He slapped it smartly a few times on the bottom, then patted it firmly on the back. Nothing. He put it on the towel I was holding, wrapped it and took it back from me. Cradling it in his arms, he blew into its mouth several times. He held it up and pressed his ear against its chest.

Then he sighed and laid it down on the bed. He tied some string on the cord and then cut the baby loose from Helen. He folded the towel up over the baby's body and then handed it to me. I reached out and took it and cradled it in my arms the way I had been doing with my dolls only a few days before. The doctor had just turned his attention back to Helen when Tommy and Aunt Deborah came into the room. She saw the wrapped up bundle in my arms and must have understood what had happened.

Aunt Deborah took my arm and pushed me toward the door. She said, "Tommy, take this girl out of here. The doctor and I will finish this up."

Tommy obediently put his hand on my shoulder and steered me out of the room. We walked into the kitchen. I stood there with the tiny bundle in the crook of my arm.

Tommy looked at me. "Did it cry a lot?"

"He didn't cry at all," I said.

Then what I was saying struck him. He sat on a chair and reached out his hands. I handed the baby to him and he laid it on the table. He pulled back the towel and stared at it.

He reached out and touched his fingertip to the little face. Tears ran down Tommy's cheek. "Look what we had, Maude. We had a little boy. Helen said if it was a boy, she would let me call him Henry Mathias, after my granddad."

Then he stood, handed the baby back to me, and went out the kitchen door to the back yard. I could hear him crying something awful. After a moment I wrapped the baby back up and held him to my chest. I took him to the rocker in the corner of the kitchen and sat and rocked slowly. I pulled back the towel and looked into his perfect little face from time to time, expecting to see him move, expecting him to make a lie out of what I knew was true.

I don't know how long it was before the doctor came to the kitchen.

"Where's Tommy?" he asked.

I kept on rocking and nodded my head toward the back door. The doctor understood. He went out to the yard and, through the open door, I could hear him talking to Tommy.

"Helen's going to be all right. She can have as many children as she wants, but she lost a lot of blood and she's going to have to rest for a long time. I don't want her out of the bed for at least two weeks and even then, she'll be weak for a while. She'll need someone to stay with her and take care of her while you're at work."

Tommy's voice sounded shrill and scared as he answered the doctor. "My Aunt Deborah has kids still at home. She can't stay here all day."

"Maude can do it. She'll be here anyway, and she's very grown-up for her age."

"Maude? Here?"

"Of course, Helen's the only family she has left. Where else would she go?"

"I don't know. I never thought of that."

"I know. It's been a horrible day. I'll talk to the undertaker and the preacher about the funerals. You try to get some rest now. Tomorrow won't be much better than today."

I got up from the rocker and took my little bundle to the room that had been all made up for the baby. Tommy had painted it a soft yellow, with white woodwork, and there was a chest of drawers and a cradle. I put the baby in the cradle and put a blanket up to his little chin. I stroked his head, still matted with the stuff of birthing.

The extra blankets off the bureau made a pallet on the floor for me. I took off my shoes and socks, lay down, and pulled a blanket up over me, and then cried for the first time, but it wasn't a sorrowful crying. I was so awful angry that the Lord had let this happen, angry right down to the marrow of my bones. It made me even more afraid to feel that way. I had been taught, and I believed, that it was a sin to be angry with God. I was afraid that God would punish me for the way I felt. The baby Helen had been so excited about was dead, my mother was dead, and my daddy was dead. How could God love us and do this to us?

The truth of what the doctor said scared me more than everything that happened. There was no one to take care of me now but Helen, no other family. For my own sake, I had to take care of her. I had to see to it that nothing bad happened to her.

After a while, the house was finally dark and quiet, and sometime after, my tears stopped coming and the anger oozed out of me, I got up and took the baby from its cradle. I lay back on my pallet on the floor and held the baby in my arms. I didn't sleep until the sun had started to lighten the room and the awful night had passed.

Chapter 2

I woke in the morning to the sound of voices in the next room. I didn't move, but listened for a while, trying to make out what was being said. The door to the bedroom opened and the preacher's wife, Sister Clark, came in carrying some clothes over her arm. She and Brother Clark served at the Holiness Church my family went to. She was a nice, mostly happy-looking young woman, not much older than Helen, with light brown hair, green eyes and a gentle touch. She laid the clothes over the side of the cradle, knelt down by my pallet, and took me by the hand. "Maude, you need to get up now. We have to get ready for the funerals."

I didn't move, only looked up at her. Sister Clark reached over and took the baby out of my arms. "I have to take him to the undertaker's, Maude. He has to get him ready. Now you get washed up. I set out some clothes for you to put on. They came from your friend Susan. She wanted to share what she has with you. Everything in your house got burnt up."

I got to my feet. "Everything?"

Sister Clark nodded, her face full of sympathy. "The whole house burned to the ground."

I thought about my pretty blue dress that Momma made me for my birthday. She'd embroidered little butterflies around the hem and the edges of the sleeves. I'd only worn it once. It was gone now, and so was my doll with the china head. I didn't play with it anymore, but all the same, it hurt to know that I would never see it again.

Sister Clark held the baby as if it were still alive, and I liked her for that. She sighed. "Under the circumstances we're not going to have a wake. There'll be a service at the church at ten o'clock."

I picked up the dress she brought and held it up in front of me. It looked a little big, but I didn't complain. She patted me on the head. "That's a good girl. I'll stay here with Helen until after the funeral. She's not in any shape to go to the service. She's going to need you to take care of her for a while. When you get dressed I'll show you what to do for her."

I dropped my head and nodded. I promised myself that I would do everything I could to take care of my sister, partly because I loved her so, and partly because, if I lost Helen, there would be no one to take care of me, no one at all.

Sister Clark left with the baby. I went into the

kitchen, pumped a basin of water and took it to the washroom. I took off my clothes from the day before and washed myself, then put on Susan's clothes that Sister Clark brought me. When I finished dressing, I went out and sat in the parlor. I watched Tommy and Sister Clark going back and forth to Helen's bedroom. I got up only one time. That was when Tommy left the bedroom door open. I walked over to the door as quietly as I could and peeked in. Sister Clark sat by the bed reading the Bible out loud. Helen lay with her eyes closed as if she were asleep. Her chest rose and fell to a regular beat, and there was a bit of color in her cheeks. That made me feel better, and I went back to my chair and sat there until Tommy walked in and told me it was time to go. He had dark rings under his eyes and a haunted look on his face.

As we went out the door, I took his hand in mine. "She's going to be all right, Tommy."

He looked down at me with a weak smile. "If you say so," he said.

The Holiness Church was different for me that day. All my life I'd looked forward to the services. They sang bright and lively tunes, except on the Sunday mornings when they had the Lord's Supper and sang "Break Thou the Bread of Life." They clapped their hands in joy. People would stand and testify about how good God was to them, and how Jesus had saved them and changed their lives.

Sometimes, someone would go down front after the sermon and repent of some sort of sin. I always wondered what it was they'd done that was so bad, but once, when I asked her, Mom shushed me and told me it was nobody's business but God's and the sinner's. That seemed fitting to me.

That day, no one was happy, no one sang brightly, and no one clapped their hands. The soft sound of women crying lasted throughout the service. Brother Clark did his best to comfort us. He was a man who made you trust him. Blond hair, blue eyes, and a handsome face, he was about thirty. His big build didn't come from studying the Bible, which I know he did every day, but from doing the chores on his parent's farm that he still tended for them.

That day, he didn't pace back and forth in the pulpit and wave his arms the way he usually did, but stood in one spot and talked about how Brother and Sister Clayborn had both accepted the Lord Jesus as their personal Savior years ago and had lived a life that testified to the truth of it. He said that he was sure that they'd attained the state of grace that every member of the church should work toward, to be able to live life in purity, no longer sinning. He said that now, this very day, they were sitting at the right hand of God. He told us how the baby was there as well, since he'd died before he could sin.

I'd done so much crying the night before that I didn't cry at the church that day. I found the comfort I needed in the preacher's words because I believed them to be true.

After Brother Clark finished, we sang another song and the three pine boxes were lifted onto the shoulders of the men of the church. It took six of them to carry the largest, which held my daddy. Four of them carried mom, and one man carried the little box with the baby, walking down the aisle with it held in two hands in front of him. A farm wagon was waiting outside. We all walked together behind it to the little cemetery on the outskirts of town, singing hymns all the way.

The boxes were lowered into the three holes that had already been dug. Brother Clark said a few more words about how we are formed out of the dust and would return to the dust and then said another prayer for the comfort of us left behind. One by one the congregation filed past the holes, each of them picking up a handful of dirt and throwing it on top of the boxes. Tommy and I went last, but I didn't pick up a handful of dirt to throw. I couldn't do it. Momma hated dirt. I hung my head, kept my eyes on Tommy's feet, and walked past the holes, not looking down into them.

When Tommy and I got back home, Sister Clark took me to Helen's bedroom and showed me all the things I would have to do to care for Helen. She was finally awake, and Helen said that she could take care of herself, but Sister Clark shushed her and told her she had to follow doctor's orders if she wanted to get well again.

She told me how to keep Helen's most private parts clean, and how to use a pan for Helen's toilet. She explained how to put clean sheets on the bed with Helen still in it. I listened close to everything she said so I would do it right.

When she was finished, Sister Clark gave me a

quick hug. "If you need help sometimes, let me know. It won't be for very long. In a few weeks, she'll be her old self, and you can go back to being a little girl again. For right now, you have to be the woman of the house."

It was as if, for the last year since Helen was married, Mom had been training me for the job I had to do. I set about being the woman of the house that very day. I gathered up the soiled bedding and took it out to the back porch where there were two washtubs, one for washing and one for rinsing. I pumped the water and heated it and carried it to the tubs myself. I took the paring knife and a block of soap and cut it up in the hot water, the way I'd seen my mother do so many times. When the bedding was washed and hung on the line, I changed the water and did the regular clothes.

After that, I put out a simple lunch for the three of us, me, Tommy and Helen. The house was full of food brought by friends. Someone had been smart enough to bring a block of ice so the food would keep fresh longer. I sliced some ham, boiled a few potatoes, and warmed up a dish of collard greens. I made a tray and took it in to Helen. Tommy took his plate in the bedroom to eat with her, and I sat at the table in the kitchen by myself.

After giving thanks for all our friends and the food, I ate alone and then cleaned up the dishes.

Tommy sat in the bedroom all that day and held Helen's hand while she slept. Later that evening, Brother and Sister Clark came over with a regular bed for me so I wouldn't have to sleep on the floor. They brought me a stack of clothes that were donated by the members of the church. Some of the things were brand new. There were a coat, three dresses, and there was enough underwear for me to go a whole week before I had to wash them. Tommy and the preacher set up the bed in the room meant for the baby. Tommy cried as he carried the cradle to the barn, and Brother Clark patted him on the back and re-assured him that someday he could carry it back in the house.

Helen was weak for a long time, and I did everything I could to take care of the house and my sister. After a few weeks, Helen's strength came back some, and she was up and about. I didn't need to help her so much in a personal way, but it was a long time before Helen started to take over the household chores. Even then she left the harder work, like the laundry and the heavy cleaning, to me. It seemed that I never did get to go back to being a little girl, but my life did start to be more normal. I went back to school and to my regular class in Sunday school. I saw my friends there, but never asked them over to the house. It wasn't my house, and besides, I didn't have time to sit on the porch the way Helen did before she married. There were too many chores to be done.

I got my first time for the monthlies when I was eleven. I picked up a basket full of laundry and felt something hot and wet run down my legs. I set the basket down and looked down to see the red streaks. No one had ever talked to me about it, but I wasn't afraid. I knew from doing the laundry that women bled once a month.

All the same, I didn't feel old enough to be a woman. I washed off the blood and cleaned myself up, then stuffed a cloth into my undies and went to talk to Helen. She said it was something all women shared. She sat next to me and put her arm around my shoulders and told me matter-of-fact what she knew about the situation. "When Eve sinned, God put a curse on her and now, every woman has to suffer for it. You'll get this once a month. It will last five or six days. You can't take a sit-down bath or wash your hair while you have it or you'll get sick. I'm sorry you got it so young. Some girls don't start until they're fifteen. They're the lucky ones."

Then Helen tore up some of the thin, older towels into strips and gave them to me with directions on how to use them and how to keep myself clean. Taking care of the house, I had a woman's job, and now I had a woman's body, and I wasn't happy about either thing, but there wasn't much I could do about it.

When I was twelve, I struck up a beginning courtship with James Connor. I always liked him, and I guess it showed, because even when I was in kindergarten, Daddy teased me about it. James mostly ignored me before.

The town had only one school, so we saw one another every weekday, and he attended the Holiness Church with his family, the same one I went to with mine. He was a few years older, and I figured out right away that now he wanted to be a different kind of friend. I was tall for my age, as tall as a grown woman, and my figure had bloomed early. I wasn't slim and tiny-waisted like Helen, but was like my daddy, sturdy built.

James had light blond hair and deep blue eyes and was tall enough that I had to look up at him. I liked that. He didn't make me feel so big. He was as plain as I was, but he was pleasant looking and had a warm smile and a winning way about him. He made me feel special. If I came into the classroom after him, when he caught sight of me, his face sort of lit up, like it pleased him for me to be there. I never saw him pay attention to any other girl. He smiled at me and seemed happy to see me each time we met. Once, he held my hand when he walked me home from school. I liked that, but the next day, someone teased us about it, so he didn't do it again.

After the birth of Helen's stillborn baby, Helen seemed to get in a family way at least once a year, but she always miscarried in her second or third month. Each time, she would go to her room for days and cry. Every time, she gave up on ever being able to carry a baby to the end. Tommy held her and comforted her and reminded her that the doctor had told them that they would have a healthy baby sooner or later.

When I was thirteen, Helen missed her period again and made it through the third month without a problem. Everyone held their breath. Doctor Wilson told her to go to bed and stay there as much as possible, and she did. For the second time, I was the only woman working in the house. I got up extra early, when the first rooster crowed, cooked breakfast for the three of us, made a sack lunch for Tommy to take to work with him, and a lunch for Helen, which I put in the icebox to keep cool. When I got home from school, I did the chores and cleaned and fixed dinner. Saturdays, I did the laundry and cooked the meal for a cold Sunday dinner, usually fried chicken, corn bread and potato salad. Except for the necessary things, even I didn't have to work on the Sabbath.

When her fourth month of carrying the baby passed without a problem, Helen became more cheerful. After the fifth month, she developed a tummy bulge, and even Tommy relaxed a bit. He would come in from work, kiss his wife, lay his hand on her big belly and talk to the baby. He was sure it was another little boy.

During the day, Helen sat propped up in bed, reading or visiting with one of her lady friends. I would have liked to join them, but I was usually busy with running the house. If I did go into Helen's room when she had company, I still got the old feeling of being an outsider, just like when I was a girl.

When I finished cleaning up after dinner, I would sometimes sit on the front porch with James. He had just as many things to do as I did. He'd graduated the last term and started a job at his father's store. While I did the housework on Saturdays, he played baseball. Saturday evenings, he visited, and we had to be careful that we kept a respectable distance between us, with our chairs not quite touching. We didn't want people to talk about us.

James couldn't keep the excitement out of his

voice when he talked about baseball. "They're opening ball parks all across the country, Maude. There's different levels of teams. The real professionals play in the majors, where they don't have to do anything to earn a living but play ball. Just imagine, getting paid money to play! Then there are what they call the minor leagues, where you still learn from real coaches and they get you ready to move up to the majors. The kind of ball we play here, one small town against another, is like the bottom level."

He'd told me all this before, but I listened anyway. I took pleasure in seeing how much he loved the game. He got a dreamy, faraway look when he said, "Once in a while they send out a man to take a look and see if there are any players who might be good enough to be a professional. One of them was here, Maude, in our town. He watched us play. He talked to three of us after the game, Henry Gray, Phil Fuller, and me. He asked us a lot of questions and said that he'd be back. That's what I want to do, Maude, I want to play ball more than anything."

James's dad ran the farm supply store, and I thought about that. "What about your dad's store? Doesn't he expect you to take over someday? Would he let you go off to play ball?"

"My dad's not like that. He wouldn't hold me back from what I love. Besides, I'd come home someday and run it for him, but not until I was too old to play anymore."

James held my hand and looked in my eyes, "What do you want, Maude? What kind of life do you see for yourself?"

I was taken unexpected by his question. I couldn't even answer him right away. After a moment he asked, "Maude?"

I laughed a little, embarrassed. "No one ever asked me what I wanted before, James, not once. I spent my whole life so far having people tell me what to do, and doing it. It's like I was out in the middle of a stream and it was better to let it carry me along than to fight it."

"Well, I'm asking you now. What is it that would make you happy?"

I smiled and looked off at some clouds in the sky. I had to think about it a minute before I could answer him. "I'd like to graduate from school and then go see other places. I've heard tell about cities where it would take days to walk from one side to the other. I read about oceans so big that it takes the biggest, fastest boat weeks to cross over them."

He was quiet and, after a few seconds, I thought of some more to tell him. "After a while, I'd like to have a home of my own, where I could make pretty curtains for the windows. I'd like to marry a good man and raise babies, and grow old with my family about me."

We sat together for a while after that without talking, both of us dreaming our dreams, until Helen came out to remind James that it was getting late, and I had chores still to do.

James's mother and father were really nice to me. They encouraged us to spend time together and told me they appreciated how I worked to take care of Helen and the house. They made me feel they thought their son had made a good choice in courting me.

James and I really enjoyed what little time we spent together. It was comfortable. Our future seemed settled. We never actually spoke about it, but I expected James would talk to me about getting married as soon as I finished school. Of course, that was three years away.

Helen's sixth month passed without any problems, then her seventh and eighth. She said the baby moved around all the time. Sometimes Helen would grab my hand and press it against her stomach. I could feel the little feet kicking away. Helen was so happy, "Henry Mathias was never like that. He hardly moved. I just know this one is going to make it."

I would smile and be happy along with her. I wanted this baby to live as much as Helen and Tommy did.

When the baby was due in another week or two, Helen started to be nervous and asked the doctor, "Are you sure it's all right, Doctor Wilson? How can you tell? Isn't it time?"

He smiled at her like she was a little girl. "You know what they say, Helen, a baby's like a ripe apple. When it's ready, it'll fall. Now, don't you worry so, I'll take good care of you. All of us will, me and Tommy and Maude."

Tommy brought the cradle down from the barn's loft and I cleaned it and polished it. I put it back into its original location in my bedroom. I shoved my bed against the wall to make room. I moved my things out of two of the bureau drawers, making room for the little layette that I'd packed away. I'd sewn enough with my mother to be a pretty good seamstress, and made little gowns and bonnets for the baby. They weren't embroidered and fancy like store-bought clothes, but they were stitched even, they would last, and they were made with love.

I came home from school one day to find Helen lying on her side in her bed. She was sweating and trying to catch her breath. "Get the doctor," she said.

I ran out of the house, and ran the quarter-mile to the doctor's house lickedly-split. He kept his office in an addition at the side of his house, one little waiting room and one examining room. The door was open, but he wasn't there. There were men I knew from the church waiting to see him. One of them had a bandage on his hand with blood leaking out of it.

"Where is he?" I yelled. "He has to come. Helen's having her baby."

They all knew what happened the first time. Their bloody fingers could wait. One of the men stood. "He just went over to the store for something not more than a minute ago. I'll go tell him."

I ran back out the door and all the way home. I was sweating and panting for breath by the time I got there. Helen was the same. "Doctor Wilson will be here in a few minutes. Is it bad?" I asked.

Helen managed a nod, her mouth twisted in pain.

I thought back to the other time, "I'll get things ready."

I ran into the kitchen and pumped a pot full of water and put it on the stove. The fire was always banked so it wouldn't go out. I ran to the porch and grabbed some of the logs that were stacked there, opened the stove door and threw all but one of them on the fire. I poked the embers with the last log until the tiny flames burst out again. When I was satisfied that the fire had caught, I slammed the door shut and then ran for the towels. I stopped and looked out the window toward the doctor's office to see if he was coming, but he was nowhere to be seen.

Helen rolled on her back, raised her knees up, and fastened her eyes on mine. "It's coming, Maude. Where's the doctor?"

I looked out the window. I still didn't see him. "Hold on, Helen, he'll be here."

The look in Helen's eyes was wild. "I can't hold on. My baby's getting born right now."

I took a deep breath and pulled back the covers. I'd already seen more of Helen's private parts than I had ever wanted to see, but I had to know what was happening. Helen was right. The baby was coming. The little round head was already out. The baby wasn't crying. I had to help it.

"You're right, Helen, it isn't going to wait. When the next pain comes, see if you can help it and push it out far enough so I can get hold of it."

Helen scrunched up her eyes and pushed hard. The baby's shoulders slid out. I pulled on it the way I'd seen Doctor Wilson pull on the first one, but it was so slippery my hands just slid off. Helen took another deep breath and pushed again. The baby slid out a little further and I took a towel and wrapped it around the baby's body and then tried again. This time, the baby came free. It was a little girl. I wrapped it in the towel. It didn't cry, and it was blue all over. I used my right hand to hold up its tiny neck while I held its feet to turn it upside down. I shook it a little. It still didn't cry. I put my mouth over the baby's and blew into it the way the doctor had the first one. The baby coughed right in my mouth and then let out a blood-curdling scream. It was the most beautiful sound I ever heard. Helen fell back against the pillows.

I looked up just as Doctor Wilson came charging in the room. The baby was letting out ear-splitting screams. The doctor pulled his instruments out of his bag and tied and cut the cord. Then he touched my arm and directed me toward the kitchen. "I need to take care of Helen. Wrap that baby up and take it in the kitchen. Clean it up, and don't let it get cold."

I was only too happy to do what he said. Holding the baby in one arm, I used my other hand to make a pallet on the kitchen table with a folded blanket. I ladled some of the warm water into a basin and washed the baby until all of the birthing mess was gone. I diapered her and dressed her in one of the little gowns I'd made, then wrapped her tight in one of the little blankets, the way I'd seen the mothers at the church do with theirs. The baby cried the whole time and the sound of her screaming made me happy because she was telling me she was alive and she was strong and she was going to be just fine. I was so proud of her perfect little body you would have thought she was my own. She was the right size and rounded out and pink all over. Her head was covered with blonde fuzz, the same color as Helen's. She was a healthy, beautiful little girl.

The doctor finally finished up with Helen and found me rocking the baby in the corner of the kitchen. The baby was sleeping peacefully, with me watching every breath she took.

"You did quite a job in there, young lady. I couldn't have done any better myself. Helen told me how you breathed the life into her."

I couldn't help but beam at the praise. In all my life, I felt it was the most important thing I had ever done.

Chapter 3

I can't tell you how much I loved that baby. I rushed home from school every day to do my work and help take care of her. Helen named her Faith, after our mother, and that made me love her even more. I washed her and changed her, and I put the cradle up next to my own bed so I could rock her and sing to her if she fussed at night. When she needed to be fed, I would carry her to Helen. I would turn away as Helen held Faith to her breast. It was the one thing I couldn't do, and it was the most important thing of all. I was jealous of Helen for it.

One day, when little Faith was a few months old, I heard Tommy and Helen talking about getting a bigger bed for her. She was outgrowing her cradle. "That room just isn't big enough for two beds," I heard Tommy say. He sounded almost angry.

The next Sunday, James Connor walked me home from church as usual, but he didn't have much to say. He'd graduated the year before and was always busy, working with his father when the store was open, playing baseball every weekend, and waiting for the scout to come back to town like he promised. I made a few tries to talk, but he decided he didn't want to, so I held my tongue and fell into step beside him, just enjoying his company. When we got to Helen's house, we found his parents sitting with Helen and Tommy on the front porch. I couldn't help but be surprised. They'd never visited us before. As James and I walked up the pathway, the men stood.

"Let's go to the kitchen," Tommy said. The four of them trooped in the house with James and me following behind. The women sat at the table, and Tommy waved James to the last chair. Mr. Connor stood behind his wife, and Tommy took up a place behind Helen.

The grown-ups all looked at each other. Tommy cleared his throat and began a speech, one I could tell he'd been practicing. "Maude, you're a young woman now, and it's time for you to make your own way in the world. We know you're fond of James, and he's fond of you. He's got a good job and can take care of you. Brother and Sister Connor are pleased with you and we all agree that it's time the two of you got married."

James looked at me with a big smile on his face. He'd known this was coming all along, and I reckoned that was why he'd been so quiet on the walk home. It riled me that he'd kept it to himself, and I took a few deep breaths while they all stared at me, waiting to hear what I'd say.

Finally I was able to whisper, "What about my schooling? I won't graduate for another three years."

Tommy shook his head. "You're almost out of the ninth grade. That's enough schooling for any girl."

It about broke my heart. I looked up at him. "But Helen got to graduate. You waited for her."

"That was your parent's doing. It was different. They had their own ways. This is the best thing all around."

I knew what he meant. He wanted me out of the house. I gave a short nod. "When do you want us to do it? Can I finish this term?"

"Of course you can. Then we can have a proper wedding for you, and the church will give you a party."

James reached over and took my hand and smiled at me. "I'll make a good husband for you Maude, I promise."

I managed a small smile for him. I would have to trust him.

It was another six weeks before the term was over. Helen took me to the general store to let me pick out the fabric for my wedding dress and I chose a light blue with no pattern to it. As we were having it cut from the bolt, Helen picked up a bolt of white lisle and laid it on the counter.

"Cut six yards of this one, too," she said. Then she stood on her tip-toes to whisper in my ear, "You ought to have some pretty underwear and a nice new nightgown."

I cut the dress and stitched it carefully, doing my best to sew it just the way Mom would have. When it was finished, I embroidered little white flower chains around the hem of the skirt and the sleeves. I was so proud of it. It was the prettiest thing I'd ever owned. I crocheted fine lace around the edges of my new nightgown and underwear. I thought I would be dressed as fine as any rich lady for my wedding.

James spent the six weeks fixing up the little one-room cabin on the back of his parent's place. Their house was quite grand for our town, with the front door opening to a wide staircase that led to four bedrooms upstairs. Downstairs was a parlor on the left and a dining room on the right. The washroom and the kitchen were at the back, and there was a wonderful covered porch, eight feet wide, that wrapped all the way around the house.

Our cabin was about twenty feet square and had a fireplace and four windows, one on each side of the door, and on each side wall. It even had its own outhouse in the back. He painted both buildings inside and out, put a new wood floor in the cabin and the outhouse, and even got glass for the windows. Mom Connor didn't understand why we didn't just live with them in the big house, but James insisted that we had to have our own place, and I'm glad he did. It was better for both of us. I didn't know then, but I was later to learn that it didn't work to have two women under one roof.

His parents gave him a table and two chairs and

a settee from their house. It was agreed that Tommy would bring my bedstead and a bureau to the cabin on the day of the wedding. The bureau would be Helen and Tommy's wedding present to us.

I finished my ninth-grade schooling on a Friday, and the wedding was set for five o'clock the next afternoon. That gave the men of the church time to get in their day's work before the service. It was that morning as I was dressing that Helen said to me, "Whatever he wants to do to you, you have to let him do it."

Every member of our little church was there for the ceremony. Brother Clark had me recite the passage from Ruth he'd given me to memorize,

"Whither thou goest, I will go, and where thou lodgest, I will lodge, and thy people shall be my people and thy God, my God."

I promised to love and obey James, and he promised to love and cherish me. I hoped that James and I would have the same kind of marriage that I thought my parents had, the same kind that Brother and Sister Clark seemed to have. I'd noticed them many times, holding hands as they stood together, the love on Sister Clark's face when she watched her husband talk. It was the way it had been for my Mom and Daddy.

The women cried at the service. At the little party at the Connor house, the men slapped James on the back, poked him in the ribs, and gave him knowing looks. It made me uneasy. I wasn't sure what-all being married involved. The only talk I'd ever heard about what happened between married men and women had come from my few girlfriends, and they didn't know much more about it than I did.

Every family brought a gift of some sort for us. There were linens, oil lamps, and bowls. None of them could afford much, but we were thrilled. I'd never been treated so warmly in my life.

After the service and the party, James and I went home to the cabin. Tommy had already brought my things, my bed and bureau and a pretty cedar chest he made for me as another wedding present. He'd carved the bottom of it into curved legs and put a leather handle on the front. It replaced the old one that I used at Helen's house. Helen packed it with the homemaking things that I'd collected over the last two years. My friends and I began our hope chests when we turned twelve, the way girls do. We talked about what we wanted and the colors and things.

As much as I loved Helen and her baby, Faith, I always dreamed of having my own home and my own family. Whatever money I was given by Helen over the years was spent mostly on fabric for linens and things to go into my chest. It was the closest thing to a dowry I had, and I was glad I'd made the effort and hadn't spent my few dollars on ribbons for my hair or candy the way some of my friends did. There wasn't as much in the chest as I would have liked, but I didn't often get cash, and I hadn't expected to marry so early.

James and I puttered around the cabin for a while, re-arranging the few pieces of furniture and placing our other things in logical locations. It was a warm evening, and there was no need for a fire in the fireplace. When the sun began going down, James lit one of the oil lamps.

I tried to keep looking busy, but finally there was nothing else for us to do. It had been a long day. James blushed and said, "I guess it's time to go to bed."

My heart began beating faster. I was afraid, and I was curious, too. "I guess so," I agreed. I took my nightgown out of the bureau and laid it on the bed. I looked around for somewhere to change. I loved my little cabin, but there was no place for me to go to and undress and put on my pretty new night gown. James realized I was embarrassed.

"Uh, I have to go out back," he said. "I'll be back in a minute."

"All right," I smiled. Even though James had left the cabin, I slipped the nightgown over my head and down around me before I unbuttoned my dress and let it fall. I hung it up, took off the rest of my underclothes, and peeled off my stockings and put them in my shoes. I folded back the covers and got in the bed, sliding over to the side near the wall.

After a few minutes, James came in. He carried the lamp to the bedside table and blew it out. In the moonlight that came through the windows I could see him getting out of his clothes. He slid in bed next to me. I thought about what Helen told me.

James nuzzled my neck. In all the time I'd known him, the only touch between us had been holding hands and the quick kiss at the church when we were pronounced husband and wife.

I liked the feel of his kiss on my neck. I tilted my head so he would know that it gave me pleasure. Then he put his hand on my breast and I thought about what Helen said, my body got all stiff. James drew back his hand. "I love you, Maude. I promise I won't hurt you."

I lay there next to him in the darkness. I had every reason to believe him. "I know you won't," I whispered, and he didn't.

Chapter 4

The next morning, I woke to the sound of wood being chopped. There was a fire in the fireplace and a pot of water boiling on the hook. James came in with his arms full of firewood and dropped it into the little box next to the hearth.

"Good morning." He sat on the side of the bed and leaned over to kiss me on the cheek. "Now that we're married, I can kiss you every day, even on Sunday."

I felt my face turn red. I smiled at him. He reached out and cupped my chin. "How you doing? Are you all right?"

I understood what he meant and blushed even more deeply. "I'm fine."

He nodded, picked up a small package wrapped in white paper from the table, and handed it to me. "Ma gave me some corn meal for us to cook for breakfast. We been invited to eat dinner at the house after church."

He stood, reached in his pocket, pulled out a handful of change, and put it in my hand. "Here's some money. You can get what groceries we need in the morning. I don't know what all else we have to have. Ma said we can share her washtub and stuff like that for a while till we get our own."

I held out my hand and looked at the money in silence. When I had fetched groceries and things for Helen, I'd just had the shopkeeper write it down in his book. It dawned on me that I was really the woman of the house now. It brought me a feeling of power.

James misunderstood my silence and crinkled up his face. "Is that enough?"

I jumped a little. I'd been thinking so hard that his voice surprised me, out of a trance almost. I looked up at him with wide eyes. "I'm sure it's fine. I don't really know how much I need. I hope I can do it right."

"I guess we've both got a lot to learn, Maude. Ma and Dad will help us with what we don't know. We'll be all right." He pulled me against him, and I leaned into his shoulder. He was only eighteen, but he felt so strong to me. My heart swelled with love for him. He was my husband, and he had already given me a home of my own. "I know we will."

Once I was dressed, I ladled some of the water into a smaller pan and boiled the corn meal. We ate it without milk or sugar. I'd get us some Monday, at the store. When we finished breakfast, we dressed and walked to church with James's parents.

I couldn't help but feel that everyone was staring at me. It was as if they expected me to make an announcement of some sort. Some of the women looked at me so sadly it made me wonder what they were thinking. James took another round of back-slapping and rib-poking from some of the men. He just smiled quietly, letting them enjoy the brotherhood of married men.

I said good morning to my girlfriends, but they looked different to me that morning. I felt that I'd gone to a place they hadn't, and that I would never be able to feel that same childlike kinship with them again.

James reached for me in the dark almost every night. I didn't understand what he was feeling or why he wanted to do that to me, but it didn't take him very long, and he was gentle, and I liked having him hold me. After we were married four months, he'd still never seen me without my underwear, but I wasn't shy about undressing in front of him. He always sort of turned his eyes to avoid embarrassing me, but he didn't leave the cabin any more.

One night, I started to unbutton my dress and he sat on one of the chairs and watched me. I waited for him to look away, like he usually did, but he kept his eyes on me. "Go ahead, Maude. I want to see you."

I know I blushed. I could feel my face and everything else go red, but I let my dress fall to the floor and then stepped out of it. I picked it up and laid it across the back of the other chair. Then I unbuttoned my shimmy. I dropped it, stepped out of it, and stood there naked, my eyes still on the wooden planks.

James stood and put his arms around me, then tilted my head back and kissed me. "Maude, you're a good wife. You've never turned me down yet, but I know this hasn't meant as much to you as it has to me. I talked to Brother Clark about it, and he said that the marriage bed is blessed and that we should both enjoy it. He talked to me straight out about the whole thing."

James stepped back and undressed himself. I had never seen his member in the light. I couldn't help but stare at it, and that didn't seem to bother him. His parts appeared to have a curious arrangement to me. He led me to the bed and took his time, practicing what the preacher had told him. That night, for the first time, I found out what it was he liked so much. I knew I'd always be grateful to Brother and Sister Clark.

Except for still being sad sometimes about not getting to finish school, I was happy, so happy I can't even tell how much. Our lives settled into a pleasant pattern. James would leave for the store each morning to work with his father. I would clean and do my chores, go to the store, and do some sewing or whatever else came to my attention. I helped Mom Connor in her garden the same way I'd helped my own mother. Our meals were simple, and I knew I was a good cook. We had corn meal mush or oatmeal for breakfast every day except Sunday, when we had oatmeal and eggs. James would come home at noon for dinner. I'd been given enough pots and pans to make different kinds of meals for him. We ate our main meal at noon, leaving the leftovers covered with a cloth on the table for a small supper at the end of the day. I dreamed of the day I could get a real stove that burned wood like the kind my mother had. There were only a few things I could make in a fireplace, mostly stews and soups. On Sundays, there was no cooking except for breakfast, but I would help Mom Connor make the meal on Saturday and when we came home from church, I helped put out the dinner we made the day before, and we ate with his mom and dad.

I prided myself on how clean and orderly I kept our little cabin. James put up a coop in back so we could keep our own chickens, and I put a vegetable garden of my own next to it, things Mom Connor didn't care to grow, like lettuce. I planted flowers around the front steps and down each side of the pathway leading to the cabin.

I was fond of James's parents and didn't mind asking his mother for advice on the garden and other things around the cabin. We women developed a genuine bond. We sometimes cooked together, and it reminded me of the time I'd spent in my mother's kitchen.

In the afternoons I often visited Helen and played with the baby. Faith looked more like her mother and grandmother every day. Her hair had begun forming soft curls. I cherished my precious little niece. When it was time for her nap, I would rock her in the kitchen where I'd rocked her the night she was born. When she became drowsy, I would carry her to her room and stroke her head until she was asleep.

Helen would buy little remnants from the fabric

bolts at the store, and I still made the gowns that Faith wore. Helen was a pretty good seamstress, just like all the other women in the town, but she didn't take the joy in sewing that I did.

The days were growing shorter, and oil was too expensive to use often, so after dinner James and I would sit on the front porch of our cabin until dusk and talk about his work at the store, the people he'd seen during the day, and our dreams for our life. On Saturdays he played baseball. He still had hopes of a professional career. It was 1906 and another league, the American, had been formed to compete with the National. Baseball was sweeping the country. They'd even begun forming teams all the way across the ocean, in Europe.

One Monday in late September, I was spooning the cornmeal mush into the bowls for our breakfast, and my stomach felt as if it were rushing up into my throat. I barely made it out the front door before I heaved up a thick yellow liquid. It scalded my throat. I leaned over the porch rail for a long time, finally just spitting out the water that formed inside my mouth to rinse away the awful taste. After a few minutes, I felt better and went back inside. I scooped a dipper of water out of the bucket and sipped it until my throat stopped burning.

The next morning, it happened again. By the end of the week I was throwing up three or four times a day, mostly in the morning. James told his mother, and Mrs. Connor came down to the cabin to see me. She stared in my eyes with a smile, "When did you bleed the last time, Maude?" she asked.

I thought it over. "About eight or nine weeks ago."

"Well, you take it easy for a while, at least until you get past the third month. Don't be fetching water or picking up anything heavy. Let James do all that for you. You don't want anything to happen to the baby."

I stared at her. "Baby?"

Mrs. Connor laughed. "Baby! Didn't you know you were in a family way? I figure by early spring you'll be a momma."

It all made sense. I remembered how Helen had been sick in the mornings the times she was that way. I grabbed Mom Connor and hugged her tight. I was so happy. I would have a baby of my own to love. I felt it was the greatest thing that could happen to me.

When James came home, I could hardly wait to run out and meet him with the news. He grinned from ear-to-ear. He had suspected as much.

"Do you think I should build onto the cabin so he can have his own room?"

I shook my head. "Not right away, maybe next summer. I want to have my baby sleeping right here where I can be close and know that it's all right."

James held me close to him and kissed my forehead. "You let me know what I ought to do to help you. We don't want to take any chances. We want him to be big and healthy."

"I'll take care. Your mom said for me not to lift anything heavy, like the water buckets, for a few months." I didn't say anything to discourage James about it being a boy. All men wanted sons, especially the firstborn, but in my heart I already knew it would be a girl. I hoped it would look like my mother and share Faith's blonde curls.

That night, when I undressed, I held my palm against my stomach. I closed my eyes and imagined my baby could hear my voice. "I'm going to love you and take care of you the best I know how. I'm going to make you little dresses and gowns with flowers stitched on them, and when your hair gets long enough, if it doesn't curl on its own, I'm going to wind it up in curls every night." I patted my tummy and the precious life inside it and smiled to myself. I was so happy.

The morning sickness passed in a few weeks. I was grateful I didn't suffer with it the way Helen had, almost until the end of her time. After a while, my clothes began to tug across my middle. I had taken to lifting the waistline a little to ease the pull. James's mother brought me some big aprons and some new fabric.

"If you wear an apron you don't have to button your dress in the middle, and that will get you through part of the time. I brought you this fabric for an early birthday present. There's enough here that you can make yourself two dresses to wear for later, when you get too big for the ones you have. After the baby comes, you can cut them over to make regular dresses."

I was so thankful. I had never in my life had two new dresses at one time. I would have one to wear and one to wash. I hugged my mother-in-law with a tear in my eye. "You're so good to me. Thank you so much."

Mom Connor patted me on the back, "You're a good girl, Maude. I can see that James is happy with you. You keep a clean house, and you're a good cook, and my boy goes around with a smile on his face. I couldn't ask for more than that from any daughter-in-law."

I couldn't help but grin from ear-to-ear. It felt good to be appreciated. I'd heard how some girls hated their husband's mother. I felt I must be the luckiest wife in the world.

It was a mild winter that year. Snow dusted the ground but didn't stay long. It didn't take much to heat the cabin, but James kept the firewood bin filled anyway. One day he brought home a smooth, wide plank about eight feet long. He propped it up on the front porch while he unfolded a brown paper pattern and drew the outline of it on the wood, then he cut around the lines, sanded the edges, and put the pieces together. I'd wrapped myself with a blanket over my coat so I could sit outside and watch him. He wouldn't tell me what he was up to, but it wasn't long before I figured it out. It was a cradle for the baby. I was so proud of him. I'd had no idea he could do such a thing. He held it up in front of me. "That ought to hold him for a while."

"It's wonderful!" I said. "I love it."

James took his time smoothing out the rough edges of the wood and then carried the cradle in the cabin and placed it in the corner by our bed. He gave one corner of it a push and it rocked for a long time before it stopped.

"That's how you can tell the bottom is even on both ends, it rocks smooth," James said, obviously proud of his work. I wrapped my arms around him and leaned my head on his shoulder. The baby was turning around in my growing tummy. He could feel it kicking against his side.

"He's about to bust out of there now. It's a good thing we got a bed to put him in."

I just smiled. Yes, it was a good thing we had a bed for my little girl. I was so happy, so very, very happy.

Chapter 5

It was almost spring, the way Mrs. Connor said it would be, when I felt the first labor pains. It was early in the afternoon, and the pains were mild and about a half-hour apart. I'd talked with some of the women at the church about their deliveries and had seen Helen deliver her babies, so I wasn't worried. There was plenty of time before the baby would be born.

When James came home from the store, I was rocking on the porch. I told him, "I been getting cramps all afternoon. I think the baby's coming." James's face went white, and his mouth fell open, "I'll run get Dr. Wilson right now."

I laughed at him. "We don't need to hurry. It'll probably be tomorrow before it happens. Go tell him it's started and tell your mom. She'll want to help us."

He said, "Mom's still up in Union City nursing

her sister. Dad thought she might get home today or tomorrow, but we don't know for sure."

"Well, go let Dr. Wilson know. He'll tell you when to come get him. Like I said, it'll probably be tomorrow. Maybe your Mom will be home by then. I know she wouldn't want to miss it. Give me your watch."

We didn't have a clock in the cabin, and I'd been guessing the timing of the pains. He pulled his watch out of his pocket and handed it to me, then he turned and took off down the path. I smiled after him as he ran full speed toward the doctor's house.

After a few minutes, he came running back. "Doc Wilson's out at the Miller farm. Sister Miller's having her baby today, too. Sister Wilson said he ought to be back soon 'cause it's the Miller's fifth baby, and she has an easy time of it."

He looked terrified. I wasn't at all afraid. I reached out and took his hand. I knew that giving him work to do would help him not to worry, so I said, "Doctor Wilson will want lots of water to clean up, hot water, and clean towels and blankets. Why don't you make the fire higher and start drawing the water?"

I could tell James was relieved to be able to do something. He ran in the cabin, got the water bucket, and made trips back and forth to the well. The first trip, he went so fast that half the water splashed out of the bucket. After that, he slowed to a normal walk. He filled the kettle that hung on the hook in the fireplace first and stoked up the logs to get them burning. After that, he went up to the main house for extra linens and piled them up on the little bedside table. Then he filled all of the pots we had and brought more from his mom's house. It tickled me to watch him, and when he gathered considerably more than I thought we would need, I finally stopped him. By then it was growing dark.

I'd still been having cramps about a half-hour apart, but they were growing stronger. I stood and stretched. "I think we should go in now, the night air is coming down."

James wrapped one arm around me and led me inside as if he thought I couldn't walk by myself. "Is there anything else we need?"

I thought it over. It would help him to stay busy, but I didn't know of anything else he could do. "I guess now we just have to wait. Let's have some supper and get some sleep."

"I'll fix it. You sit down and rest."

"I'm all right," I said. I laid the watch on the bed table and started dinner. I'd had James kill a chicken that morning, fried it for the noon meal, and left it covered on the table. I pulled the cloth off and got out some cornbread. We had that with a mess of greens left warming in a pot next to the fire, and even though I wasn't hungry, I made an act of eating so James wouldn't notice and miss his meal. I tried not to show it when the pains came, now a little closer together and harder. I didn't want to worry him.

After we'd eaten, I cleaned up and changed into a nightgown, not one of my best, just something that would do.

"Leave the lamp burning low," I told him, "just enough so I can see the watch."

I folded a blanket and placed it under my hips so if my water broke during the night the mattress wouldn't get wet, then we went to bed. In only a few minutes, James's breathing told me he'd fallen asleep, so when the next few cramps came I pulled my knees up and kept quiet. They were worse than before, but I was still able to doze off between them.

About two in the morning I woke with a pain so sharp I couldn't catch my breath. The nature of the pain had changed altogether. It wasn't a cramp anymore. No wonder Helen screamed. I held back a cry, rolled over on my side and rode it out, staring at the watch. After another five minutes, another one washed over me. When it eased up, I shook James. He was awake in an instant. "It's time to go get the doctor. I'm not going to make it until morning. Tell him I'm sorry to get him out of bed."

James pulled on his shirt and pants, kissed me on the forehead, and ran out the door. I realized he was barefoot. I hoped he wouldn't catch cold.

After only a few minutes, he ran back in the cabin. "Are you all right? Doctor Wilson will be here in a little bit. He just got back from the Millers."

He pulled a chair up next to the bed and clutched my hand. Another pain came, and my whole body went stiff. Even though I didn't cry out, James's face went white. Finally, it passed, and I relaxed.

The doctor came and James jumped up out of his seat, "The pains are real bad, doc."

"Why don't you wait out on the porch while I look her over, James."

James stopped at the door and looked back at us. I could see that he wanted to stay, but I was glad to have him gone.

"Go ahead, now," the doctor said, waving his hand towards the door. "I don't need you here to tend to."

James shuffled out of the room and to the front porch. I could see him standing there, almost pressed up against the screen, straining to hear and see what was happening inside.

Doctor Wilson sat on the chair and pressed his palm against my stomach. "How far apart are the pains, Maude?"

"Every few minutes, and the last ones were awful hard."

"Looks like it's time. You'll be fine."

I thought his speech was slurred a little, and I was sure I smelled liquor on his breath. I thought that I must be wrong. He was a deacon at the church. He would never drink alcohol. It must be the pains making me think that. I looked hard at him. There were dark circles under his eyes, and his hair hadn't been combed. "You look tired. Is the Miller baby all right?"

"He's fine, he just took a lot longer than we expected. He was breech, and it took a time to right him."

I wasn't sure what that meant, but if it was all right now, it couldn't be too bad. I would ask James's mother about it later.

Another pain hit me. Doctor Wilson pressed his hand harder against my stomach until it let up again. "Let's take a look," he said, and pulled the covers back.

Even though I knew Dr. Wilson delivered babies all the time, it was embarrassing to have him see my privates. I turned my head and looked at the wall until he was finished. He said, "I can see his little head now. When the next pain comes, I want you to push it on out, Maude."

I just nodded my head a little. The doctor put the covers back up over my stomach, leaned back in the chair and closed his eyes. It looked to me as if he'd fallen asleep. It was only a matter of seconds until another pain came, this one the worst of all. I pulled my knees up and took a deep breath. I pushed as hard as I could, and felt it slide out of me. The pain stopped. Doctor Wilson was sound asleep.

"James," I called.

James ran back in the room.

"I think it's here, James. Wake up the doctor."

James cursed, the first time I had ever heard him do that, and shook the doctor's arm. Doctor Wilson jumped, and his eyes popped open.

"I think the baby's here," I said.

Doctor Wilson pulled the cover back down and picked up the baby. "Sure is. I wish they were all that fast."

My heart raced. "It isn't crying, is it all right?"

"She's just fine. Not all babies cry, Maude." He held her up so I could look at her. The little face was all scrunched up and she was blue, but she was waving her little clenched fists in the air and seemed to be breathing fine. Doctor Wilson tied off the cord and cut it. He pressed on my stomach again, first on one side and then on the other.

He looked the baby over and then wrapped it up in one of the cloths and handed it to James. "She's fine, James, and I'm so tired I'm ready to fall over. I'm going home. You'll have to clean the baby up yourself."

Then he picked up his bag and left. James held the baby away from him as if it were hot. He gaped after the doctor's back. "What do I do, Maude?"

"Just dip a cloth in the warm water and wipe her down over and over until she's clean. Keep her covered up as much as you can so she doesn't take a chill."

I longed to do the job myself, but I was so spent I couldn't even lift my head. James began the job of washing our baby. He'd barely started when another pain grabbed at me. I couldn't help crying out. "I think there's another one coming, James. You better run after Doctor Wilson and tell him."

James laid our half-washed baby in its cradle and pulled a little blanket up over her chest, then ran out the door. He was back in a few minutes. "Sister Wilson tried to get him up, but he just told her that there's no other baby in there, and you were fine. He said he'd stop by tomorrow."

Another pain came, not as strong as the ones before the baby had come out, but a big pain just the same. I felt the need to push again. I caught a deep breath and bore down. Another mass slid out of me.

"Here it is, James. See if it's all right."

He pulled the covers back. "That's not a baby. I don't know what that is."

I tried to lift my head but I was too weak. "Run up to the house and see if your mother's back yet."

He ran out of the room and was back in a minute. "Dad says she's not back yet, but he'll send her as soon as she gets here. Should I go get Helen or one of the other women?"

"It's the middle of the night, and they've all got babies of their own to tend to. What does that thing look like?"

"It's almost as big as a baby, but it's like a big bag, and it's blue and red and white and it's got the baby's cord hanging from it. Lord Almighty! It's awful!"

I could hardly catch my breath. "It must be my womb. It's fallen out. What should we do?"

James paced back and forth and ran his fingers through his hair, "I guess we should just try to get it back in there."

He worked at it and finally got it back up in me, but after just a few minutes it slid back out.

He started pacing back and forth. "What are we going to do, Maude? It won't stay in there."

I started crying. "I don't know. Try to get back again."

James managed to shove the thing back up inside me again, but it slid right back out.

I knew I had to get hold of myself for his sake. He looked so scared that my heart ached for him. The baby had started to cry. "We'll just have to wait until morning. It's only a few hours until sunup. Help me sit up, James."

He leaned over me, and I put my arms around his neck. He got me to a sitting position.

"Give me the baby, she wants to eat." He picked up the bundle and handed it to me. I uncovered my breast and held the baby to it. She shook her head from side to side and finally latched onto the nipple. She rooted at it and began sucking and grunting.

James beamed. "Look at her go. She's going to be just fine, Maude."

The nursing hurt, and that surprised me, but I was so happy to see how lively the little one was that I ignored the pain, and after a little while it let up. I looked up at James.

I guess he was surprised by the expression on my face. "What's the matter, Maude? She's fine."

"She's wonderful, but if I've lost my womb, we won't have any more babies. We won't have a little boy for you."

"Little boy? I don't care about that. Look at her Maude, she's beautiful, and she's healthy, and she's got everything on her just perfect."

"James, look at my womb again."

He pulled the cover back and looked between my legs. "What am I looking for, Maude?"

"Is it still attached to me?"

"No, it's just lying there by itself."

I couldn't help crying. "Then I guess you might as well go bury it. We can't keep it here. It'll never be any good again."

James nodded, picked up the mass, and wrapped it in one of the cloths. He carried it outside.

I kept nursing the baby, switching it to the other side after a few minutes the way I'd seen Helen do with Faith. She was her father's child, with blond fuzz on her head just the way Faith had when she was born. My heart swelled inside me. I hadn't known it was possible to love a thing so much.

When James returned, I was lying there sound asleep with my baby sleeping on top of my stomach. He told me the next day that the two of us made the most beautiful picture he'd ever seen. He would have liked to have a lot of children, but this one would be enough.

We were still sound asleep in the late morning when the screen door banged open and James's mother came in. "Where's my grandbaby?" she said so loud we both jumped.

I opened my eyes and smiled. I was full of pride for the beautiful baby I'd made. "Right here, isn't she beautiful?"

Mom Connor picked up the child, unwrapped her, and examined her from head to foot.

"A little girl. She's perfect, just perfect. Look at that blond hair, just like her daddy. She looks exactly like he did when he came, only not as big. He was a whelp for sure. Did you have a hard time, Maude? How long did it take you?"

"It started easy in the middle of the afternoon and didn't get real bad until around two this morning, but she came quick after that, around four."

James sat up. "I'd get up, but Mom hasn't seen me in my underpants in years." He just sat there, a big grin on his face.

"Get up boy, get that fire stirred up. We don't want Maude and this baby to freeze to death."

He got his pants off the floor where he'd dropped them and stepped into them, then pulled on his shirt and went to stoke the fire.

Mrs. Connor rocked the baby in her left arm. She reached over and smoothed my hair with her right hand. "The first one's always the hardest, Maude. The next one will come real fast. You've got a good body for it."

I shook my head and started crying. James put his hand on his mother's shoulder. "I'm sorry, mom, there won't be any more babies."

"Why? It couldn't have been that bad. Your daddy said the doctor got here in time. Did he say there wouldn't be another?"

"No, he didn't say that."

"Then what makes you think you won't want more?"

I wiped the tears off my face with the blanket. "Because I lost my womb."

"What? What do you mean, you lost your womb?"

"The doctor left right after she came and James had to wash her off. My womb came out and we couldn't get it to go back. James had to bury it out back."

Mrs. Connor took a minute to figure out what had happened. "Maude, you were there when Helen had her babies. Did you see the whole thing?"

"No, they gave me the babies to clean up as soon as they came out. I took them to the kitchen to wash them."

"Well, no wonder. What came out of you after the baby was a natural thing. It's called afterbirth. You still have your womb. You're going to be just fine. You can have as many babies as you want."

"Really?" Then Mom Connor and I began to giggle. James stared at us. I took my mother-in-law's hand. "You mean, it was supposed to come out like that?"

"Of course, that happens with every baby. You wait until I see that doctor. I'll give him what-for for leaving here without finishing the job." We laughed louder.

"What in the world are you two laughing about?" James asked. "That isn't funny. We thought Maude was dying."

I shook my head, unable to stop giggling. "We kept trying to put it back." I was so relieved, so happy to know that someday I could still give James the son he wanted.

"Lord have mercy!" Mrs. Connor said, practically doubling over with the laughter. The noise woke the baby, who began crying. Mom Connor handed her to me. "Has she nursed yet?"

James was beaming. "She sure has, Mom, watch her."

My embarrassment was overcome by my pride in the fine job I was doing at being a mother. I opened the front of my gown and put my baby to my breast. She fastened herself to it right off and began working for her breakfast.

My baby's grandmother looked at her and smiled. "Look at her. She sure is a lively one. She'll be strong and healthy. You did real good, Maude, real good. What are you going to name her?"

I smiled and gazed down at my daughter. "I don't know. I had three or four names picked out, but I never did make up my mind."

"Well, she sure is a lulu of a baby. She needs a name."

It was James's turn to laugh. "Then that's what her name will be, Lulu."

Mrs. Connor looked at me. "Is that all right with you, Maude?"

The name hadn't been on my list, but if James liked it, it was good enough. "That'll be fine, if that's what her daddy wants."

Mom Connor turned to James. "Fetch me the Bible on my front table, James, and something to write with."

He was gone only a minute and returned carrying the Bible, a pen and a bottle of ink.

It was a beautiful, big Bible, not the kind you carry to church, but the kind that sits on the table in the hallway of a big house, with gold leaf on the edge of the pages and a thick, black leather binding. Mom Connor sat at the table and opened the book in front of her. She took the lid off the ink bottle and dipped the tip of the pen. Then she paused and turned to me. "Will she have two names or just the one?"

I thought it over. "Let's call her Lulu Helen Connor."

Mrs. Connor smiled as she made the entry on the line under James's name. She looked a little sad and said, "I wanted to add more names of my own children to the Connor bible, but none came after James was born. I waited nineteen years to write on this page again."

When she finished, she blew on the ink until it dried and then carried it over to show me. I read the entry. "You sure have a beautiful hand, Sister Connor."

"Don't call me that anymore, Maude, call me Mom, if you're of a mind to."

Tears welled up in my eyes. "Thank you, I'd like that. I'd like that just fine."

Mom Connor turned to James. "You get on to work, boy. We women have things to do here that don't include having a man around. For one thing, my grandbaby needs a proper bath."

James kissed me on the cheek and kissed his daughter on her fuzzy head. "I'll see you tonight, Lulu," he said to the baby, and he left for the store and bragging time.

Chapter 6

I was so happy. Everything was just as I dreamed it would be. I kept my baby clean and dressed in the fancy cotton embroidered dresses just like I'd promised her. I gave her a bath every day and changed her diapers the minute she was wet. Lulu grew fast. She ate like she was starving every time I put her to my breast. The nursing was painful for only the first two days, and my milk came in fast and I had plenty of it. I had to keep towels under my dress to soak up the extra milk. Before long, Lulu was so chubby, I had to make sure I got into the creases when I gave her a bath.

When she was a few months old, I began to carry her to Helen's in the afternoon where we would sit on the porch and sip iced tea while we watched our little ones. Faith was toddling around and getting into everything. Helen had to keep an eye on her every minute to keep her from eating bugs and dirt or falling off the porch. Lulu slept in the crook of my arm or sometimes we brought out the little cradle that Faith had outgrown to the porch so I could have my hands free to sew.

Helen looked at her like she was a little jealous. "She sure is a peaceful baby. I don't remember Faith ever sleeping that much. Doesn't she ever cry?"

"Not much, only when she's hungry. I fed her before I came over here, so she's got her usual afternoon sleep time. She won't wake up now 'til four o'clock. Then I feed her again, and she'll sleep 'til her daddy gets home. You ought to see him. He wakes her up and carries her around talking to her 'til dinnertime. He's going to spoil her rotten."

"That's nice, Maude, that's real nice. She won't be a baby for long. Next thing you know, she'll be tearing up the house."

Helen's girl, Faith, was petite like her mother, and Lulu was sturdily built, like James and I were. I could tell it wouldn't be long before the girls were the same size, even if they were almost two years apart. There we were, Helen and Maude, the sisters who looked so different and whose ways were so opposite, rocking and sipping our iced tea together, watching our babies and taking great satisfaction in our peaceful lives.

For the first time in my life, I didn't envy anyone in the world.

Chapter 7

I turned sixteen in the summer of 1908. Lulu was one year old and learning to walk. James and his father were building onto the cabin to make a room for Lulu to have for her own place. I hadn't conceived again yet, but Mom Connor told me that as long as I was nursing Lulu, I probably wouldn't start another baby. That was all right with me. I wanted more children, just not right away, at least not for another year or two. It wasn't unusual for the other mothers in the town to breast-feed for three years or more to put off getting another baby. Sometimes that worked, and sometimes it didn't.

I was enjoying each part of Lulu's growing up. James loved to watch her and see her learn to crawl, sit up, and then take her first steps. She was the light of our lives. When James was home, he carried her around or played games with her almost the entire time she was awake.

He was away from home some Saturdays, playing baseball against the teams from other towns. I took Lulu to the ball field on the Saturdays they played at home, and she and I cheered him around the bases. Lulu would clap her little hands together and whoop along with me. James would tell Lulu that he loved her the most, me second, and baseball third. I wasn't jealous of that, because as much as I loved James, I loved Lulu more.

Even if she did take after me in the way she was built, she was a beautiful little girl, with a pink complexion, long fingers, and rosy cheeks. Her hair by then formed soft curls around her neck, and her big round eyes were the same bright blue of her father. I was glad that she took after James. I hoped that if any of our children inherited my own looks, it would be the boys. My daddy was a handsome enough man, but I'd known my plain looks all my life. James told me I was beautiful, and it made me feel wonderful, but I knew it wasn't true. I still compared myself to Helen.

Neither one of us had ever received a single piece of mail in all our lives. One Monday afternoon that spring, James came running in the cabin with a letter in his hand. He waved it back and forth in front of me, dancing around. He grabbed my shoulders, hugged me, then held me away from him far enough to kiss me all over my face. "It's from the St. Louis Browns, Maude, they're sending a man down here to see us play. We beat every team we played so far this year, and they want to take a look at us. This could be it for me. If I can hit like I've been doing, maybe they'll sign me up to play professional."

He looked so happy. I set aside my thoughts of him being a real baseball player, for money, and being away from home all the time. "Oh, James, it's your dream come true, isn't it?"

We laughed and danced around the house. "I got to tell Mom and Dad," he said, and ran out of the cabin. I couldn't hold back the tears, both happy and sad. Of course, they would hire him. My James was going to be a real baseball player. He was going to have his dream.

He and the rest of the boys on his team gave up their evenings all week so they could get in practice time. I hadn't seen him so excited since Lulu was born. That Saturday, he fidgeted all morning, pacing back and forth, running up to his parent's house, changing his socks three times. When it was finally time for us to leave for the ball field, he gave me a big hug. "This is going to be the best game you've ever seen. All the boys are going to put out their best, including the team from Union City."

James's parents were waiting for us, and we all trooped out to the ball field together. James carried Lulu, Mr. Connor carried a picnic basket, Mom Connor carried a few hooked rugs for us to sit on, and I carried supplies and toys for the baby. All five of us, including Lulu, were quiet during the walk, we grown-ups were thinking on what the day could bring for James's future, and Lulu, well, she must have picked up on our serious mood.

Mom and Dad Connor and Lulu and I took our seats on the benches built by the field. As the family of a player, we didn't have to bring our own chairs. I sat in the second row with Lulu on my lap, and the Connors sat in front of me. I looked around the crowd, looking for strangers, trying to spot the man from St. Louis. Word of the scout coming had spread to both teams that were playing, and there was a bigger crowd today than I'd ever seen before.

Lulu was always a quiet baby and used to being at the games. The noise when someone made a home run didn't bother her at all. She dozed off right away.

My heart swelled with pride when the hometown team took the field. James was the tallest of them, and his blond hair helped me spot him right off. I thought he was so handsome.

Out in left field, James caught the ball to end the first inning. At his first turn at bat, James got a hit that took him to second base and was taken the rest of the way to home plate by a teammate's home run. We all cheered as loud as we could. Lulu wriggled a little in my arms, but settled back to her nap.

I knew James was nervous by the way he kept picking up a handful of dirt and rubbing it between his palms, but no one else would have been able to tell it. James was playing like he was already on the big-time team. I was so proud of him. By the third inning, his team was already two runs ahead.

James got his second at-bat in the fourth inning. He gave me a wave and a big smile as he stepped up to the plate. He took his position and focused his attention on the pitcher. The first ball was wide and counted as ball one.

The second ball was wide again, but James swung and clipped the outside of it, sending it out to right field, but short of the first base line. It went foul, and it was called as strike one. The third pitch was again wide and called ball two. The catcher stood and walked out to the pitcher and put his arm around his shoulder. They both lowered their heads, talked for a few seconds, and the catcher went back and squatted down behind the plate.

The pitcher took some time before the next pitch. He stared at James and finally wound up, leaning back as far as possible, and threw the ball as hard as he could.

It traveled so fast that it was just a blur to me. James moved his bat back for his hit. The ball connected with his left temple with a loud crack, jerking James off his feet and into the air. His body fell to the ground with a thud and lay face-down. The dust clouds billowed up around him and then faded away into the air. James lay there and didn't move at all. The people held their breath and waited for him to get up, but he didn't. It was so quiet, you could hear the leaves rustling.

His mother was out of her seat and running to him in a split second, his father a heartbeat behind her. I told my body to move, to get to him, but I was frozen. I turned to look into the face of the woman sitting next to me, and the last thing I remembered was the blue sky over my head.

Chapter 8

The faraway sound of a pitiful wail woke me. I didn't open my eyes right away until the horrible memory of what I'd seen rushed back to me. When I looked around, I was in my own bed at home, and Sister Clark was sitting next to me in a chair.

"James?" I asked.

Sister Clark bit her lip. "I'm sorry, Maude, he's gone to be with the Lord."

I sat up and looked for Lulu. "Where's Lulu, is she all right?"

Sister Clark patted my hand. "Mrs. Hopkins was sitting next to you and caught her when you passed out. Helen took her home with her. We didn't think you'd be up to looking after her for a spell."

I tilted my head and listened to the mournful keening coming from the main house. "Mom

Connor?"

"She's in a bad way, Maude, James being her only child and all. The doctor wanted to give her something, but she wouldn't take it. I've never seen anyone grieve so. If she doesn't start leaning on the Lord soon, I'm afraid she'll lose her mind."

I jumped out of the bed. I was wearing a nightgown, and I pulled it off with no modesty at all and dressed in a top and skirt as fast as I could. I pushed my feet into my shoes, called, "Thank you," over my shoulder, and ran out of the house. Sister Clark went after me, expecting me to go to the house, I guess, but instead I ran right out of the yard and down the street. More than anything, I needed to hold my baby in my arms.

I ran up the steps and through Helen's door without knocking. Helen was in the kitchen with both of the girls. She turned when she heard me and was about to say something when I grabbed up Lulu and started to leave. "I'll be at Mrs. Connor's," I cried, slowing up just enough that I didn't upset Lulu.

I was back at the Connor house in only a few minutes. I went in the front door and followed the sound of the crying to the Connors's bedroom. Mom Connor was sitting up in the bed, her face swollen and her long hair mussed around her shoulders. Sister Clark was trying to get her to drink something, but she turned her head this way and that to refuse it.

I walked to her and stuck Lulu in her grandmother's arms and then went and stood against the wall. Mom Connor looked down at the little round face and the blonde hair. Lulu looked up at her with a curious expression. She had never heard such a sound come out of a person, but instead of being scared, she tilted her little head and watched her grandmother's face to see what was happening. Mom Connor stopped the wailing and gulped some air. She stared down at the little girl who looked so much like her father, then she held Lulu's cheek up against her own and began rocking her. The baby reached up and patted her grandmother's cheek and then twined her fingers in Mom Connor's long, soft hair.

Sister Clark held the glass back up to Mom Connor's lips, and she sipped a little of the mixture the doctor had left. I left Lulu with her grandmother and went back to my cabin alone. Sister Clark sat with the two of them until they'd both fallen asleep. Then she came to check on me.

She found me rocking on the cabin porch, wearing one of James's shirts on top of my dress. It was a heavy, red wool plaid that he wore on chilly mornings. I guess I was staring off in the distance and didn't notice the preacher's wife until she spoke to me. "You knew just what she needed, didn't you, Maude? She's going to be all right now. The two of them are sleeping. How are you doing?"

"I don't even know. It's like this isn't real, like it never happened. He was here just this morning. The cabin is still full of him being here. I had to fuss at him to get him to eat his breakfast because I didn't want him to try to play ball on an empty stomach. Now he's gone. I've been sitting here in this shirt with the smell of him still in it. He's never going to run up the walk at the end of his day, never going to play with Lulu like he always did, never going to---," my voice failed me and I had to struggle to catch my breath, then I gasped so deep my whole body shook. "I'm never going to see him again. You don't know what he was to me. Nobody knows."

"I got an idea, Maude. I know how he loved you."

"I don't know why he did. I'm not pretty, no matter what he said about it. He could have had any girl in town. Why did he pick me?"

"He saw into your heart, Maude. He knew what was real when he saw it."

I stopped rocking and sat up. "Where is he?"

"He's at the undertaker's in Union city. They'll bring him to the house when he's ready. It ought to be a few hours."

Sister Clark patted my hand. "I'm going back up to the house to sit with his mother. I'll send someone down for you when it's time."

I nodded a little. "Thank you," then I put my arms around Sister Clark and hugged her before I went in the cabin.

Helen, Tommy, and Faith came and walked back to the house with me. I was calm.

In the parlor, James was lying in a plain pine box with a satin lining, looking for all the world like he'd just fallen asleep. I looked down at him for a while, but it was still like it wasn't real, and I'd wake up any minute, and he'd be lying next to me and tell me it was only a bad dream.

Looking at my young husband in his coffin, I began to feel like I was going to pass out. When I sat next to Dad Connor, he looked at me with relief on his face. I think he was already depending on me to hold them all together. I gave him a small smile, linked my arm through his, and made a nod that told him his confidence was in the right person. In a minute or two, my head stopped spinning, and I went to the bedroom to wake James's mother.

Mom Connor was sleeping with Lulu nestled in the crook of her arm, her curls on her grandmother's shoulder. I watched them for a while before I reached out and touched Mom Connor's hand. "He's ready, Mom, it's time to get up."

Mom Connor opened her eyes, but didn't move. She stared hard into my face. "All right," she said at last.

"Do you need any help getting dressed?"

"No, I can do it."

I picked up Lulu and left. When I got back to the parlor, the chairs from the dining room and the kitchen had been set up in rows. Helen and Tommy sat in the second row. Holding Lulu in my arms, I sat in front of them. Lulu stirred and woke. She started crying. Helen handed Faith to Tommy and took Lulu out of my lap. "I'll take her to the cabin and feed her something and change her."

Mom and Dad Connor sat next to me. The inside door was open, and no one had to knock. The friends and neighbors opened the screen door and came on in. For the next few hours, just about everyone in town came and went. Some paid their respects in only a minute or two, and some sat and talked for a while. The boys from James's team all came by, and every one of them cried like the world was coming to an end. For me, the world had already ended. Helen came back with Lulu, and I held her for a while, but finally Helen and Tommy took the two girls home with them.

We sat up for the watch as long as we could, but finally, we went to bed.

In the morning, the body was moved to the church, and the preacher held the same service for James that he'd held for my mom and dad and Helen's little Henry eight years earlier. It was the same one he preached for every funeral. I recited it in my mind as he spoke it, and I took comfort in knowing what he was going to say and the promises from God. James had accepted the gift of God's salvation several years before, and I knew I'd see him again. It made the whole thing tolerable, to know that.

After the preaching, singing, and prayers, we walked behind the undertaker's wagon to the graveyard. Mom Connor was calm, and her face showed enough steel to get her through the day. I'd been back to the cemetery only a few times over the years since my parents' burial. When we got there, I was surprised by how sharp the memories were in my mind. I had bad dreams about the fire that killed them all my life, but not a one since Lulu was born.

Our family, friends, and fellow church members clustered around the hole that had been dug, the preacher said a few more words, we all dropped in our handful of dirt, and then we prayed and left. As we walked away, I could hear the sound of the dirt thumping against the box as the men shoveled it into the hole. The thud-thud of the work followed me all the way down the path.

Neighbors brought food, and the house was full of people for hours. The women of the church made a fuss over us, and I finally made a show of eating something, pushing food around on a plate. I realized that James's mother was doing the same thing. Finally, everyone was gone. Helen and Tommy were the last to leave. Helen hugged me. "I'll be by tomorrow, hear?"

I watched her back as she went out the door and then Mom Connor and I exchanged looks. I could see my reflection in the mirror that hung by the door, and both of us had dark circles under our eyes. Our faces were lined with grief, and we were both worn out. I gave her a hug. "I'm going back to the cabin unless you need me to do anything for you."

"I guess we're all right, Maude. The Lord will take care of us. We can face what we got to face. We both need some sleep. You go take care of that baby, and we'll talk tomorrow."

I carried Lulu back to the cabin and got her ready for bed. Once she was sleeping, I took James's shirt back off the hook where he always hung it. I held it up against my face and breathed deep. I always said he smelled better than any man I'd ever been around. My daddy smelled of leather and hay and the horses. James smelled of the supply store, oats, alfalfa, soap and grass.

I held the shirt to my face for a few minutes, then put it on over my dress again and went back out to the porch. I sat in the rocker and looked up at the sky. It was getting dark. The moon was out early, and I could see it on the tree line to my right, like it was stuck on the top of a pine. The last rays of the setting sun filtered through the tops of the trees on my left and made a pattern of shadows on the yard. It was such a pretty night, like the nights when James and I used to sit out and talk until time to go to bed.

I sat there for a long time, rocking now and then, sitting still some, crying at last. I had no idea what would become of me and my little girl. I'd already been an orphan, a wife, and a mother. Now I was a widow. I was only three months past my sixteenth birthday.

Chapter 9

In 1908, there weren't many things a young widow with a toddler could do to make money and support herself. I didn't want to be a burden to James's mom and dad or to Helen and Tommy either.

In my sixteenth year, I knew enough to know the whole world was changing. I'd heard of automobiles but never seen one. People were talking about a man named Edison who'd invented an electric light that was being used in the big cities, but not one house in our town had electricity. Homes like Helen's, with a pump from the well that brought water right into the house, were the latest thing in being modern and up to date.

The Connors treated me like their own daughter, and they just showered their love on Lulu. They told me I could stay in the cabin forever if I wanted, and they said they prayed that we would. They even gave me spending money when they could, but the year after James died was a hard one, and a lot of the farmers couldn't pay their bill for the things they bought at the store.

Dad Connor's health began to fail, and he had to take on a hired man to replace what work James had done. It made for a tight budget. I knew they weren't having an easy time of it, and I didn't have the heart to ask them for more money. In my brother-in-law's store, he kept a book with what everyone spent and they paid him at the end of the month. I know he put down half of what he should for what I bought. We didn't talk about it, but I was grateful.

One day after church, Sister Clark was telling me how adorable Lulu was and going on how much she'd grown. "You made her a little dress just like your blue calico, Maude. You should have worn them at the same time, it would be just precious."

"We can't do that, Sister Clark. I made that up out of my old dress. She's growing so much I have to make her new things every time I turn around."

"Well, you certainly have a beautiful hand with a needle. Look at that smocking on the front and the little flowers you embroidered. It's as fine as any dress you could buy in St. Louis."

Sister Clark took a closer look at the dress I wore. The fabric was getting thin at the elbows and shoulders. It looked ready to come apart any minute.

"You're having a hard time of it, aren't you, Maude?"

"We make do. Mom and Dad Connor take care of us the best they can."

"If I could get you some work sewing, would you be interested?"

I had to hold back how excited I got when she talked about work, but couldn't think of how that would happen. "Of course I would, but all the women here can sew their own clothes. They don't need me to do it for them. Even if they did, I don't think they could pay me for it. It's been a hard year for everyone."

"I don't mean here. I have friends up in Union City. My sister, Dora, lives there. Some of them are doing very well. You know, I go up there to visit Dora about once a month. Give me the best thing you've made, and I'll show it to some of the ladies who hire out that kind of work."

I went through every piece of my own and Lulu's clothing. I finally decided on the nightgown I'd made for my wedding night. I'd worn it only that one time, then washed it and put it away for the next special occasion.

James and I had talked about taking a trip someday when we had more money, and I planned to wear it again when we went. We thought we might even stay in a hotel if we could afford it. When he signed up to be a professional ball player, he'd said, we would have money to burn.

I ran my fingers over the tiny, even stitches and the little embroidered flowers. It was almost like brand-new. I pressed the nightgown and wrapped it in the white paper I saved from a package of fabric that

Helen gave me. I took it down to the parsonage and handed it over to Sister Clark.

She said, "I'll show this to the ladies and see if we can get some work for you, Maude."

A few days later, Sister Clark was standing on my front step with the good news. She had an order from one of her friends. She wanted me to make the gown exactly. She'd sent enough money to buy the fabric and thread, and I would have two dollars left over to keep for myself.

After that, I got a lot of work as a seamstress. For the next few years, I made dresses and fancy underwear for the ladies. Brother and Sister Clark drove me and Lulu up to Union City in their buggy so I could measure the women, and they could get to know me. It was the first time in my life that I had set foot outside of my little town. Union City was a hundred times bigger. A lot of the buildings had three or four stories, and there were all kinds of automobiles.

The ladies at the Union City church were all very kind, making a fuss over Lulu and taking turns holding her while I measured them in the preacher's study.

One day, one of them asked me if I would be interested in doing the wash for her delicate clothing. She gave me a pillowcase full of her undies, and I brought them home with me. I washed, pressed, and folded them neatly. I bought a roll of white paper and string from the store and wrapped them. Then I gave the bundle to Sister Clark, who delivered it to her friend. She sent back another bundle that included her fine table and bed linens to be done up along with a new bundle of lacy garments.

Pretty soon, I had enough coming in from my sewing and laundry that I didn't have to take money from the Connors. After I tucked Lulu into bed at night, I knelt on the little rag rug by my bed and said my prayers, thanking God for my family, my home and my work, and asking forgiveness for the times that I'd failed as a Christian.

Dad Connor never really recovered from losing James. He spent less and less time at the store and let his hired hand run it. He went for days without saying more than a few words to Mom Connor. She told me that losing James had taken the heart right out of him, and the only time she saw his eyes light up was when I brought Lulu up to the house.

Lulu liked to pull a book off the bottom shelf and carry it to him. He'd put her on his knee and read to her from the same storybooks he'd read to James. She listened close, following his finger as it moved across the pages, making the animal noises when he told her about a chicken or a cow. She never got tired of hearing the same stories over and over.

By the time she was three, she'd memorized most of the words and could read them along with him. It was proof to her grandfather that she was the smartest little girl ever, and Mom Connor and I agreed. She told me that when I took Lulu back to the cabin, Dad would fall right back into his gloomy mood.

He caught the flu in the winter of '09 and didn't fight to get well. The whole family was sick with it. I fussed over Lulu and waited on Mom and Dad Connor hand and foot until I came down with it myself, and then Mom Connor nursed me in return. We all had a fever and were coughing and aching for a few days. The doctor couldn't help much. "Drink lots of water and stay in bed," he said. "Everyone in town has it."

Dad Connor's fever never went down. He mumbled as he tossed around in his bed, with me changing his sweat-soaked sheets twice a day. Mom Connor was in her own sick bed in the other room. Somehow, I didn't get sick with it, but Lulu did. I worried something awful, but in only a few days, she was back on her feet and getting into everything.

The doctor put a poultice on Dad Connor's back, but it didn't help. One night, he went to sleep and didn't wake up. He was only fifty years old.

After that, we women grew even closer than before. Mom Connor wanted me and Lulu to move up to the house, but I knew I would be happier in the cabin I'd shared with James.

Chapter 10

A few of the single men in town started paying attention to me, but I wasn't interested. The thought of another man touching me in the way James touched me made me shiver. I didn't see how I could ever share that part of myself with anyone else.

The years passed. In 1915, Lulu was ten, and I was twenty-four. My life fell into a nice routine. I walked Lulu to school every day, even though she didn't want me to, cleaned my cabin every morning, did my laundry and sewing, and then did the housework that Mom Connor had grown too weak to do for herself.

In the afternoon, I fixed dinner at the main house. Every evening, Lulu and I ate there. On Sundays, we went to church. Mom Connor couldn't walk the distance anymore, so Helen and Tommy picked us up in their buggy, and we all rode together. Helen's family sat in the front seat and mine in the back. As Faith and Lulu grew, the buggy became more and more crowded.

John Stuart, that I'd known all my life, was one of the men who failed in his attempts to court me. I liked him well enough, I guess, but wasn't interested in him the way he was in me.

He went to visit some of his family in Kennett, Missouri, a town across the Mississippi River. He was gone longer than expected, but he sent a letter that he was fine, and had been held back by an "unexpected turn of events."

After being gone an extra three weeks, he came back with a wife. I met her at church the next Sunday. She was even taller than I was, with jet black hair and warm brown eyes. She had a pleasant face and a friendly smile. When John introduced her to me he grinned and said, "Maude, this is Elizabeth Foley Stuart, but she'd like it if we all called her Bessie. Bessie, this is Maude Connor that I told you about. If she'd of had me, you'd still be single."

I was afraid Bessie wouldn't take kindly to me and would be jealous, but Bessie grabbed my hand and held it in both of hers. "We'll be great friends, won't we, Maude?"

That's the way it turned out. Bessie became part of the circle of females that made up my life, Mom Connor, Helen, Lulu and Faith. We all sat in the big Connor kitchen once a week, stitching a quilt that was stretched out tight on a big wooden rack, talking and drinking iced tea.

Bessie brought something new to the group, a lot of laughter. Her sense of humor was contagious, and soon, our usual seriousness was lit up by her joking and foolishness. The children rolled on the floor laughing at her while she played with them and acted silly. The sound of Faith and Lulu laughing was like music.

I was content. I didn't want for anything, and except for Mom Connor getting older, my loved ones were well. It was only that, in the night, when I'd gone to bed, I still missed James, missed the warmth of his body lying next to me, missed the smell of him, and missed his touch.

Bessie became my best friend outside of Helen. One Sunday in late spring, Bessie and her husband John brought a visitor to church, a nice looking, tall, slim man. Helen and Tommy had barely stopped their buggy before Bessie led him over to me, tugging his hand. "Maude, this is my brother George Foley. He's here to visit for a week."

He was handsome, and you could tell right off he was related to Bessie. He had the same warm brown eyes. He took off his hat to show the same jet-black hair. He grinned at me. "Pleased to meet you, Maude."

Bessie introduced him to the rest of the family, and he greeted them each in turn without taking his eyes off me. I could feel my face turning red. We all chatted outside the church door for a few minutes before we went in for the service. Bessie and her husband sat in the row across from me and my family. During the preaching, I looked over at George a few times. He was always looking right at me and smiled when he caught my eye. I felt myself blush again.

After the service, he came over to our buggy, took off his hat, and said, "I'd like to come calling on you some time, Maude, if that's all right."

Helen held back a giggle. I looked at Bessie for help, but Bessie was grinning from ear to ear.

"I-I-I- guess so," I said in a voice so low, I'm sure he could barely hear me.

Early the next afternoon, I was hanging clothes in the side yard when I saw George Foley drive up to the Connor house in the Stuart's buggy, but it wasn't the Stuart horse pulling it. He didn't see me in the yard, and he went up the steps and knocked on the door at the big house. It was quite a while before Mrs. Connor answered.

I heard her say, "Sorry it took so long for me to get to the door, but my arthritis is getting the better of me these days."

"I'm here to see Maude," he said.

"She lives around back."

It was a warm day, and my door was propped open. I hurried inside before he saw me. He tapped on the frame. I'd been expecting him, but I had mixed feelings about the visit. I came out to the front porch.

He took off his hat. "I brought a buggy, Maude. It's such a pretty day, I thought maybe you'd like to go for a ride."

I said, "I have to wait for Lulu to get back from school. Let's just sit here and talk a spell. I'll get us some tea."

"That would be real nice, Maude." He led his horse over to the water trough and let it drink. He stood next to it and patted its neck. The horse nickered and rubbed its nose against George's arm. I liked the way he treated his horse. I disapproved of the rough ways some men had with their animals.

He came back up the steps and sat in the rocker that had been James's favorite place to spend warm evenings. I almost asked him to move to the other chair, but thought better of it. I nodded toward his horse. "That's a beautiful animal, George," I said.

"His name is Pawnee. He's been in my family for sixty years."

I'd never heard of a horse older than thirty. "Sixty years? How is that possible?"

He laughed. "What I mean is, his bloodline. This one is only four years old. My grandfather was in the cavalry and rode Pawnee's great-great-grandfather into battle in the Civil War."

Tennessee and Missouri had been split, brother–against-brother, during the terrible war. I asked, "Which side did he fight on, George?"

"Why, he fought for the North, of course."

"I was just wondering." I fetched two glasses of cool tea, and we sat there and talked for over an hour. I told him a little about my childhood and my marriage.

He told me a little about himself. "I live in Kennett, Missouri, Maude. I'm the sheriff there. I used to be a deputy, but when Sheriff LeBeck retired a few years ago, they elected me to the job."

"We don't have a sheriff here. The mayor fills in. It's such a small town, we never needed one. I don't know what they would do if anything really bad happened. I guess they could call the marshal from over at Union City. Is that dangerous, being the sheriff there?"

"Not really. The most we have is a fight at the saloon sometimes. I generally go over if they call me and talk to the boys and they give it up. Sometimes I have to throw one in jail until he sobers up. We never had any real trouble."

"What would you do if that happened?"

He pushed out his lower lip and rubbed his chin. "I don't know. I guess I'd have to think up something."

"We don't have a saloon here. I guess that's why we don't need a sheriff."

"What does a man do if he wants a drink?"

"I've heard that some of the farmers have stills. I've never seen one, but I know for a fact that there's more than one man in town who finds liquor when he wants it. Almost all of us who live here go to the Baptist or the Holiness church. Drinking isn't very popular in these parts."

I thought about the night Lulu was born and the smell of whiskey on the doctor's breath, but I didn't mention it.

"Well, I like a drink every now and then myself. I suppose it's just as well I live in Kennett."

That didn't sit well with me, but I didn't say anything more about it. "How big a town is Kennett?"

"We got a real nice place there. Got a bank and a

hotel, new schoolhouse. It's a good place to live."

"I like it here. It's what I'm used to, I guess."

When Lulu came up the walk, George stood to greet her. "Good afternoon, Lulu. I'm George Foley, Bessie's brother."

She looked up at him with a frown. "I remember you."

I was a little embarrassed. "Be polite, Lulu."

Lulu stood there, waiting for the grown-ups to say something. When no one spoke, she asked me, "Is it all right if I go visit Gramma?"

I nodded. "Go ahead."

Lulu wheeled around and ran up to the house. I said, "I'm sorry, George, she's a little shy."

"That's all right, Maude. She'll get to like me after a while. Most folks do."

I stood. "It's been a nice visit, George. Say hello to Bessie for me when you get home."

He stood and reached out and took my hand and kept hold of it. I wanted to pull it away from him, but I just stood there. He smiled at me. "I'd like to come visit again tomorrow, Maude, if that's all right."

I wasn't very impressed with him, but was too polite to refuse. "I guess so, I'll be here."

After he left, I went up to the house to talk it over with Mom Connor. "He wants to come back tomorrow, but I don't really like him all that much, Mom. What should I do?"

"Give him a chance, Maude. You haven't found anyone here in town who pleases you, not that there's much to pick from. Most of the unmarried men here are two, three times as old as you. You can't be a widow forever. You're only a girl. You ought to have a life of your own.'

"I'm satisfied with what I have, Mom. Why do I need a man?"

"I'm getting old. I won't always be here. What are you going to do when I'm gone?"

I'd never thought about such a thing, and it scared me. I'd come to think of my mother-in-law as a permanent part of my life. "You're fine. It's going to be a long time before you get old."

"No, it isn't, Maude. It's not only my arthritis anymore. Doc Wilson says my heart is getting weak. My sister over in Nashville has been after me to come live with her. She lost her husband last year. Her children are all married and moved away. You and I, both of us, need to think about the future."

I wanted to cry. "I'll take care of you, you know that. I'll move up here to the house like you asked me before."

"That wouldn't be fair to you. You're young. You and Lulu deserve more than nursing an old woman. It could be years before I die. By then, you'll have lost your chance to find someone."

I tried to think of other arguments, but there weren't any. After Lulu was asleep, I spent the rest of the evening sitting on the porch and staring at a sky that was looking the same way I was feeling. There wasn't a star to be seen.

The next afternoon, George showed up again. I decided I would give him another chance to court me, but I still had my doubts. I don't know what I was thinking, but this time I agreed to go for a buggy ride. He drove me out over the rolling Tennessee hills for several miles. It was a beautiful day, and we talked about everyday matters like the weather and Lulu's school work. He got me back to the cabin in time to meet Lulu coming home.

My ten-year-old girl knitted her eyebrows together and ducked her chin down into her chest. She looked at him with a sour face and ran into the cabin without even saying hello.

That embarrassed me, and George saw the look on my face. "Don't worry about Lulu, Maude. She'll warm up to me. I mean, if we see more of one another. Can I come by tomorrow?"

I was still looking after Lulu. It wasn't like her to be rude like that. "I don't know, George. I'll have to think about it."

He put his hat on. "Well, I'll stop by, and if you got other things to do, you can tell me, and I'll be on my way."

"All right, George."

I went inside and hugged Lulu to me and kissed the top of her head. "You don't think much of Mr. Foley, do you, Baby?"

"He isn't going to stay here. He's going to go back to Missouri where he lives. If you married him, I'd have to leave all my friends. Tell him he can't come here anymore."

I thought it over. "Maybe you're right. I'll tell him tomorrow that it would be best if he stopped coming here."

Lulu hugged me and craned her neck to kiss me on the cheek. "I'm going to see Gramma. Holler if you want me."

"All right, Baby."

I made up my mind I would tell George that I didn't want to spend any more time with him. I went up to the house. Lulu and Mom Connor and I began fixing dinner. We were a family already, the three women of the house, and didn't need a man to make us whole.

Mom Connor sat in a chair stringing the green beans that Lulu brought in from the garden. The sound of the snap-snap as she broke off the ends of each one was so regular it was almost music. Lulu peeled potatoes while I breaded the chicken. Lulu tilted her head and smiled a little. "Mommy is going to tell Mr. Foley that he shouldn't come around here anymore," she said with satisfaction.

Mom Connor looked from Lulu to me, her eyes wide with surprise. "What do you mean, child? Your Mom can't do that."

"She can if she wants to."

Mom Connor dropped the bean she was stripping back in the bowl. She lifted the bowl off her lap and plopped it down on the table so hard it almost broke. Both Lulu and I jumped, startled by the bang of glass against wood. Mom Connor shook her head. "You can't do that, Maude. You have to marry him now."

I was dumbfounded. "What on earth are you talking about? I hardly know him."

"You went out in that buggy alone with him, clear out of town. Half the women in the church saw you. They been planning the wedding party all day."

"Wedding party? But he hasn't even asked me to marry him. What if he doesn't want me?"

"He wants you. Just look at him. He gets all mushy-faced when he's about you. If he hasn't asked you yet, he's going to before he leaves."

Lulu jumped up. "No! We're not going to marry him and go live in another town in another state with people we don't even know."

Mom Connor frowned at her granddaughter. "Sit yourself down and be quiet, young lady. You don't know anything about this. This is grown-up business here. Your Mom went out in a buggy with a man and out of town, and was gone for two hours. It doesn't matter if she never so much as touched his hand. She's *got* to marry him now. If she doesn't, she'll be put out of the church, and no decent woman in this town will speak to her."

Lulu's eyes popped open, and she plunked back down in her chair.

I began pacing the room. My hands covered with the flour from the breading smeared the front of my skirt. "I don't want to marry him."

"I'm sorry, Maude, but you have to, and you know it's true. There's no way you can live here if you don't. I hate to see you leave as much as you hate to go. Maybe you can talk him into staying here with you. You can keep the property. Live in the house and rent out the cabin or do it the other way around if you want.

I'm leaving all this to Lulu anyway. I already told the preacher where my will is and what's in it. I'll put in there that she won't get it if you leave town. Maybe that will make him want to be here."

Lulu felt better, thinking she wouldn't have to move away from her friends, and relaxed a little. I could feel her watching me for my reaction.

I knew Mom Connor was right. The town was too small for me to outlive the gossip. If George asked me, I'd have to marry him. If he didn't ask me---? "Oh, my God, Mom, what if he doesn't ask me? What am I going to do then?"

"If he hasn't asked you by tomorrow night, I'll pay a visit to Bessie. She'll make him see what he has to do. If he doesn't, she won't be able to live here either. All the women will blame her for bringing him here."

I couldn't say anything. I just stood there with my head down, staring at the planks in the floor as if I were looking for an answer to the mess I'd gotten myself into.

When George drove up the next day, I managed to smile. I refused his offer of another ride and invited him to sit a spell. I talked with him about things that didn't matter, and all that time, what really was important was running through my mind. I pretended to pay attention, but inside I wanted to scream. I forced myself to sit on the porch with him and sip tea and chat as if nothing at all hung on what he had to say. The only words I needed to hear were the ones that concerned getting married, and even if he said them, I would hate to hear them. I tried to ease my mind. I told myself he was very handsome, that the other women would envy me his tall, slim build and his cheerful manner. They would think I was crazy if I didn't want to marry him.

As it got close to time for Lulu to get home, he hadn't even talked a bit about the future. I began to panic. He stood and made polite references to leaving. I stood, too. George reached out and took my hand and clasped it in both of his. Other than taking my elbow to help me into the buggy, it was just the second time he'd ever touched me. I braced myself, waiting for the proposal. "Well, I'll be leaving tomorrow. I sure have enjoyed knowing you, Maude. If I ever get back over this way, I hope I have your permission to call again."

I just nodded a little and pulled my hand away from his. He smiled that warm smile of his and turned to go. I watched his back as he walked away and climbed up in the buggy. I stood there without moving a muscle. Mom Connor, who'd been leaning against her back door listening for the sound of the buggy driving off, popped out the door. She met me on the pathway and gave me a questioning look. I looked up at her with the saddest eyes she could have ever seen and just shook my head. Mom Connor gasped. She asked me to go over every word that was said, and I told her there wasn't anything to be gone over but talk about the weather and such.

Mom Connor pinched her lips together. "I'm not one to interfere, and you know that, but I have to do something about an intolerable situation." She turned around with more energy than I'd seen in her for years, went back in the house, and let the door slam behind her. She loved me too dearly to see me hurt, even if I had done something wrong when I should have known better.

But how could I have known? My mother would have taught me the customs of courting a man if she'd lived, but she didn't live. I never really had the opportunity to be courted by anyone. Our families had arranged my marriage to James before I was old enough to think seriously about what it meant.

After about an hour, she came back and found me in the yard, hanging up clothes. She said, "Sit down, Maude. Let me tell you what I saw." We went up on my porch and sat down.

"I marched right over to Bessie's as fast as these old knees would let me. The front door was propped open, and I could see Bessie moving about in the kitchen. I didn't knock on the screen door, but called out loud enough for her to hear me, 'Bessie, you and me got to have a woman-to-woman talk.'"

I sucked in a breath. "Did the neighbors hear you?"

"No neighbors around that I could see. Bessie smiled at me that way she has that makes you feel happy, wiped her hands on her apron, and hugged me. 'Come on in,' she said. 'We'll sit a spell and have something to drink. We can talk about the wedding.'"

"I was flabbergasted she didn't know. I told her, 'I'm not in a sitting frame of mind, and there doesn't seem to be any wedding coming up. Is George back here yet?'"

"She said, "I heard him ride up. He'll be out in the barn. I guess he's putting the horse away." She caught the way I was upset and asked me, "Did Maude turn him down?"

"I told her he left without asking, so you couldn't have turned him down if you wanted. Bessie's face turned white. She'd talked to the other women and knew what would happen if her brother left town without marrying you. She said, 'He didn't even ask her?'

"Not a word about it. Matter-of-fact, he told her pretty-as-you-please that he was leaving tomorrow and asked if he could call again should he ever get back here.

"You should have seen her face! She looked like she was about to bring down the wrath of God on George's head. I almost felt sorry for him. Her face turned beet-red, and she pressed her lips together, put her hands on her hips, and nodded her head up and down while she glared out in the direction of the barn. She said, 'Don't you worry about it, Sister Connor, George isn't leaving tomorrow. He'll be back over to see Maude in the morning.'

Mom Connor patted my hand. She told me, "You rest easy, girl. Bessie and I will see to it that this turns out the right way."

I was surprised by the mean look on Mom's face, like one of those tigers in picture books, and at the same time it made me feel better. If Mom said it would be all right, it would be all right.

Chapter 11

A few years later, George told me what happened that night. I thought part of it was funny, and part of it was sad how Bessie made him marry me.

As best I can remember it, this is what he said:

"When I came in the house that night, I was whistling my favorite song, all relaxed. Bessie put dinner on the table while John dried his hands on a towel, ignorant of what'd been going on around him.

"I told John, 'I'm going to miss seeing the two of you when I leave tomorrow. It's been a real nice visit.'

"John's mouth was open and his lips were making an answer he never got to say. Bessie pulled back her right arm and landed a tight-fisted punch on my face. She was no little flower, and it knocked me back against the wall. I managed to stay on my feet and leaned there, rubbing my chin.

"John grabbed Bessie's arm and pulled her away. He said, 'Lord Almighty, Bessie, what're you doing?'

"Bessie ignored him. She kept her eyes on me. She jerked free, ran over to me and began punching my shoulder and trying to land another one on my jaw. I held up my hands to push away her fists aimed at my face.

"I was able to defend myself without hitting back. I didn't know at the time what I did that made her so mad, but since I grew up with her temper, I wasn't the least bit surprised. John ran over and grabbed her in a bear hug and lifted her off the floor so she couldn't break free. He said, 'Stop it, Bessie, what in the world has got into you?'

"Bessie kept staring holes through me. She shouted, 'Maude Connor was my best friend from the day I got to this town, and if you think you're going to disgrace her by taking her out on a buggy ride with no chaperone and then leaving her here without marrying her, you got another think coming. I'll cut your throat in your sleep before I'll let that happen, even if I have to come all the way to Kennett, Missouri to find you.'

"I knew very well she meant it. I held up both hands in front of me. 'All right, Bessie, all right.'

"Bessie was on fire. 'You get your pitiful self over there in the morning and ask that girl to be your wife.' She jerked one arm free from John's grip and pointed her finger at me, wagging it so close to my nose it almost touched me. 'Or else.'

"I nodded and smiled to myself as if I found my sister's meanness to be funny, but I didn't argue with her. It doesn't do to cross her when she's like that. Bessie glared at me awhile and, satisfied I'd follow her orders, sat at her place at the table and held out her hands on each side, calm as anything. 'Now, let's sit down and give thanks for this meal."

"John ate with his face down, like he was afraid to speak. After we were through, he and I went outside for a smoke while Bessie cleaned up the kitchen.

"John cleared his throat, like he was halfway afraid to bring up the subject. 'George, are you really going to marry Maude?"

"I have to. You heard what Bessie said."

"Well, yes, but you're not afraid of Bessie, are you, George? She loves you. She wouldn't really hurt you. She couldn't anyway. She's only a woman."

"I looked at John for a minute and asked, 'You two never had a bad fight?'

He shrugged. "We argue about this and that, just like any married folk do."

"Well, if you ever see that look on her face she had tonight, don't argue, just do what she says."

"But, like I said, she's only a woman, and either one of us could knock her down without even working hard at it."

"I don't believe in a man hitting a woman, no matter what she does, and besides, she's not a regular woman, John. There are times she's going to be just like our mother. You'll live happier if you know when that is."

John laughed at me. "Come on, how bad could they be?"

"Bad enough that I'm going to saddle up in the morning and ask Maude to marry me. I been thinking about it anyway. I like her. She's got a way about her."

"Bessie behaves just like your mother, you say?"

"Almost, but not as mean."

"How did your father put up with it? Didn't he ever do anything to stop her? I don't think I would tolerate it if she hit me like she did you."

"Dad was afraid of her, just like I am."

"Right up until he passed away?"

"I guess so."

"Guess so?"

"We don't know for sure what become of him. One day, about ten years ago, he was there in the evening when we went to bed, and the next day he was gone."

"I'm not surprised. He probably ran off so he wouldn't have to live with her anymore."

"Maybe so, but he didn't take any of his clothes, and he didn't take his horse."

After telling me this, George threw back his head and laughed. He said, "We both know for a fact, John never looked at Bessie in the same way again. As long as they lived together, they got along just fine."

Chapter 12

The next day, it was around nine in the morning when George rode up. When I saw him, I felt like one of the four horsemen of the apocalypse had come to call. He tied Pawnee to the post and knocked on the cabin door. I came out to meet him, with no smile and nothing to say.

He said it right out. "Maude, I want you to be my wife."

I felt like I was falling in a deep pit and there wasn't one thing I could do to stop it. I looked away and nodded. He leaned over and kissed me on my cheek. I didn't tilt it up to make it easier for him. He said, "I know how you like your church, so if we can get the preacher to say the vows tomorrow morning, I'd like to get an early start home. I'm late for my job already, or I'd stay a few days longer. John brought my wagon here when he came home with Bessie, so we can take it back to Missouri and carry what you want with us."

I looked up at him. "I was wondering if you would think about staying here to live, George. You'd be close to Bessie, and Lulu wouldn't have to leave her friends. Mom Connor said we could stay in the cabin as long as we wanted."

"That's right nice of her, Maude, but I got a good job at home. I got a house to take care of, and livestock, and I have to see after my mother."

It hurt my heart to hear that, but what could I say? I nodded. "I'll talk to the preacher about tomorrow. I have a lot to do today. I'll meet you at the church in the morning. Ten o'clock ought to be all right."

I stood for a minute on the porch after he left. When I turned around, Lulu was standing inside the door, tears streaming down her face. I could feel my heart breaking for both of us. I sat on the rocker and pulled Lulu on my lap. I held and rocked her for a long time. From time to time, I cried some, too.

I went to the parsonage and told Sister and Brother Clark and he said he could perform the ceremony the next morning. I cried on my way home. Having the time set made it real to me. I went back to my cabin to get ready to move to Missouri. While we packed, Lulu sobbed off and on the whole afternoon. We both wiped away tears as we folded our things.

I looked over my few dresses, thinking about what I should wear for my wedding the next day. I ran my fingertips over the dress with the embroidered white flowers that I made for my wedding to James and laid it out on the bed. There was no way I could bring myself to wear that. It would be like committing adultery on James.

I took James's plaid shirt I'd worn the day he died. I hadn't washed it since. I held it up to my face and breathed in deep, hoping to catch a trace of his scent, but it had faded away. Then I folded it up inside the wedding dress and packed them in the cedar chest Tommy made me. They were the only parts left of the dream James and I had lived. I finally chose an everyday blue calico dress that I'd worn many times for my second wedding.

I told Mom Connor about the wedding, and I suppose Lulu told her friends. The Clarks might have mentioned it to someone, and maybe Bessie said something to a neighbor. The next day, there wasn't an empty pew in the Holiness Church when the preacher gave George and me our vows. The gossipy women of the town came early and sat right down front to make sure George did the right thing. Even some of the Baptists came to see.

The preacher used the opportunity to preach to all the married couples in the church without the usual sermon, just by reading the Bible. I'd taken him aside and asked him to leave out the passage from Ruth that I'd memorized for my wedding to James, so he quoted from Ephesians 5, 22-33, about how husbands and wives are supposed to act toward one another.

I did agree to love, honor and obey. George promised the usual. I took my vows in my church in front of God and we were man and wife. It was done and done, no going back, ever. As we left the church, the preacher handed me an envelope. "Here are the letters of membership for you and Lulu to give to your new church. We're going to miss you, Maude."

We had a quick meal with Mom Connor and Helen's family at Mom's house, and George loaded Lulu's and my clothes and personal things on the wagon. There wasn't much room for anything else. George told me his house was completely furnished, so I left behind all the furniture except the little cradle James made for Lulu. I expected I might need it again. I hoped George would be the tender lover James had been.

After hugs all around and promises from Helen and Bessie that Kennett was only a few miles away from home and they would visit back and forth every chance they got, George helped Lulu and me up on the wagon seat. Mom Connor handed us a picnic basket she'd filled for our dinner.

As we drove away, I looked back and gave a little wave to my family. All the girls and women cried. I wrapped my arm around Lulu's shoulders and patted her back. Lulu's tears let up a little, and after a few hours on the road, she fell asleep leaning against my side.

The only life I'd ever known faded in the background, and I steeled myself to face my future. I'd have to find my way in a strange place, with only Lulu, my few belongings, and the stranger who sat next to me on the wagon seat.

Chapter 13

It was late afternoon when we stopped on the banks of the Mississippi to spend the night across the river from Caruthersville, Missouri. We could see the Powell Ferry on the other side. It would take us across in the morning. I'd lived all my life only a few miles from the river, but had never seen it before. It was a wonderful and frightening thing to me. I learned in school that it stretched all the way to the south end of the United States. I watched the boats with their cargo pass by and thought about the places they would stop before they found New Orleans. I daydreamed a little about what it would be like to get on one of the boats with Lulu and sail away from the life that faced me.

We ate our dinner from the picnic basket and rested for a while. George unhitched Pawnee to let him drink from the stream and nibble at the long grass.

"Aren't you going to hobble him?" I asked.

"I don't have to hobble him. He always stays within forty or fifty feet of me. I brought him into the world. I raised him as much as his mother did. When he was only a few hours old I started handling him and brushing him every day. I put a halter on him right off and trained him gentle. I had him following a lead when he was still a baby."

"How many horses do you have?" I asked.

"He's the only one now. We used to keep four or five, his daddy, Rascal, and some mares. When Rascal died, we sold the mares to save on feed. I don't need them now, so it's only him. Someday, I'm going to buy another mare and put him to stud, but he's young, and there's plenty of time for that."

"He's so good. How do you train a horse like that?"

"Like I said, I brushed and handled him from the day he was born. When he was a few months old, I started out by tying a loose rope around his middle. After he got used to that, I put a blanket under the rope. You can see he loves being brushed, so I would brush him and lean some weight on his back each time. When he was old enough, I put a saddle on him. When he got used to that, I put more of my weight on him until he was three years old. Then I got up on his back."

"And he just let you ride him?"

George laughed. "No, he threw me off every day for three weeks. I'd leave the saddle on him for a few hours before I took it off, and I tried again the next day."

"And he finally let you ride?"

"One day he threw me, and I landed flat on my back. It took all the wind out of me, and I had to lay there for a while until I could breathe again. He got all worried and came over and tried to get me up. He kept pushing at me with his nose and whuffing in my face. If it's possible for a horse to get a guilty look, he had one. The next day he didn't buck when I got on him. He stood stock-still. I finally got him to walk and then every day I took him out a little farther down the road. After a week or so, I got him to canter. He's been good as gold ever since. He does anything I ask. A lot of saddle horses would never pull a wagon, but look at him. He's just fine with it."

Pawnee chewed on the long grass for a while and then acted as if he wanted to play. He came up behind George and bumped his nose against George's back several times, harder each time, until George finally stood and paid him some attention. He took a brush out of his bag and brushed Pawnee's long, bushy mane and the tail that almost reached the ground.

This inspired Lulu, and she found a bag of hair ribbons in her things and began sectioning off the mane and braiding it. She tied a different color ribbon to the end of each braids. Pawnee stood perfectly still, closing his eyes while she worked. When she finished, she patted him on the neck and said, "There, now you're beautiful." Pawnee turned his head, and that big powerful stallion nuzzled the girl with his nose and nickered to her. She wrapped her arms around his neck and hugged him.

George built a fire to keep the snakes and animals away, rolled out some blankets in a grassy spot, and we slept on the ground. The next morning, after we ate, George hitched Pawnee back to the wagon and drove it on the ferry. Blocks were put under the wheels to keep it from rolling around during the trip across the water. The driver seemed to know George right well. He pointed to Pawnee's braids. "Got him all dressed up for church, George?" he laughed.

Lulu and I stood next to the wagon and held on the side rail, and Lulu held onto my waist with her other arm. George stood next to the driver, telling stories and making him laugh. The river pushed the ferry this way and that, and I held on so tight that after a while my hands went numb. The helmsman struggled to steer as best he could to get us across the river without going too far downstream. It seemed to me that we would never reach the other side, but we finally did. George drove the wagon onshore, and we waved goodbye.

George's horse perked up his ears like it knew where it was going by then. We rode all morning and afternoon and only stopped once to let the horse eat a little while we finished up what was left in the picnic basket.

As night set in, Lulu fell asleep with her head in my lap and George and I leaned against one another and dozed off and on for the rest of the trip. I was jolted awake when the wagon came to a stop in front of a large, two-story house. Several dogs began barking. It was very early in the morning. There was no moon, and the sun hadn't begun to rise. The sky was so dark it was hard to make out what the house looked like.

"Here we are, Maude," George said, climbing down from the buggy. He walked around to my side and took the sound-asleep Lulu in his arms. I climbed down and followed George up the path to the front door.

As we reached the top step, the door opened, and a scowling old woman stood there in the glow of an oil lamp. She held out the light, and I could see she had a large dog on each side of her, baring its teeth and rattling a growl.

George took a deep breath. "Ma, this is my wife, Maude." He nodded down at the sleeping Lulu, "and this is her daughter, Lulu."

The old woman's mouth fell open. She stepped right in front of me and stared hard at my face. She was almost as tall as I was, even with a bent back. Her stringy gray hair hung over her shoulders.

I almost cringed at how she glared at me. Then George's mother turned her attention to Lulu. She looked down at my child asleep in George's arms and reached out a hand. My motherly instinct made me take a step forward, but the old woman just ran a finger down Lulu's cheek and smiled sweet as anything. "Put her in Bessie's room," she said.

She held the door open for George so he could carry Lulu inside, then slammed it shut. That left me standing on the porch with the two dogs, which still showed their teeth and growled even louder. It hurt my feelings and made me mad at the same time. I thought, "So, that's how it's going to be."

I pushed the door open, stepped inside, and kicked it shut before the dogs had a chance to get in behind me. I followed George and his mother up the stairs. He carried Lulu in one of the bedrooms. His mother pulled the covers down on the bed, and he laid Lulu down.

"I'll get the rest of the things out of the buggy and bed down Pawnee," he said and left.

The old woman stood in the corner without saying anything. She watched as I took off Lulu's shoes and socks and undressed her down to her underwear. I pulled the covers up, kissed her cheek, and turned around.

"I'll show you George's room," the old woman said with a sharp voice.

She led me to the large corner bedroom, stepped aside for me to go in, and slammed the door shut as she left. She took the lamp with her. I stood there in gloom, barely able to make out the shapes of the furniture.

One window faced the back yard, and one was to the side. As my eyes got used to the dark, I looked around. There was a good-size bed against one wall, with a small table and lamp next to it, and a chest of drawers on the opposite wall. I looked around the table for matches to light the lamp, but here weren't any. A chair sat by the window facing the back yard. There were no curtains. I walked to the window and looked out. I could see the outline of a few small buildings.

One, I recognized as the outhouse. Another looked like the chicken coop, and one more towards the back of the property with a chimney that I figured was a smokehouse. A row of trees looked like an orchard.

In the light coming from the open door of the barn, I saw the dogs walking around and the shadow of George moving about. After a minute, he came out carrying my cedar chest and brought it as far as the back porch, then returned to the barn, fetched the oil lamp, and headed for the house. The dogs followed his every step. He stopped to stroke some cats that gathered around his legs and rubbed against him. I watched as he made his way to the outhouse. I knew I would need to do that before I went to bed. After a few minutes, George came in the room with the lamp. He set it on the table and then went back to bring the chest. He said, "The wagon is in the barn. I'll get the rest of your things tomorrow."

I stammered. "I, ah, I need to--go before I go to bed." I could feel myself blushing.

"Do you want to go to the outhouse? You can use the slop jar. It's right under the bed there."

I couldn't bring myself to do that right there in front of him. "I think I want to go out."

I picked up the lamp, went downstairs, and found my way to the kitchen and the back door. The dogs were lying on the porch. As soon as I stepped outside they ran up to me, heads lowered, ears back, and started snarling. My stomach turned over with fear. Then I was angry again. I was so worn out, I was ready to fall over, and I'd taken about as much as I could stand.

I glared at them, pulled back my lips, and showed my own teeth. "Sit yourselves down, and be quiet, or I'm going to kick you both 'til you can't walk." The dogs sat right down and were quiet.

I made my way down the path singing and stomping my feet a little to run off any snakes. The dogs followed me and sat outside the door when I went in. The lighting was dim. I wasn't pleased by what I smelled. What little I could see in the dark, it looked clean enough, but my family and the Connors had kept a fresh outhouse, moving it to a new spot from time to time, and dumping lime in the pit often enough to kill any odor. I thought, "I'll have to talk to George about this in the morning."

The dogs followed me back to the house, and when I opened the door, they started to go inside. I shooed them back. "No dogs!" They lay down on the porch, one with his head across the other's back, and settled in for the night.

I went back upstairs to the bedroom, dreading what was coming. I thought about what Helen said to me the morning I married James, "You're his wife, and whatever he wants to do to you, you have to let him do it." I hoped that my relations with George would work out as well as it had with James, but I'd known James all my life before we married. I'd only known George for five days.

George was already in bed, his clothes lying in a heap on the floor. "Everything all right?" he asked.

"Fine," I said. I opened the cedar trunk and took

out a nightgown, slipped it over my head, and undressed under it. George watched me without saying anything. I walked around the bed and slid in next to him. He leaned over and gave me a quick kiss on the cheek. I couldn't help it. I went stiff as a tree from head to foot.

He said, "Maude, it's been a long day. Let's get some rest," and he turned his back to me. Within a minute, his breathing told me he was fast asleep. I lay next to him for a while before I relaxed and drifted off to sleep, wondering what manner of man I'd married.

Chapter 14

When I woke the next morning, George had already gone downstairs. I dressed and went to check on Lulu. Her bed was empty, too. I heard the sound of Lulu laughing and followed it to the kitchen. Lulu was sitting at the table eating a breakfast of hotcakes. George's mother was at the stove. She turned around with a smile on her face that disappeared as soon as she saw me standing in the doorway.

I smiled at her. "Good morning, Mrs. Foley."

The old woman turned back to her cooking. I sat at the table and took a deep breath. To Mrs. Foley's back, I said, "I must have been really tired. I don't know when I ever slept so late. I was wondering what you'd like us to call you."

Lulu piped up, "I'm going to call her Grandmother. She said I could."

I waited for an answer, but none came. "Should I call you Mom Foley, or Mom, or Mrs. Foley? What would be best?"

George's mother put some hotcakes out of the pan and onto a plate, then sat and began eating them without giving me an answer. I saw that Lulu could sense the situation. She tilted her head. "Grandmother, I think my Mommy should call you Mom Foley, don't you?"

Mrs. Foley smiled at the child. "That'll do as well as anything else," she said, still not looking at me.

I hadn't eaten since the picnic supper the night before, and I could see there wouldn't be any hotcakes made for me by my new mother-in-law. I stood and went to stove.

"This is my kitchen," Mrs. Foley said.

I don't know where I got the backbone. It was like with the dogs the night before. I turned and looked her in the eye. "It *was* your kitchen. Now it's either yours, or mine, or we can share it. I'm a pretty good cook, so they tell me. Maybe you'd like having someone to help around here. Taking care of a big house like this must wear out an old woman like you."

I could see her teeth like one of the dogs. "I been taking care of it just fine for forty years, ever since my husband brought me here."

I bit back a sharp answer and decided to make an effort to be friendly. "Where are you from?"

Mrs. Foley sat up straight in her chair and jutted out her chin. "I am from Oklahoma, born of the Big Hill Osage tribe, the Wazhazhe. There was a time when my people owned what is now three states. We had many more horses than any of the other people."

I was surprised. George had said nothing about being Indian. I nodded, "I have some Indian blood myself. My great-grandmother was Cherokee, from eastern Tennessee, but she died before I was born. I never got to know her. Tell me about George's father."

Mrs. Foley scowled. "He was a fool, a white man, from a line of fools. He promised me many things, but he lied. I should have married one of my own people."

She bent her head and went on eating. It was clear she didn't want to talk about it anymore. In the daylight, she didn't look any less scary than she had the night before. Her skin was like dried-out leather with deep lines, especially her forehead, as if a frown was her permanent look, and there were lines like trenches running from the sides of her nose down to the corners of her mouth. Her hair was thin, and she had pinned it in a bun at the back of her head. It was a mixture of gray and white. I tried to picture her as a young woman. I could see right off that George and Bessie had to resemble their father, who must have been quite handsome. Mrs. Foley was probably attractive at one time, or she would never have caught his attention.

What struck me as odd about her was that she had beautiful hands. Even though they were rough and calloused from work, they had long, tapered fingers that reminded me of the woman who played piano at our church.

My stomach wanted to be fed and poked at me. I

looked through the pantry until I found some corn meal and a small pan. There was a bucket of water sitting on the sideboard. The stove was still burning high, so I dipped enough water in the pan and mixed in the meal. When my mush started cooking, I poured a cup of coffee out of the pot on the stove and took a sip. It was so strong I winced. I spooned a little water into my cup, and then I asked, "Where is George?"

"He went to his job. He said to tell you that if you need him, ask anyone you see in town and they will take you to him."

I looked at Lulu. "I think I'll go see where George works. He said it was only two miles into town. Do you want to go with me?"

Lulu had finished eating and jumped up. "Yes, it'll be fun to see the inside of a real jail."

Neither of us had ever seen one. "All right, but first, let's unpack our things and put them away." I turned to my mother-in-law. "Do you take a lunch to George?"

"No."

"Well, I think I'll ask him if he would like that."

Mrs. Foley almost jumped to her feet. "I have to feed the chickens," she said, and went out the back door, letting it slam.

I told Lulu, "Let's see what this house looks like in the daylight." We started by looking around the downstairs. There was a staircase built in the center, right in front of the door, with a parlor on one side and a dining room on the other. The parlor was furnished with a settee and two chairs, tables, oil lamps, and a few pictures hanging on the walls. I looked closely at the pictures. One of them was a yellowing print of what must have been George's mother when she was a young woman. I'd been right. She looked nothing like Bessie, but was moderately attractive. The others were of George and Bessie, but there was no trace of his father.

Across the hall was another room that would have been the dining room, but it had no furniture in it. In the back of the house was the large kitchen, and a small room lined with shelves that served as a pantry. There was also a wash room with a small cabinet that had shelves underneath for the towels, which were neatly folded and stacked, but well-worn and threadbare, and an ewer and pitcher on top. I wondered where the well was.

None of the walls had been papered, but were covered half-way up with planking and painted so long ago that I couldn't tell for sure what the color had been. I thought it would be nice to put up paper and re-paint the woodwork.

The house was clean, but everything in it was shabby and worn. It didn't look as if any effort had been made to re-cover any of the upholstered pieces or refinish any of the wooden furniture in years.

"Let's look around upstairs," I said to Lulu, and we trooped up. There were four bedrooms, the one I'd shared with George, the one where Lulu slept, another one with no furniture at all and nothing on the walls, and one with the door closed that I thought must be his mother's. I didn't open the door and look inside.

Lulu's room, the one that had been Bessie's, had a large bureau for her clothes, and there was plenty of room for all of Lulu's things. Clean white curtains with a lacy edging hung on the window and there were pretty pictures hanging over flowered paper. The spread on the bed was also white, quilted beautifully, and large enough to touch the floor on both sides. There were several fluffy pillows on the bed, and hand-tied rugs on the floor. It was by far the nicest room in the house.

"You've got the prettiest room," I said, hugging my daughter to me. "Mom Foley told me last night that it was your Aunt Bessie's room."

"Let's go see your room," she said.

The room that I was going to share with George wasn't at all attractive. The bedclothes were clean, but like the towels, well-worn, even shabby. There were no pictures on the wall.

Lulu looked a little sad. "It isn't very nice, Mom."

I smiled at her. "Men don't care about things like that the way we do. It'll be fun fixing it up, won't it? I'll see if it's all right with George for me to buy some fabric for a new spread and to make some curtains. Let's leave the unpacking for later and go on in to town and see how the stores are. Maybe we can pick out some pretty paper, too."

When Lulu and I left the house, we walked across the road to get a look back at it. It was badly in need of painting, and the steps were sagging in the front. I would have to talk to George about that also.

I measured the distance to the next house, only a

short way down the road, counting the steps from my front door to theirs. George told me his homestead was about five acres and ran back to a stream on the rear property line, but the houses were so close together, I figured that they were both built on one corner of the lots.

"Which way is it?" Lulu asked.

"I don't know." I started to go ask Mrs. Foley, but thought better of it. "You run ask George's mother."

When Lulu came back, she pointed to the right. "That way."

As we walked toward the main part of town, I thought about George's father. My new husband had never let on, and neither had Bessie, that their mother was full-blooded Indian. I knew that many people would have been ashamed to be half Indian, but the truth was that nearly everyone I'd ever known had some degree of Cherokee blood. I knew the tribe had been friendly to the white man. Their daughters married freely with frontiersmen of the time. Women were in scarce supply, and the Cherokee people were a handsome group.

George's house was about a quarter mile from the taller buildings that signaled the heart of town. Kennett was much larger than my home town. Lulu and I talked about our plans for decorating as we walked. School was out until after the crops were gathered, and I hoped I could keep Lulu's mind off having lost her friends. We passed a livery stable, several homes on lots much smaller than George's, and a Baptist church. I could see several spires in the distance that told me where the other churches were. I was comforted by their presence. I hoped one of them would be Holiness. Maybe Lulu would find new friends there.

When we reached the center of town, we were amazed by the number of city buildings and businesses. There was a bank and a regular city hall, a barber shop that also served as a dentist, a fire station, a hotel, a restaurant and at least six stores.

I looked up and down the street but didn't see any sign that said, 'jail,' or, 'sheriff.' A young woman coming out of a general store stopped and smiled at us. She looked friendly, so I asked her, "Excuse me, but could you tell me where I can find the sheriff?"

With a big, pretty smile, the woman said, "You must be Maude, and this must be Lulu. Aren't you a pretty little thing? I'm Sarah Graham. My husband is George's deputy. The whole town wants to welcome you. Everyone likes George. We couldn't believe he finally found himself a wife. There's going to be some mighty disappointed young women in Kennett. I'll walk with you to the sheriff's office. It's right down the street."

She fell into step beside us and linked her arm in mine. It gave me a really warm feeling to be welcomed like that. She was pretty, and neat, and dressed in clothes that didn't look homemade. I told her about wanting to fix up the house, and as we walked, Sarah pointed out the best place to buy groceries, the store that carried the most fabric, the doctor's office and other important locations. She put a little local color in her information. The banker's wife had consumption.

The mayor was thirty years older than his wife. The town had hired a new schoolteacher for the coming year because the last one got married.

When we got to the jail we found George's horse hitched up out front and George inside with his feet up on the desk and his deputy pouring a cup of coffee out of a big pot. George was wearing a vest that I hadn't seen before. It had his badge pinned to the front of it. The badge was a circle with a star inside. The word, "Sheriff," circled the top arc and, "Kennett, Mo." circled the bottom. It made me feel a little proud when I saw it.

"Look who's here, George," Sarah said. George jumped up and introduced Lulu and me to his deputy, Doug Graham.

Sarah and Doug said goodbye and went home to have some dinner. George pointed me to a chair beside the desk. "How did you get along with Mom this morning?" he asked. He sounded half-afraid of the answer.

"We'll work things out," I said. "It's hard to have two women under the same roof. We just need to find out our own property lines is all. I looked around inside the house. Would it be all right if I got what I need to fix up our bedroom?"

"The bedroom? What's wrong with it? What did you want to do?"

"I'd like to put up some pretty paper and get enough fabric to do up some curtains for the windows and a new spread."

"How much does all that cost?"

"I'll go over to the store and find out."

George looked doubtful and rubbed his chin. "Let me know before you order anything. We aren't rich you know."

I couldn't help it, this rankled me. First, I had to face down those growling dogs, and then I had to face down Mrs. Foley, and now George was treating me like a child. I'd spent the first twenty-six years of my life doing as I was told. I wanted that to be in the past. "I'm just finding out things as I go along, George. You have a good-sized house and a lot of property. You own your own horse when a lot of men don't. I'm not one to waste money at all. I spent my life so far stretching every penny, and I'm not going to change that now. I'm just trying to find out what I can do."

He leaned over with his hands on the desk. "I'm sorry, Maude. I didn't mean that you couldn't fix up the place, just that we ought to plan it ahead of time. Ma never cared much how things looked as long as they were clean. Bessie's the only one who liked to make things pretty. Go ahead and find out how much you need to spend. I get paid every month. If I can't afford it all at one time, you can do some things this month and more things next month. Would that be all right?"

I put my hand over one of his and he looked up at me as if my touch surprised him. "That will be just fine, George. I'll check with some of the stores and see what they have."

I stopped in the doorway and turned back to face him. "Mom Foley said that you don't bring a noon

131

meal with you. Do you want to come home at noon or do you like to eat at the restaurant?"

"I don't usually eat until suppertime. I just have my big breakfast and coffee in the morning and go on through the day 'til I get home."

"That's not good for you. Would you like me to bring you something? I don't mind a bit, and it would give me and Lulu something to break up our day."

"That would be nice, but don't feel like you have to. I'm used to doing without."

I smiled at him. "I'll see you later." As we went out the door, I heard him start whistling a soft, tuneless song.

Lulu and I visited several stores. We priced the fabrics and looked through samples of wallpaper. It seemed everyone already knew who I was, and everyone we met told me how much they liked George. I noticed that not one of them told me they liked his mother. In fact, they never even mentioned her.

I wrote down the number of the wallpaper I liked best, and the shopkeeper told me how much I would need for the size of the room. It had a pattern of big cabbage roses on it, and I found some light green fabric that picked up one of the colors in the leaves that would make a nice bedspread. There was a store that sold ready-made bedding, but I just looked around for ideas about what I wanted to do. I'd never even had a ready-made dress and wasn't about to waste money on what I considered rich people's things.

We stopped back by the sheriff's office to report

on how much money we wanted to spend. George had his feet propped up on the desk again and was sound asleep when I opened the door. He stood and smiled sheepish at me. "Not much crime in Kennett," he said.

I laughed a little. "Good, I wouldn't want to live where there was." I told him what the figures were going to be for the paper and the fabric. I could see that he was pleased I could sew my own things.

"Go ahead and order it, Maude. I guess we can afford it all right. It's about time we did something to fix up the place."

Lulu and I went back to the store and ordered the wallpaper and fabric and headed home, happy with the day. More people stopped to greet us on our way out of the downtown area. There were a few ladies with girls Lulu's age, and they made friends right off. School wouldn't start for a few more weeks, and they promised to see one another then. It seemed like the friendliest place on earth. In my home town, strangers were sometimes looked at suspiciously until we got to know them. Both Lulu and I were feeling better about things.

As we neared the house, we could see George's mother in the backyard. The clothesline was hung with laundry, and she was standing next to the back porch, twirling a chicken around her head. It was an ordinary sight to anyone in a country area, but the look on the old woman's face gave me a start. She enjoyed what she did. I put my arm around Lulu's shoulder and hurried her to the front door. "I guess we're having chicken for supper," I said.

We took turns visiting the outhouse. When I came out, I found Lulu and Mom Foley sitting together on the back porch. There was a tub of steaming water in front of them, and they were plucking the feathers out of the chicken, the old woman pausing every now and then to dip the carcass in the hot water. She had the sleeves of her shirt rolled up past her elbows, and I was surprised to see tattoos on her forearms. I tried not to stare. Lulu was laughing at something her new grandmother was telling her. The old woman fell silent as I came near. "Can I peel some potatoes or do anything to help with supper?" I asked.

Mom Foley got all stiff. "I got almost everything done. There's plenty of time to get it ready."

"All right. I think I'll get some things ready for the wash for tomorrow."

"Tomorrow? I just washed today."

"I know, but I didn't have our things out yet. I don't like to let them sit around dirty."

Mom Foley nodded a sharp approval. "I'm glad to hear it. I like things to be clean. Go ahead."

"All right. I will."

As I walked toward the kitchen, I heard my mother-in-law's voice take up the story where she'd left off. "My grandfather stole twenty horses from the Kaw that day. One of the horses had a dog that followed it home. The dog was in love with the horse and never left its side. Whenever my grandfather rode the horse, the dog would run behind them and go everywhere they went."

Lulu laughed again as her new grandmother

134

elaborated the story of the horse and the dog. I was thankful that the old woman at least seemed to have taken a shine to my girl, if not to myself. I could cope with the way she felt about me as long as Lulu was treated right.

I gathered up the things that needed washing and then got out my big sewing box. The box was a pleasure to me, and I added to it over the years until I had a large collection of thread and buttons, patterns for myself and Lulu, and even some that I'd used for James. When a shirt or piece of clothing got too frayed to wear, I always took the buttons and hooks off and saved them. The fabric made dust cloths.

George was much taller than James had been. I'd have to remember that when I cut his clothes. It was my habit to look over each piece of laundry before I washed it, checking for missing buttons and torn seams. The familiar routine was comforting to me, and when I finished with my own and Lulu's clothes, I looked in the bureau drawers at George's. He didn't have many clothes, but they were clean and neatly folded. A few of them needed the attention of a seamstress. Several of his socks needed darning, and I took out my darning egg and the soft yarn I used just for socks and sat by the sunlight coming in the bedroom window to repair the holes. I was proud of the quality of my work. When I was done, the socks looked almost like brand new. I thought I would knit him some new ones for his birthday, whenever that was. It occurred to me I had no idea how old he was, but guessed him to be in his early thirties.

When George came home, we ate supper at the kitchen table with polite but forced conversation. Lulu and I were pleased with the plans to redecorate the bedroom, and we went on about that. George's mother wore her usual sour expression. The only time her face softened at all was when Lulu spoke. It was a curious thing to me how the old woman had taken to Lulu. I wondered why, and decided to ask George about it when we were alone.

All evening I had the thought in the back of my mind that it would soon be time for me to spend my second night in George's bed. I was grateful he hadn't wanted to have relations with me the first night and wondered if he would this time.

We finally went upstairs. I made sure I had my own lantern so I wouldn't be left in the dark again. I listened to Lulu's prayers, tucked her in, and kissed her goodnight. I couldn't help but let her see my mood, and Lulu wanted somehow to comfort me. She caught me by the hand before I turned to leave. "It's going to be all right, Mommy. Mr. Foley seems very nice, and I'm having so much fun with grandmother. You wouldn't believe how many stories she has about the old days."

I smiled at her and kissed her again before saying goodnight.

In our bedroom, I sat on the edge of the bed as George undressed, again just dropping his clothes in a pile on the floor, and climbed into bed in his long-johns.

"I was wondering about your mother, George.

She doesn't care for me, but she took to Lulu right away. Why is that?"

"Her people love all children. It's their way."

"Her people? Oh, you mean the Indians."

"I hope it doesn't bother you that I'm half-breed Osage. I should have told you before we married."

"I don't care one way or the other. I got some Indian blood too--Cherokee."

He looked relieved. "I guess most folks around here do, but there's some would hold it against you."

"I never met anyone who did. My town was all Christians. We treated everyone with the respect they showed us."

He stared at me for a minute. "I always thought that's what a Christian should be, but they don't all live up to it. When you're a kid, and church-going people call you names, it cuts deep."

I thought that over. "Well, I guess there's say-so Christians, and there's real Christians." I took my nightgown off of the hook on the back of the door where I'd hung it. George took my hand. "I'd like to see you, Maude."

I felt my face turn red, but nodded, laid the gown on the bed and started undressing.

As James had so long ago, George watched me undress, and I pretended it didn't bother me. When I finished, I got in the bed next to him and he said, "I don't want to hurt you, Maude. You tell me to hold back if you need to."

I didn't expect that he would hurt me. He'd been so considerate and seemed to be such a gentle person.

If he was as good to me as he was to his horse, we'd get along fine.

It had been so long since James, I wanted him to touch me the same way, but he began the relations right off, without so much as kissing me. He did it very gently, but I could tell something wasn't right.

"It's all right, George."

"I don't want to hurt you," he said again.

"I don't think you will."

He pushed further into me and it took my breath away. I gasped and he pulled back.

"Are you all right?"

"It's been ten years, George. Let's just go slow for a while."

He started again but I could tell he was holding himself back. I tried to relax, but couldn't. He got done in just another minute, still holding himself away from me. Then he rolled over. I heard him let out a long sigh, and in a minute he was asleep.

I was relieved. It hadn't been satisfying to me, but he was a kind, considerate man, and I was sure that after a while we would work things out.

The next morning I woke when he got out of bed. I sat up and smiled at him. "I'm going to do the wash today. Why don't you put on a clean set of underwear, and I'll throw those things in the tub with the others."

"I just put these on Sunday morning."

"That's all right, I don't mind."

He unbuttoned the long-johns and dropped them to the floor, stepping out of them and standing there naked. I tried to hide my surprise, but couldn't help staring at his member. It was three times as long as James's had been, reaching halfway to his knee. I guess he'd been waiting for my reaction, and it was his turn to blush. "That's why I was afraid I would hurt you, Maude. I'll always try not to."

I looked down at the quilt. "I know you will, George. It'll be all right. We'll get better with one another after a while."

He got a clean set of underwear out of the drawer and slipped into it. "Ma won't know what to think of it, me changing right in the middle of the week."

"I always did like to do the wash twice a week. That way it doesn't pile up." I took a deep breath and jumped into the subject that had been worrying me ever since I got there. "I can see right out that your mother doesn't want me here, George. I don't want to get off to a bad start with her. Is there anything that I can do to please her without giving up my rightful place?"

He took a step back and held up his hands like in surrender. "I can't help you much there, just don't make her too mad. She's not a woman you can cross much." He rubbed his chin. "Let her spend time with Lulu. I see that it soothes her to have a child about the house again. She hasn't been the same since Bessie left. Just feel your way with her until you two can work out your territories, but don't let her push you around."

"I'll do the best I can, George. I spent most of my life doing what I was told, but I'm a grown woman now. I'm not going to let her run all over me."

"I wouldn't want you to, Maude."

He went on to the kitchen, and I got dressed. I looked in Lulu's room. She wasn't there, and her bed was already made. I went to the kitchen and found her sitting at the table, watching her new grandmother making coffee. The old woman had been telling Lulu another one of her stories, but stopped talking when I came in the room, and she only grunted in reply when I said good morning to her.

She had a big iron coffee pot that looked as if it held a half-gallon, and she spooned coffee in. I couldn't believe how much she put directly in the water. She got out a big iron skillet and filled it with thick strips of smoked bacon.

I went to the pantry and got the plates and cups to set the table. Lulu stood and helped without being told. It had been her job at home to set and clear the table, and she enjoyed the grown-up responsibility. The old woman didn't miss what Lulu was doing. She patted her on the head, "You're my angel, aren't you, little one, and such a good girl."

Lulu beamed under the praise. I smiled at her as well and looked at Mom Foley. "Is there anything else I can do to help?"

"Sit yourself down and watch. When I die, you'll want to know what George likes to eat for breakfast and the right way to fix it."

I pressed my lips together, but did as I was told. George didn't say a word. I watched as the old woman fried up the bacon until it was almost burned. She took the skillet off of the stove and set it in the middle of the table, then put a plate of thick-sliced bread next to it and poured about two cups of coffee into the skillet of bacon grease.

The coffee was so thick it looked like black molasses. It formed globs and floated around. George saw me staring at it. "Black-eyed gravy," he said. "My favorite thing." He put a slice of the bread on his fork, dipped both sides in the mixture of bacon grease and coffee, and lifted it to his plate. Lulu and I both watched.

George ate several pieces of the greasy bread and drank several large cups of coffee. I admired a healthy appetite, but I wondered how he kept his slim waistline after eating all that. I sipped at my coffee, but it was so strong I couldn't drink it. I added enough water to thin it out a bit, but that cooled it off too much.

Turning to George, I asked, "Do you have a teapot, George?" I hadn't noticed one in the pantry, but I hadn't taken a really good look through what was in there.

"We have one somewhere, don't we, Ma? Bessie used to water down her coffee, too." He laughed, "She said it wasn't fit for humans to drink."

His mother went to the pantry and came out carrying a regular teapot, whistle and all. She slammed it down on the stove. When he was finished eating, George stood and stretched. "Well, I guess I'll be getting to the jail. You know where to find me if you need me." He headed to the barn. His mother hadn't eaten with us, and I asked her, "Aren't you going to eat, Mom Foley?"

"I'll eat when I'm of a mind to," she said with a

growl.

"Can we clear up the dishes here?"

"Me and Lulu can clean them up. You go do that laundry you been wanting to do."

I held back a smile. "All right. I'll do my laundry."

I went upstairs and gathered the bundle of clothes. The well was right next to the back porch. Two tubs and a washboard hung on the back wall of the house, a large tub for washing and a smaller one for rinsing. I would have to draw a lot of water to fill the old, galvanized tub. I heated the first bucket of water in the big pot on the stove, and when it was boiling, I poured it back in the washtub, and cut the bar of Fels-Naptha soap, and added it to the water.

All the time, whenever I looked back at the kitchen, I could see the old woman watching me. I think she wanted to see if I was doing the job right.

It was a warm, sunny day, and I knew the clothes would be dry in only a few hours. Both dogs sat and watched me, and when I was finished with the wash and picked up the basket, they followed me out to the clothesline.

I was hanging up the last of the dark things when I saw a slim, young, redheaded woman come out the back door of the house next door and head toward me. She was carrying a dish and followed by a girl with flaming hair that matched her mother's, who was just about Lulu's size. I was so happy to see my neighbors coming to greet me that I had to hold back tears. It had only been a few days since I left Bessie and Mom

Connor behind, but I was already missing the companionship of other women. I doubted I would ever grow close to George's mother.

I dropped the shirt I held back in the basket and greeted my neighbor with a real smile from my heart. She smiled back just as warmly.

"Welcome to the neighborhood," she said. "I'm Clara Taylor, and this is my daughter, Maggie. That's short for Margaret, but she doesn't like that, so she asked me to have everyone call her Maggie. I think that's because her favorite teacher was named Margaret but used Maggie for her name. My husband is Alfred Taylor. He owns the feed store in town." She held out the dish in her hands. "I baked you an apple pie."

I took the pie from her. "I can't tell you how happy I am to meet you and Maggie. There's coffee on the stove, please come in, and let's sit and talk."

Clara looked toward the house and frowned doubtfully. I couldn't help it laughing out loud. "I see you've met my mother-in-law."

This drove Clara into a fit of giggles. "I would never have said anything, but she isn't exactly friendly. How's it going with the two of you?"

"Not too good, but I set my mind the first time I saw her that she wasn't going to run all over me. We got home in the middle of the night and there she was, standing there on the front porch in the moonlight looking like a 'haint with those two dogs next to her. I've always been a quiet and easy-going person, but I knew right then and there that if I didn't stand my ground I could never live with her."

"Looks like you're getting along with the dogs all right. I've always been a little afraid of them."

"They just needed to know who was boss. I growled at them that first night, and they been good ever since. 'Course, they love Lulu, my little girl, and so does George's mother."

"Maggie can't wait to meet her. With school out for the summer she's been missing her friends. We don't get into town all that often."

"Well, come on in. If the old lady bothers you, I'll protect you."

Clara laughed again, and she and Maggie followed me to the kitchen. Mom Foley and Lulu were nowhere to be seen. I set the pie down on the table and called out, "Lulu, come here, I got a surprise for you." I heard Lulu's feet coming down the stairs, and she popped in the kitchen. When she saw Maggie, her face lit up. I was so happy for her, "This here's Maggie Taylor, and she lives right next door. Maggie this is Lulu."

Maggie grinned at Lulu. "Want to come over to my house and play with my dolls?"

Lulu's bobbed her head so hard, I thought she might get dizzy. She grabbed Maggie's hand and the two of them ran out the back door without even asking permission. I almost cried to see Lulu so happy. I got cups and what else I needed to fix the coffee, and Clara and I sat at the table. I looked in the hallway and could see George's mother walk by. She stopped at the sound of our voices, gave me a hateful look, and then went on her way. I didn't care. I had a new woman friend to share things with. I could survive.

Chapter 15

The rest of the week passed without any big problems. There was a small daily struggle over territory between us women of the house, but nothing that I wanted to bother telling George. Another attempt at nighttime relations was just as unhappy as the first for me, but we didn't talk about it. George's mother kept the house clean and, needing to keep busy, I made another trip to town to get some in-stock fabric for a new shirt for George. It would be a month or so before the wallpaper and the amount of fabric I needed for the bedroom arrived.

Clara Taylor and I found some time each afternoon to sit on Clara's porch and talk while we sewed. At Clara's, we were out of earshot of Mom Foley. Lulu and Maggie played with their dolls or on the swing hanging from one of the big oak trees that bordered the back of both yards. Lulu was so happy with Clara's friendship that she didn't even talk about missing Tennessee.

I hadn't met Clara's husband yet, but knew I would see him at services on Sunday. I was happy to learn that Clara was a member of the Holiness Church. It was one of the spires I'd spotted when I went to town that first day. It stood quite a distance away from the house, on the other side of the jail.

I was looking forward to Sunday. At the end of the service the preacher would give the invitation, and Lulu and I would go forward with our letters from our home church and ask to move our membership to the Kennett church. The church members would vote and approve them. We would belong.

When Sunday came, I was awake with the first rooster crow and dressed in my best dress. George didn't stir right away, but I woke Lulu, who was almost as excited as I was.

We went downstairs to the kitchen. There was no sign of George's mother. I looked back upstairs. The old woman's door was still closed. I thought that maybe they made it a practice to sleep in on Sundays.

I made the coffee and some cornmeal mush and Lulu and I ate. By then I was getting anxious. If George didn't get up soon, we would be late for the service. I'd been looking forward to it all week.

I went upstairs. George was still sound asleep. I shook his shoulder gently. He stirred a little, but then went back to sleep. I shook him a little harder.

He opened his eyes. "What?"

"If you don't get up now, we'll be late for church, George."

He sat up in the bed and started rubbing his chin, but didn't look me in the eye. "I don't go to church, Maude."

"What do you mean? Everybody goes to church."

"Well, I don't. I'll hitch up the wagon and I'll drive you, and I'll wait outside for you to bring you home, but I don't go to church."

I was shocked. I'd never heard of such a thing. "Why not?"

"Ma doesn't believe in it. She keeps the old ways, and I just never started up."

"What does that mean, the old ways?"

"It's the religion of her people. They call their idea of God Wakondah."

"What does that mean, their *idea* of God?"

"It's not like we think of our God, but more like a spiritual force that directs their lives. The holy man is kind of like the preacher and he teaches the people how to act and what to do to honor Wakondah."

"But Bessie never missed a meeting."

"When she was a girl, Bessie went to church with one of her girlfriends, and when she came home she said she'd been saved and she got baptized and that was that. She went to church every meeting from then on."

"But you came to church with her."

"When you're in Bessie's house you do what she tells you to do, but this is my house, and I'm not going to church."

"You said that they don't think of God the way that we do. Does that mean you believe in Jesus, like us, or in this Wakondah, like your mother?"

"I guess I believe in both of them. I believe in God and I believe in Jesus being his Son and all that, but *I don't go to church*."

"You never accepted Him for your Savior or got baptized?"

"No."

I thought about this for a few minutes. Finally, I said, "Well, Lulu and I will go to church every Sunday, and I'd appreciate it if you hitched up the wagon and drove us, but if you don't want to do that, we'll walk."

He got up and in a few minutes, he pulled the wagon to the front door and waited. Lulu and I had been watching for him, and we went out and climbed up. George made no move to get down and help us.

I thought about the tattoos I'd seen on the old woman's forearms. "Do those pictures on your mother's arms have something to do with her religion?"

"Sort of, her people all wore them in the old days. I'm surprised she showed them to you."

"She didn't. I saw them when she was cleaning chickens."

I didn't speak another word on the way to church. My mind was turning over what we'd talked about that morning. If I'd known George wasn't a born-again Christian, I wouldn't have married him, and I wouldn't have cared what anybody said. Besides, no one would have blamed me then for turning him down, even if I had gone for an unchaperoned buggy ride.

It was too late. I would have to live my life as an example to him and hope that someday the Lord would call him, the same way He called me, back when I was only eleven years old, and Lulu, when she was nine.

The way to the church was straight through town. I couldn't help but notice how everyone we passed greeted George with a smile and a wave. It seemed to be true what his deputy's wife, Sarah, had told me. Everyone liked George. He stopped a few times to introduce us to people, and they were all friendly to both Lulu and me.

When we got to the church, several people came over to say hello. Our neighbors, the Taylors, were with them. Clara's husband wasn't at all what I'd pictured. Clara was a few years older than I was, but her husband looked to be at least fifty, and was as plump as an October hog. Her being so slim, that surprised me. He met us with a cheerful expression. "I'm happy for Clara to have a woman friend right next to us," he told me.

George got down from the wagon and helped Lulu and me down, but then he climbed back up on the seat. He looked down at me. "I'll be back here to pick you up when the service is over."

I'd hoped he would change his mind and come inside for the meeting, but I could see that it wasn't going to happen--today--so I just nodded. Clara smiled up at George. "You go on home, George. Our buggy is big enough for us to bring them home. There's no need for you to sit out here three hours with nothing do to."

He tipped his hat. "If you say so, Clara. Is that all right with you, Maude?"

I was embarrassed and I just nodded. Clara hooked her arm in mine and took me to meet some of the other women. Maggie pulled Lulu's hand and led her over to meet some other girls their age. I looked back and saw George was driving off.

It was time for the service to begin, and we filed inside and took our seats. Lulu and I sat next to the Taylors, about halfway to the back. We sang and prayed for a half-hour and then the preacher took his text from Matthew 25:34, his voice rich and full, rising and falling as he read the words of Christ about welcoming strangers.

The words were a happy challenge to me, and I was sure they were the same to every Christian in the church that day. Every person I'd met in the town of Kennett, Missouri, had greeted me with Christ's attitude, except, of course, George's mother. I couldn't help but wonder if Wakondah wouldn't rebuke the old lady for being so rude.

After the preaching, we sang some more songs, and a few people repented of unexplained sins. Several people testified to God's goodness in their lives. Finally, the preacher gave the invitation, and Lulu and I went forward, handing him the letters of membership my home pastor had given me. He asked for a vote, and we were accepted into the church. We stood at the front with the preacher while another song was sung, and every member walked around in a circle to shake our hands and welcome us. I was so happy I cried. I didn't yet feel that the house I was living in was mine, but I did have a church home there in Kennett.

Chapter 16

Things at the house settled into a sort of miserable peace between me and George's mother. I was satisfied to let the old woman do the chores she had always done, the cooking and most of the cleaning. I did my own laundry separately and spent my extra time sewing for myself or Lulu and George. I talked to Clara for a while every day and gave thanks to God for sending her to me and sending Maggie to Lulu. It was only a few weeks before she filled the hole left in my life when we moved away from Bessie.

I saw Clara hanging out her wash one Wednesday morning and went over to chat for a while. As I came close to her, I saw she had dark circles under her eyes.

"Are you feeling all right?" I asked.

She didn't look at me. "I'll be fine. I didn't get much sleep last night."

"I hope you're not taking sick. Do you have a fever?"

"No, no fever. Really, I'll be all right," Clara said, shaking out a sheet before hanging it on the line. I took the other end of the sheet and held it up while Clara pinned it. Something wasn't right. I could tell, but I didn't want to be nosy, so I held my peace.

"I never knew you to do your wash on a Wednesday," I said. "Maybe my odd habits are rubbing off on you." I did my own clothes any time it struck my fancy. Clara shook her head, "It isn't that, but I do like how you wash clothes any day you want."

I laughed. "That's just because Mom Foley does hers on a Monday, and I don't want to mix in on her routine."

Clara looked over at my back door. "I wouldn't want to upset her, either."

Clara and I finished hanging up the sheets, and Clara stretched her back. "Let's sit for a spell and have some tea."

She and I fetched the drinks from her kitchen and sat in the twin rockers on Clara's back porch. I knew that she needed to unburden herself of something, but I didn't want to force her to talk about it before she was ready. We sat quiet for a few minutes and then Clara began, "If you don't want to answer this, don't, but I was wondering, how are things with you and George, I mean, you know, in private?"

I knew what she meant, but my private life was something I'd never talked about much with anyone, even my husbands. I swallowed hard and stared out at the oak tree like I was examining the branch arrangement. Normally, I wouldn't think of talking about so personal a thing to anyone, but maybe it would be all right to confide in Clara. I trusted her, and she had something on her mind that she needed to talk about with another woman. I said, "Not like it was with me and my first husband. James and I fit together, you see, and George is, --is different. He can't do all he wants because he's so big it hurts me."

"Well, that part of my married life isn't what I expected with Alfred and me, either." Clara stared off in the other direction, neither of us wanting to look one another in the eyes. I waited for her to go on, and when she didn't, I asked, "Is that why you look so peaked this morning?"

"Yes, he bothered me last night."

"Is he too much for you, like George is for me?"

"No, he isn't so big he hurts me," she sighed and took a deep breath. "I been wanting to talk to someone about this for fifteen years, but I was always afraid to, Maude. You're the first one I felt close enough to that I can tell it, and I've only known you a few weeks."

"Go ahead, Clara. It'll be between you and me."

Clara took another deep breath. "Well, he's older than I am, so he doesn't bother me as often as he used to, and that's some help. It's just that when he does, he won't wear anything, so he does it naked and he wants me naked, too."

I waited. Being naked didn't seem like a problem. James and I almost always had relations without any nightclothes, especially in the warm days of summer.

When Clara didn't go on, I urged her a little. "That doesn't seem bad, Clara."

"No, not by itself it isn't, it's just that when he--, ah, when he--, oh, I don't know how to say it."

"Just go ahead and tell me, Clara."

"When he gets done, he passes out and messes the bed. It gets all over him and the bed--, and Maude, it gets all over me."

I tried to think of some sort of words that might comfort Clara. "He doesn't hit you or hurt you, or anything like that, does he?"

"Oh, no, he's never hit me once in all the years we been married. But,--it's awful, Maude. When he passes out like that, he's so heavy I have to push him off me, and I can't get him out of the bed to clean up after him until the morning."

"What do you do?"

"I get up and clean myself and then go sleep on the sofa. I asked him to wear his underwear, because that might help keep things cleaner, but he refuses."

"Has he always messed the bed like that?"
"Ever since the very first time we did it. Back then, he was younger and not so heavy and he wanted it a lot more. When we were first married, he bothered me almost every night."

I nodded, kept my eyes on the oak tree, and considered that there were worse things than going to bed with George. Finally, I looked at Clara, who still had her head turned, and reached out and took her hand, "We all got something to bear, Clara. At least he doesn't want it as much as he used to. Maybe someday soon he'll get to where he won't want it at all."

"That would be an answer to prayer, Maude. There's just that one thing wrong with him. He's a good husband to me. He treats me kind, and he loves his little girl, and he gives us anything we need."

"There's a whole lot of women would wish for that from their husbands, Clara, a whole lot."

"I don't know if they'd want to take what comes with it, Maude."

I reflected that they probably wouldn't. After that day, I could just look at Clara and know by her face when Alfred had bothered her the night before.

Chapter 17

It was on a Monday, about a month after I came to Kennett, when I walked to town to check on my order for fabric and wallpaper. I was excited when the shopkeeper told me they'd finally received what I wanted for the bedroom. He gathered up the paste and brushes and other things I would need, added them to the bill that George paid once a month, and said he would hold them in the back room until George came to bring them home.

I stopped by to tell him that my order was in. I found him like I always did, with his feet up on the desk, his chin on his chest, and sound asleep. I put my hand on his knee and shook it to wake him. He opened his eyes and smiled at me. "Maude, what brings you to town?"

"My things are in at the store. You can pick them

up on your way home. I can't wait for us to start work on the bedroom. It's going to be so nice, George."

He smiled at how excited I was, nodded a little, and closed his eyes to go back to his nap. "I know you're going to have a good time with it, Maude. I'll see you for supper, like always, unless someone robs the bank or something." Before I could answer him, he was asleep.

I left the office and stopped to talk to several people on my way home. They all asked after George and smiled when I said he was just fine. Again, I thought how nice it was that everybody liked George.

I'd been looking forward to the decorating ever since the day I had George's permission to place the order. When he came home that night, I almost ran out to meet him, but he hadn't brought the supplies home with him.

I tried to hide my disappointment. "I thought you'd be bringing my things home with you, George."

"I'll have to hitch up the wagon one day. I can't bring all that on the horse."

"You'll do that tomorrow?"

"Sure," he said.

But when I saw him ride off to work the next morning, he wasn't driving the wagon. He was riding his horse like he always did. I asked him again that night, and again, he said he'd forgotten, but would do it the next day, but he didn't.

On Friday morning, when George rode his horse into town again, I went over to Clara's.

"I'd like to borrow that little play wagon of

Maggie's if I could, Clara. Looks like the only way I'm going to get my things here is if I go get them myself."

"Go right ahead and take it, Maude. We haven't used it in a long time. You can keep it. I'm not busy now and it's such a pretty day. I'll walk in to town with you."

After the storekeeper loaded my decorating supplies into the wagon, I wanted to show George what I'd chosen. "Let's stop by the Sheriff's office on our way home," I told Clara.

She chuckled. "All right."

As usual, George was napping when we arrived. I shook his leg a little harder than usual. He smiled sheepishly at us when I told him why we'd come, and rubbed his chin that way he always did when he needed a minute to think of what he was going to say. "I kept intending to bring it, but I forget."

There were no smiles from me this time. "I'll get it home by myself. We brought Maggie's little wagon to put it in."

"All right, Maude. Just let me know if you want anything else. Nice to see you, Clara. Say hello to Alfred and Maggie for me." He closed his eyes.

Outside, Clara saw my frown and noticed that my lips were pressed tightly together. She knew I was angry, so she kept quiet while we began the walk home. It was such a pretty day, like Clara had said, and it wasn't long before my anger went away. I finally had my things, but even though we talked happily about my plans for the bedroom, in the back of my mind, I kept thinking about George.

He slept soundly every night and was asleep every time I saw him at work. How in the world could anyone sleep that much? When I left home that morning, the dogs and cats were all lying around the back yard taking their morning naps. It would be about an hour before they woke for lunch and settled down to take their afternoon naps. *He must be part dog or cat.*

On Saturdays, George didn't stay at the office all day. His habit had been just to go in to see the deputy, who was in charge for the weekend, and after chatting with one person or another, he would have a few beers at the saloon and then ride home. I didn't approve of drinking anything with alcohol, but after he told me he didn't go to church, I wasn't surprised.

Most Saturdays, he was back at the house by noon for his dinner. I'd been thinking we would start putting up the wallpaper after we ate. When he didn't get home at the usual time, I walked out to the road and looked to see if he was coming. I did that every half-hour until five o'clock, but there was no sign of him. His mother was putting supper on the table at six, the usual time, when he finally rode up. I watched out of the upstairs window as he went to the barn and began his nightly ritual of taking care of his horse.

I was jealous of Pawnee. He paid a lot more attention to that horse than he did to me. We ate in silence, the usually chattering Lulu picking up on my mood. After supper, Lulu went to play in the yard with Maggie, and I went upstairs and sewed for a while until it was dark.

George didn't come upstairs until I was in bed. I waited until he got under the covers to say anything. He settled his body down with his back to me. I lay on my back, not touching him. "I was thinking that we'd put the paper up today, George. Did something happen in town to keep you there?"

"I had a few beers with some of the boys from one of the farms that I hadn't seen for a while, and time got away from me. We can start on the paper tomorrow."

It would never occur to me to raise my voice but I couldn't help tell him how disappointed I was in him. "You know good and well that I'd never do such a thing on the Lord's Day, George."

He yawned loudly. "Suit yourself, but I can't do it by myself you know. It takes two people to hang wallpaper."

I sparked at that. "I've seen Tommy hang paper at Helen's house all alone and do a fine job of it, too, but I won't ask you to work on Sunday, even if you're not a Christian."

He sat up in the bed and sighed deeply. "Maude, it isn't that I'm a heathen, just because I don't go to church."

"What about your Wakondah?"

"He's not my Wakondah. He's my mother's Wakondah. I believe in God and I believe that Jesus was His Son and all of that. I just don't go to church. I never saw the need for it. That doesn't make me a heathen."

"How can you be saved and not go to church?"

"Saved--who said I was saved?"

"You just said you believe in Jesus."

"Well, I didn't mean it like you mean it."

I would have to think that one over. It somehow comforted me that at least he admitted he believed in Jesus in some way or another. I would pray twice as much that God would save him.

I turned my back and he lay down. Over my shoulder I asked, "Will you promise me that we'll put up the paper next Saturday?"

He sighed again. "If someone doesn't rob the bank."

When two more Saturdays passed and George found excuses to stay in town all day, I gave up hope of his helping me. Clara and I walked into town and talked to the storeowner about the right way to hang paper. He chuckled to himself and wrote down directions for me. As I left the store, he shook his head and said, "That George."

On Tuesday, following the storekeeper's directions, Clara and I managed to get one wall of the bedroom papered. It took us all afternoon, but I was very happy about it, and thought it came out wonderful. I waited for George to tell me how nice it looked. If he noticed it at all, he didn't say. He went to bed without a word.

On Wednesday, Clara and I did the second wall, getting better at the work and picking up speed as we gained experience. We did the third and fourth walls on Thursday and were finished. The difference in the room was amazing. It had gone from drab and dull to bright, pretty and cheerful. George either didn't notice or pretended not to notice.

I set up my little round quilting frame by one of the windows in the bedroom and spent my afternoons working on the new bedding. With Mom Foley still doing most of the housework, I was happy to have something to fill my spare time. George's mother and I had worked out a truce concerning that. She made him his bacon-grease/bread/coffee breakfast every morning, and she allowed me to help her with supper. She had a large garden planted in the back yard, surrounded by chicken wire to keep the poultry out. I made and fenced my own garden on the other side, planting the things I enjoyed that weren't grown in the other plot. I took cuttings from Clara's roses and lilacs and other shrubs and coaxed them into rooting. I planted them in the front yard and hoped they would make the front of the house pretty for the next summer.

I bought bulbs in town that would grow the next spring and planted crocus, tulips and hyacinth in rows down the walk from the front step to the road. I left the downstairs cleaning to Mom Foley and cleaned my room and Lulu's room and did our laundry. It still wasn't enough work to fill my day. Sewing the bedding and curtains gave me a great sense of satisfaction, and I almost dreaded the time when they would be finished.

When it came time for Lulu to start back to school, George's mother brooded like an old hen. For some reason that I didn't understand, she and my girl had really taken to one another. They worked together in the garden while the old woman told stories about her people, about the Holy men, the councils that had included her grandfather and her father, the Big Hill Osage and the Sky people. Lulu loved hearing them.

On the day that school started, Lulu and Maggie went off hand in hand, swinging their lunch pails. They joined a few other girls walking by on their way to the schoolhouse. They were all really looking forward to classes. To celebrate the occasion, I'd made two new dresses for Lulu and stood on the porch to see the girls off. George's mother watched from the side yard as they disappeared down the road. I almost felt sorry for her.

In the afternoon, I saw her walk down to the road several times and peer into the distance until the girls returned. When she finally caught sight of them coming home, she went back to her cleaning without saying a word.

Chapter 18

I asked George several times to fix up the outhouse. He always agreed to do the work, but he never got around to it. I borrowed Maggie's little wagon again and walked into town to buy a bucket of paint, a paint brush, some thinner, and a bag of lime. The storekeeper loaded it into the wagon because the bag was too heavy for me to lift, so when I got started, I used a bucket to scoop the lime out of the bag and dump it into the hole a scoop at a time. I wouldn't allow Clara to help me on a project that was clearly not woman's work. I started by dumping the lime into the pit. It took a while to get the work done. That took care of the stink.

I found a hammer in the barn. Whatever nails were beginning to pop out of their place, I pounded back in, straightening and fastening down some of the boards that had come loose at the bottom and gone crooked. I used a scrub brush to clean the walls inside and out, and once they were dry, I painted both sides in white. The difference was really satisfying.

Again, George made no comment, except to ask how much it cost. When I told him, he began whistling his non-tune and rubbing his chin, but he didn't object.

It was the same when it came to painting and papering the living room. He promised he would do it the first chance he got, but after waiting several weeks, I ran out of patience and did it myself. Again, I didn't ask Clara to help. That would mean her being in the house with Mom Foley all day, and I didn't want to put her through that. It was a lot harder to work alone, but since there was boarding on the bottom half of the walls, the paper strips weren't so long that I couldn't handle them.

I'd planned to get George to run a water pipe and set up a pump in the kitchen like Helen's house, but after asking him over and over, I just gave up completely on that idea. I would ask him, and he would say that he'd think about it, but he made no move to start the job. The longer he put it off, the more resentful I got. After a while I suggested he hire someone to do the work.

"Hire someone? To work here in my own house? I can't spend money for that."

"You don't want to do it, and I can't do plumbing. How else are we going to get it done?"

"My mother's been getting water out of the well without a pump for forty years. It's right at the end of the back porch. If a well and a bucket are good enough for her, it's good enough for you."

His mother stood listening and smiled to herself. I threw up my hands in surrender. I hadn't brought enough money of my own to the marriage to pay for anything myself. I would have to make do with the well and the bucket, at least for the time being, but I began to think that maybe I could do something else to have more of my own money.

I told Clara I would like to do some sewing for other people, and she put out the word. In a few days, I had work. I knew George would find out and wondered what he would say. I was afraid he either wouldn't like his wife working for other women, or that he might take the money from me, which as my husband, he had the legal right to do.

When we got into bed a few nights later, he asked me, "Doug Graham said that Sarah told him you were doing some sewing for some of your friends at the church. Is that right?"

"Yes, it is George. Do you mind?"

"Sure, it'll help pay for all these improvements you're making around here."

I kept my money in a little bag with a drawstring top in the back of the drawer with my underwear. George never mentioned it. It didn't amount to a lot, but it gave me a good feeling to have it.

It was the second week in November. I'd overslept and jumped out of bed, thinking that Lulu would be late to school. I dressed in a hurry, but when I went to Lulu's room, the bed was made and Lulu was gone. Downstairs, I could hear her chattering away. *She must be eating breakfast with George and his mother.*

I was glad Lulu was up, no matter who had wakened her. I walked into the kitchen. George was sopping up the black-eyed gravy with a thick slab of bread. He lifted the bread out of the dish and the grease made a string as it slid back down into the bowl. I leaned over and threw up all over the kitchen floor.

I straightened up and leaned back against the doorframe, so weak I could hardly stand. George looked at me wide-eyed. "What's the matter with you?" he said.

His mother actually cackled. "It's about time," she said.

Lulu's eyes grew wide. "What's the matter, Mommy? Are you sick with the flu or something?"

I stood there, my eyes squinched shut, my throat squeezed so tight I could hardly get a breath, and my mouth filling with water that I couldn't seem to swallow. It was a familiar feeling, and I realized what it was right away.

"I'm all right, baby, just a little sick to my stomach, is all."

George's mother laughed. George and Lulu looked at her in surprise, and she said, "Your mother's going to have a baby, Lulu."

I was angry at the old woman for saying it so blunt. I wouldn't have put it out like that. I'd have waited until my stomach grew, and then would have set Lulu down for a mother-daughter talk and broke the news gently. Mom Foley had no such refinement in her.

Lulu's eyes opened even wider and her jaw dropped open. "A baby? When are you going to have a baby?"

Again, I didn't get to answer first, Mom Foley butted right in. "I'd say about May or June."

I did a little math in my head and nodded in agreement. I hoped the news wouldn't upset Lulu, but I needn't have worried. Lulu jumped up from her seat and grabbed me in a bear-hug. "Have a little girl, Mommy, so I can have a little sister."

Mom Foley got up and walked up to me. She put her own face just a few inches from mine and gazed into my eyes. Then she stuck out her hand and placed it with her fingers spread apart on my stomach, never flinching in her stare, "She's going to have a boy, Lulu, and we're going to see to it that it's a big, healthy one, aren't we?"

My throat began relaxing so I was able to swallow the water that had filled my mouth and I stood straight. "I'm sorry. I'll clean up this mess."

With her hand still pressed against my stomach, the old woman smiled and said, "You go upstairs and lay down. I'll clean it up."

George, Lulu, and I were all speechless. I thought that maybe the world would stop turning, but I was still shaky and glad of the opportunity to rest. I went back upstairs and dozed for another hour. I heard the front door slam behind Lulu as she left for school. I thought maybe George would come upstairs to talk to me before he left, but I heard his horse trotting around the house as he rode for town.

A stubbornness took hold of me. I waited for George to talk about the baby, but he didn't mention it, and I wasn't about to bring up the subject with him. I didn't know if he was happy or not. I was sick every morning for the next three weeks, but had learned when to expect it and always made it to one basin or another before it came over me.

I was almost down to the kitchen one morning when I heard George's mother say to him, "You leave her alone at night, George. You're made just like your father and she doesn't need that going on with her carrying a baby."

George didn't answer. I hoped he would listen to his mother. He hadn't reached for me since that morning I'd thrown up in the kitchen. I wouldn't mind a seven or eight month rest from the painful relations. As much as I longed for him to kiss me or even hold my hand in some sort of tenderness, I hadn't missed his nighttime attentions at all in the last few weeks.

What I did miss, what I pined for, was affection. James had held my hand when we walked together, stopped to kiss my neck when he passed behind my chair, sometimes just wrapped his arms around me and gently held me next to him. I would relax my body against his and feel that I understood the true bond of marriage. George never touched me for anything but the relations. Not anything. It seemed to me that he went out of his way to keep from touching me.

I put on a lot of weight and couldn't do much

without getting tired. I gave up work on any restorations to the house, fearing that lifting things and dragging the wagon back from town filled with supplies might be too much for me. I knew it was useless to ask George to do anything to help. I went to church every Sunday until my stomach was too big and might be an embarrassment.

I'd bedded my garden for spring before the winter set in, and I looked forward to working it after the last frost. Lulu would have to help me. I talked to her about it, and she was excited about it.

Everything seemed to make Lulu happy those days. She loved her teacher, loved her new friends, loved the idea of helping with the garden and especially loved the idea of the baby. She and I sat sewing a layette for him and little coverlets for the cradle in the few daylight hours left after she got home from school. I remembered how I loved sewing with my mother, and now, I loved sewing with Lulu.

Lulu and I both shared our relief when winter passed and the days began growing longer so we could have more light to work.

I'd given up asking George to do anything at all around the house, but realized that if I worked it right, there was a way to get things done. At the kitchen table one morning in April I said to Lulu, "I'll have to ask George to get your cradle down from the attic so we can clean it up."

Lulu was happy at the prospect, but she'd also figured out that George wouldn't ever get around to doing the small chore. "I'll get it down after school,

Mommy," she said. "We can get it cleaned up and ready. It'll be fun."

George walked in just then. His mother fastened her glare on him. "Get upstairs to the attic and bring down that cradle, George."

"I'll get it later, Ma, I'm running a little late right now."

She strode over to him and stuck her face up to his, "Get it right now," she hissed. He jerked his head back away from her. His eyes grew wide. "All right, Ma, I'll get it."

He went out of the room. Lulu looked down at the table in shock. She'd never seen the grandmother like that. I smiled to myself. *There's more than one way to skin a cat around here.*

George's mother didn't miss my reaction, and for the first time, she smiled at me. "You just don't know how to handle a man," she said, then went back to her work.

George was back in the kitchen in a few minutes, cobwebs hanging from his head. It was all I could do to keep from laughing at him. He started to put the cradle in the corner.

His mother glowered at him, "Put it out on the porch so we can clean it up," she barked. He did as he was told, then went straight out to the barn to get his horse and leave for town.

Chapter 19

June second, a Wednesday, in 1915, just before dawn, the first pain woke me. It wasn't an easy pain, like the first ones I had when Lulu was coming, but sharp and strong. I gritted my teeth until it passed and then poked George in the back with my elbow. It took considerable pokes to wake him, but he finally sat up. "What is it?" he asked, as if it had never come to him that it was time for his son to be born.

I took a deep breath. "It's time, the baby's coming. Go fetch the doctor."

He rubbed his chin. "Doctor? Why would I get the doctor? Is there something wrong?"

"George, I told you, the baby's coming."

"My mother's here. She'll take care of it."

"Your mother?"

"She can do it. There's no need to pay a doctor

for something when my mother can do it just as well as he can."

I could see that there was no use talking to him. Maybe his mother could do it. A lot of women had babies with a midwife instead of a doctor. "All right, let her sleep until the pains are closer."

George lay down and went back to sleep right off. I shook his shoulder. "I need for you to get my things. I need the pads to keep the bed clean and the linens and such for the birthing." He answered me with a snore.

I was fed up with his sloth. I thought about hitting him with the flower vase that I kept on my bedside table, but instead got up and gathered what I needed myself. I got the bed ready for the birth and lay back down. Another wave of pain hit me about a half-hour after the first. I rode it out, and after a minute it eased up. When the next one came, it was a little sooner and a little harder than the first two. The sun was coming up, and the rooster crowed. George was sound asleep. I prodded him again with my elbow.

He finally woke enough to look at me. "What?" he asked.

"Go tell your mother it's time, George." Just as he stood to pull on the trousers he'd dropped in the floor the night before, his mother opened the door and came in. She was carrying a bundle of rolled up cloths in one hand. She laid them on the bed and gave an order to her son. "Get out. See to it that Lulu eats and goes to school. We don't need her here in the house while this baby is being born. It might scare her. Just say her mother is too tired to get up, and I'm sitting with her in case she needs anything."

George pulled on his shirt and shrugged into the vest with the badge that he wore to work. I knew that he would do what his mother told him, and for once, I agreed with the old woman. Lulu didn't need to see the birth and didn't need to sit in another room worrying while it happened.

The pains came off and on all morning, coming harder and closer together as I expected. I was getting more and more tired. I wondered if I would have any strength at all when it came time for the baby to be born.

Mom Foley did her work around the house, looking in on me from time to time. Around noon she came in carrying a bucket of water. The pains were close together and awful by then, but I tried to hold on, telling myself it would be over soon.

Mom Foley unrolled the bundle of cloths she had brought in earlier. Inside it were two knives, one I recognized as being from the kitchen, and one I hadn't seen before. It had a short, thin blade. She laid the strange one on the table and stuck the kitchen knife under the mattress. She said, "This is to cut the pain."

There was also a cloth bag that smelled of herbs and a small roll of new string.

A really bad wave of pain rolled over me. I sat up a little and braced myself with my hands behind me. I pulled up my knees. Mom Foley pulled back the covers, then sat on the side of the bed, giving me a single command, "Push!"

I took a deep breath, held it, and pushed as hard as I could. Mom Foley nodded in satisfaction. "One more will do it."

I relaxed as the pain let up, but it was followed right away by another. Again, I took a deep breath and pushed. I could feel it when the baby slid free of me. The old woman laughed sharply and held it up for me to see. "Look at him, a big fat boy, just like I told you," she said, her eyes shining. The baby had long, thick black hair. His grandmother rubbed the herbs over him and began chanting in a low voice. He let out a scream and then began crying shrilly as most newborns do. His grandmother laughed again. "Listen to him!"

She laid him down and picked up the roll of string, cutting off two lengths and tying them on the cord. Then she picked up the small knife and cut the cord between the two knots of string. She wrapped the baby in a blanket, picked him up, and left the room.

I waited for her to come back, but she didn't. After a while I began having sharp cramps. I knew this time that it was the afterbirth. After a few minutes it came out and the cramping stopped. I lifted my head far enough to look at it.

There was more blood than I expected. I waited and waited for George's mother to come back and do something to stop the bleeding, but there was no sign of her. I tried to call out, but I was so weak I couldn't raise my voice. I finally closed my eyes and let myself sink into the blackness.

It was still daylight when the sound of the baby crying woke me. I wasn't sure how much time had passed or where the sound was coming from. I struggled to get up, but was too weak. The best I could do was prop myself up on the pillows. The crying kept on and grew louder.

Mom Foley came in the room with him in her arms. She stood over me and stared at me with a look that could freeze water. I reached out my hands for my baby, but the old woman waited, her look changing to one of satisfaction as I struggled to reach my screaming child. She finally stuck the baby in my hands and stormed out of the room. I held the baby with one arm while I unbuttoned the neck of my nightgown. When I was finally able to hold him to my breast, he latched on right away.

When he was finished eating, I inspected my son. His grandmother had cleaned him up, and I could smell the sweet herbs she'd rubbed on his body. He had thick black hair, almost two inches long, and his skin was the color of new strawberries. I didn't have any idea how much he weighed, but knew it had to be well over nine pounds. Lulu had been only two-thirds as large when she was born, and they told me Lulu weighed a little under seven pounds.

I unwrapped his blanket and examined his body. He was long and thin and had beautiful hands with long fingers and long feet.

I waited, but it didn't happen. The feeling of love that came over me when I had Lulu didn't come. He went to sleep. I gazed at him, waiting for it, and waiting. There was something missing. I held him in the crook of my arm and dozed off again myself, still lying in the bloody, wet, and now cold, bedding.

The slamming of the screen door told me that Lulu had come home from school. She came running up the stairs to my bedroom and grabbed up her little brother. "Look at him, Mommy, he's beautiful. He's just like a little papoose." She ran her hand over his hair.

They weren't words I liked, but they were true. I took hold of Lulu's arm and said, "I need for you to go fetch Clara for me, Lulu. Give the baby to George's mother to take care of until you get back."

Lulu minded me and went to get the neighbor. In a few minutes Clara was there. She had a joyful face that faded to worry as soon as she saw me. "Are you all right? Did you have a hard time of it? I didn't see the doctor's buggy, or I would have come over and helped."

I tried to talk in my normal voice but a whisper was still the best I could manage. "George's mother brought him by herself, but I need you to help me clean myself."

"Didn't she clean you up after he was born?"

"She just took him and left me here. I think I bled a lot, Clara, because I'm so weak, I can hardly move."

Clara pulled back the blankets and gasped. "You mean she didn't even deliver the afterbirth? Good Lord, Maude, you could have died!"

I put my finger over my lips. "I don't want Lulu to know."

Clara nodded. She pulled the chair next to the bed and took a blanket off the stack of linens that I kept nearby. She shook it out and then draped it over the chair. She leaned over me, "Wrap your arms around my neck and hold on, Maude, I'm going to sit you in the chair so I can clean the bed."

I shook my head. "I'm too heavy for you, Clara. You'll have to get George's mother to help you."

"After the way she left you, I wouldn't ask her help for anything."

I wrapped my arms around Clara's neck, and she put her left arm under my knees and her right arm around my waist and half-lifted, half-slid me into the chair. She cleaned the bed, and then she washed me. I was so embarrassed. "I hate it that I can't do this for myself, Clara."

"Nonsense, I may need you to take care of me someday."

"Where's the baby?"

"He's down in the kitchen with Lulu and his grandmother. The way they're making over him you would think they never saw a baby before."

"I'm glad they love him, Clara."

"Of course they love him. Everybody's going to love him."

"Clara, can I tell you something awful and you won't hold it against me?"

Clara stopped her washing. "You can tell me anything, Maude."

"I fed him and looked him over and I waited, Clara, but it didn't come."

"What didn't come?"

"When they put Lulu in my arms for the first

time, my heart swelled up with so much love that I thought it was going to bust right out of me."

"I felt the same way."

I looked in Clara's eyes. "I didn't feel any of that with this baby, Clara. What's the matter with me?"

"You're just wore out, is all. When you get back on your feet you'll be fine. He's a beautiful, healthy boy. You'll come to love him in no time."

I nodded, but I knew in my heart that I would never feel the way I ought to feel for this baby. Clara finished her cleaning, slipped a fresh nightgown over my head and guided it down over me. She pulled up the covers.

"There, good as new. You rest now. I'm going downstairs and get you something to eat."

"I'm not hungry."

"I don't care. You have to eat something, and you need some water to drink or you won't be able to make any milk for that little boy."

Clara went out and I dozed off. It felt wonderful to be clean and dry and warm. She brought me a tray with dinner, and I ate like I was starved and fell back to sleep. When I awoke again, Clara was sitting in the chair next to the bed. It was dark outside.

"What time is it?" I asked, still half asleep.

"It's almost eight o'clock. You had a good sleep."

"I need to pee."

"All right, do you think you can get up to use the chamber pot or should I get something to slip under you in the bed?"

"This is embarrassing, Clara. I don't think I could

make it outside. I'll try to get up and use the jar."

Clara pulled the ceramic bowl out from under the bed. Once again, Clara helped me out of the bed, then held my nightgown up so I could squat over the bowl. It took a few minutes, and Clara was relieved when I was finally able to pass water. It was an important sign that things were all right 'down there.' She helped me back in bed in a sitting position and tucked me in.

"Now, I'm going to fetch the soup I made special for you."

She was back in a few minutes with a bowl of chicken soup and some slices of bread. I hadn't realized it until I smelled the rich broth, but I felt hungry again.

She said, "You eat that and I'll take the pot out and empty it. I'll be right back." I finished my meal and drank a glass of water.

When Clara came back, I asked, "Where's George?"

"He's downstairs. He joined them in admiring that baby. He wanted to see you, but I ran him off. I told him you needed your rest."

The sound of the baby's crying reached us, and Lulu brought him to me this time. "Grandma said that he wanted his supper, and you were the only one that could give it to him. It looked to me like that made her mad."

She handed me the baby. I held him to myself and fed him again. My milk was in, and this time it didn't hurt. As soon as he went to sleep I handed him back to Lulu. "Put him in his cradle, Lulu."

The cradle had been cleaned and furnished with the bedding that Lulu and I made together and placed in the corner of the room, but when Lulu picked up the baby and started in that direction, the cradle was gone.

"Where is it, Mommy?" Lulu asked.

I pursed my lips. "I think Mom Foley has put it in her room. Take him to her."

Lulu left, cooing to the baby. Clara stood and stretched her back. "All the better that he's in her room. You can get more rest that way. I'll go on home now, Maude. If you need me for anything at all, send Lulu to get me, and I'll be here in a minute. I don't care if it's the middle of the night."

I caught hold of Clara's hand. "I don't know what would have happened to me if you hadn't come, Clara."

She smiled and leaned over me and kissed my forehead. "Us women got to stick together, Maude. I'll tell George he can come up now."

In a few minutes George came in. He sat on the bed next to me and took my hand in his. He looked awkward, as if he were embarrassed to be touching me. "He's a fine boy, Maude. You did good. I've never seen Ma so happy."

I decided to keep his mother's treatment of me quiet. "That's good, George. I'm glad you're happy with him." George undressed and got in bed. He was asleep in a few minutes.

Chapter 20

It was several days before I felt well enough to go downstairs. Mom Foley took care of the baby, bringing him to me only when he cried to be fed. He was always clean and seemed to be well cared for. When Lulu came home, she visited me and then went to see her baby brother.

Clara came over twice a day to look after me. She became my lifeline, bringing me my meals, listening to me, praying with me and seeing to my needs. George came and went as he always did. His life didn't change one bit.

One day, about a week after the baby came, I woke feeling stronger. I got out of bed and dressed. The effort tired me, so I sat and rested for a while. I could hear my family chattering downstairs in the kitchen. I made my way down, hanging on to the bannister and sitting down to rest for a few minutes every few steps.

When I finally reached the kitchen, Mom Foley was holding the baby and rocking it. Lulu was eating her corn meal mush, and George was eating his black-eyed gravy. Lulu jumped up and hugged me. "Look, Mommy's here."

Worn out by the trip down, I plopped in the chair. Lulu patted me on the back. "Do you want a bowl of mush?'

I smiled at her. "That would be nice."

Lulu got a bowl, spooned it out, and put it in front of me. Between bites I said, "I guess we ought to name the baby."

George's mother looked down at her grandson with love. "His name is William, after my father."

I was shocked and a little angry. It had never occurred to me that I wouldn't get to name my own baby. "I thought your father would have had an Indian name, him being pure-blooded and on the council and all that."

Mom Foley glared at me, and answered hatefully. "Many of my people took English names years ago."

I looked at George, who ducked his head and kept on eating. Lulu chimed in. "We've been calling him William all along, Mommy. Can't he keep it?"

I sighed. "It'll do. We'll call him William." I looked at George, who still had his head down. "William James Foley."

George looked up in surprise, but I returned his stare, and he dropped his head without objecting and went back to his greasy breakfast.

I really surprised myself with my speaking up like that. After I had time to think it over, I hoped that calling my baby James would help me to come to love him the way I did Lulu. I realized it wasn't natural, the way I felt. It wasn't that I hated him, or even felt bad about him. I didn't feel anything at all about him. He was only another person in the house. I went back upstairs, and when I had taken my Bible out of the bottom drawer of the bureau, I wrote the name on the line under Lulu's.

I fed William and held him every day, but it was as if I were doing it from a distance. Each time Mom Foley came to take him back, I felt relieved that he was out of sight. It bothered me that I wasn't growing to love my own baby, but I didn't know what to do to make it happen. I prayed about it every night for several months and then just gave up. I thought if I did my duty to the child, maybe in time I would love him, but deep inside myself, I knew it would never be the way I loved Lulu.

Chapter 21

A year later, William was toddling around the house. George had taken to calling him Willie and Lulu called him Bud. Since the name Bud appealed to me, that's what I used, too. George's mother still called him William.

His doting grandmother had been urging him to give up nursing and drink milk from a cup. She gave him a cup at every meal, and although I would have rather nursed him for another year or so to help keep from getting in a family way for a while I didn't say anything to her. I didn't see why my mother-in-law kept giving William the cup and almost gloating when he would accept it, until one morning in October.

It was still my habit to do my own laundry on a Tuesday, and I'd changed the bedding and gathered up my wash in a basket to take outside. George hadn't gotten around to running a water line inside the house yet, and I still had to do the wash on the back porch. I held the large basket against one hip with my right hand and the bannister in my left as I started down the stairs.

I heard quick footsteps behind me and then I was hit hard in the middle of my back with such force that I went rolling head-over-heels down the stairs, bouncing off the landing, and then crashing to the floor by the front door. The breath was knocked completely out of me, and I lay there on my back wondering if anything was broken. I opened my eyes and there was Mom Foley at the top of the stairs, grinning down at me.

The old woman went back to her room and came out carrying William. She walked down the stairs, stepping over the laundry that had scattered, and went right past me. By then, I was able to sit up. I seemed to be all right and grabbed at the skirt of the old woman as she swept past. "Why did you do that?"

Mom Foley gave an evil smirk. "I was hoping you'd break your neck, and I'd be rid of you."

I let go of her skirt, and she went to the kitchen, smiling and humming a song to her grandson. I sat still for a while and then bent first one leg and then the other. I tried out parts of my body until I was satisfied my bones were all right and then got up and gathered my laundry from the steps. I picked up the basket and went to the kitchen. George's mother was holding William on one hip while she stirred a pot on the stove. I couldn't stand it anymore. I slammed the basket down on the table. "I've never been anything but nice to you. Why in the world would you want to hurt me?"

The old woman didn't turn around, just kept stirring. "I don't want to hurt you."

"If you don't want to hurt me, why would you push me down the stairs like that?"

"I don't want to hurt you," Mom Foley said, finally turning to look directly at me. "I said, I wanted to be rid of you."

I know my face went white and tried to catch my breath. I lived right in the house with someone who wanted me dead, and I believed she would keep trying until she killed me or someone stopped her.

My heart pounded so loud I could hear it. I ran out of the house and over to Clara's. I beat on the back door. Clara opened it, and her eyes grew wide when she saw the look on my face.

I grabbed Clara's hand. "She tried to kill me, Clara, and I don't think she's going to stop trying until she does it. She told me right out that she wants me gone."

Clara pulled me into the kitchen and sat me down at the table. "Oh, Maude, what are you going to do?"

"I don't know what I can do. Tell George? He won't do anything."

"Maybe you should tell Doug Graham. As deputy, he can arrest her."

I shook my head. "Then what? It'd be my word against hers."

Clara stood and stomped her foot, her fists clenched as tight as her teeth. "You'll just have to take the children and leave him."

I looked up at her. "Where would I go? I can't make enough money sewing and doing laundry to take care of myself and raise two children."

"Oh, God, Oh, God, this isn't right," Clara moaned. "What are you going to do? You can't just wait around to see what else she tries. She might feed you poison, or God knows what else."

"I don't know, Clara. Let's try to think up every possible way she might do it, and maybe I can just be careful not to give her the chance."

So, we two, kind-natured, Christian women sat at the table and discussed ways to kill someone and make it look like natural causes, then listed ways to keep from being a victim. When we were sure we'd thought of every possibility, we both knelt by the table and took turns asking God to keep an angel on guard over me and to change the old woman's heart.

Satisfied that we'd done all we could, I hugged Clara. "I don't know how I could live in that house if you weren't here," I said to my friend, and then I went back to the house, sick with being afraid.

I stayed in my room and sewed until George came home. When I finally went downstairs, my family was sitting around the table, looking for all the world like a normal family. No one would have thought that one of them wanted to be a murderer.

Mom Foley was dipping the stew out of the pot and putting the plates on the table. She sat my plate down last. I gave the old woman a challenging look and picked up the plate and exchanged it with

George's. He gave me a puzzled look, then caught the expression that went between me and his mother. He ate without saying anything about it, and I acted as if nothing had happened.

When he came to bed that night, he turned out the lamp, put his back to me, and yawned as if he were sleepy. I lay in a shaft of moonlight, "Aren't you going to ask me about it?"

George sighed. "Ask about what?"

"Your mother pushed me down the stairs this morning and told me right out she's going to kill me."

George finally said, "What can I do about it, Maude? She's my mother, and she's an old woman. You can't expect me to put her in jail. You'll just have to be careful around her."

"That's pretty much what I thought you'd say."

After that, I was as careful as I could be, looking around me before I went down the stairs, eating only the same food that George ate, being as careful as I could. I knew that, if it happened, it would be something that looked like an accident or something natural, like bad mushrooms. The old woman didn't want to go to jail. She just wanted George and the house and the children to herself, and she would do anything she could think of to get rid of me.

Chapter 22

There was talk everywhere of the war in Europe, but I didn't pay much attention to it. Once in a while, I would get my hands on a real newspaper, not just our little hometown one, and read it from front to back. I would have liked to have a newspaper every day, but the big one was printed in St. Louis and cost too much money.

I didn't see what the war had to do with me. I was fighting my own war right in my home. Sometimes I would catch George's mother looking at me in that way she had, and it would give me a chill. I could tell she was trying to think of a way to get rid of me without getting caught.

In April of 1917, America got in on the fighting. President Wilson, who'd been saying all along that America was staying out of it, finally declared war on

Germany. He started up the draft, and we sent 10,000 men a day to go fight over there.

Almost every one of the young men from the town joined the army without waiting to be drafted and went off to what they were sure would be a great adventure. They were saying it was the war to make the world safe for Democracy, or the war to end all wars. I didn't know what to think about that. I knew that the Bible said there would always be war and rumors of war.

A few of the young men never came home at all. Some were buried in cemeteries across the ocean, some at a place called Flander's Field, and some at Arlington in Virginia, where I read they were laying a lot of our boys to rest. Some died in the forests of France, and they never did find them. Some came home without arms or legs, or blind from the mustard gas. The war finally ended on November 11, 1918, and the rest of those who could, came home. One of them, Johnny Parker, came home with the Spanish Influenza.

I read later that it swept around the world twice in two years, killing between ten and twenty million people, changing as it went. Many people died within hours of coming down with the symptoms. With so many doctors away at war, those on the home front made do with nurses, or medical students. Some had no one to help them. It didn't matter much. There was no treatment except prayer. If a person got the flu, he either lived or died.

As the sheriff, George closed public places, and everyone stayed home as much as possible. When it came to the Parker house, Johnny Parker died, his mother lived, and his father lived. One of the marks of the terrible disease was that it was more likely to take the young and strong than the old or infirm. No one group was spared.

Toward the end of the outbreak in Kennett, there were no coffins left in the town. No one who knew how to make them was well enough to do the work. They wrapped the flu victims in canvas or bedding and buried them as fast as they could. With a shortage of workers, family members who were able, dug the graves in the cemetery themselves, and put up wooden markers that would have to do until they could get a proper stone.

Influenza ran through the town, killing one out of four. The preacher at the Holiness church visited as many sick as he could and then caught the flu himself and died. There had once been three doctors in town. One was away to the hospitals for the soldiers, one was still working twenty hours a day, and one died from the flu.

George was the first in my house to get sick. I kept cold compresses on his head to ease the fever and washed him all over several times a day with cool cloths. In a week he was over the worst of it, but still weak and bedridden.

At three years old, Bud had outgrown his cradle, but still slept on a mattress on the floor in his grandmother's room. She was the next one to get sick, and he was sick right along with her. I tended both of them as I had George, stroking them with the cool cloths and changing the soiled bed linens. Mom Foley was so weak she could barely move, but as I cleaned the vomit and the runny stool from her body and washed her, she looked hard at me, her eyes shining with hatred. It was pitiful, and I pretended not to notice. I talked to her as I worked, "I'm praying for you, Mom Foley, praying that you'll accept the gift of Jesus's salvation for your soul. I don't think Wakondah would hold it against you. I think Wakondah is just a different name for God."

Bud's fever finally broke, and after a few days, he grew stronger, but George's mother slipped away one night. I tried to comfort George and Lulu, but they were both grief stricken and would not be consoled.

I hoped my prayers for the old woman's soul had been answered. George sent a telegram to his sister Bessie, but he knew she couldn't make the trip home. He wrapped his mother in a blanket, and Lulu tended to her little brother at home while I rode with George in the wagon to the cemetery. He had to dig the grave himself, and I read some verses and prayed over it.

Clara's family got sick next. Maggie was the first, but Clara nursed her hand and foot, and she made it through.

Alfred came home one morning just a few hours after going in to work at his feed store. The last thing he said to Clara was that, sick or not, people had to have feed for their animals, and he felt it was his duty to provide it. When he came home, he left his horse tied to the front door and staggered inside. Clara ran to meet him. His weight was more than she could support, and he keeled over in the living room, a red foam running out of his mouth. Clara ran next door to us to get George to help her get him in the bed, but by the time they reached the house, he was dead--that fast. He'd looked fine when he left that morning.

George went into town and got Doug Graham and another man to help him. They rolled Alfred up in a bedspread and loaded him in the back of the wagon. Leaving Lulu home to see to Bud, Clara and I sat in the back of the wagon and rode to the cemetery.

Maggie's bedroom was upstairs in the front of their house. She was still too weak to go to the cemetery, but sat up in her bed and watched as the wagon with her daddy's body disappeared down the street.

Clara woke with a fever the next day. Still weak herself, Maggie dragged out of bed and came to get me. Clara tried to wave me away. "You'll get sick yourself, Maude. You go on home, I'll be all right."

I paid no attention. I bathed her and sang to her and prayed over her. "Remember how you took care of me when Bud was born? This is my time to take care of you."

After a few days, Clara was over the sickness, and Maggie was strong enough to help.

Then I got sick. Clara and Lulu nursed me until I was better. Except for Lulu, everyone in both houses had battled the flu and either won or lost.

Lulu went to bed healthy that night. The next morning when I called, she didn't come downstairs.

Chapter 23

When his mother died, George had taken to cooking his own breakfast and stood at the stove, turning the bacon.

I called Lulu again, but she still didn't answer. As I recall, it seemed as if it all happened in slow motion. George turned to look at me. I met his eyes. Panic flooded through me, and then my insides went cold. I walked out of the kitchen and to the stairs, willing myself to climb them. I pulled myself up the bannister one step at a time. When I reached the landing, I was shaking all over. I stopped and called Lulu's name again and waited for an answer. No answer came.

I kept on, finally reaching the top. George stood in the kitchen doorway, looking up at me. I pushed myself forward one foot at a time to Lulu's room and opened the door.

My beautiful blonde girl lay there, her hair curling down her shoulders, one hand thrown up over her head. Except for a thin trickle of bloody foam running from her mouth and down the side of her face, she looked for all the world as if she were asleep.

George came in the room carrying Bud. I stood there, staring at my precious daughter. I was frozen, and made no sound. George stood next to me, and I looked down at Lulu for a long time. George didn't say anything. It was like he knew nothing he could say that would console me, any more than he could be comforted when his mother died. Bud sensed something wrong. He leaned his head against his father's chest and whimpered.

Finally, George wrapped his arm around my shoulder and patted my back. "I'll take Bud over to Clara's, and we'll see to burying her."

I didn't take my eyes off Lulu. "I want her buried in a coffin, George. I won't have her put into the ground in a blanket."

"Maude, you know there aren't any coffins to be had. We'll have to do what we can."

With my head lowered like a charging bull, I turned to look at him. Grabbing his shirt with one hand, I pushed my face into his and almost growled, "You'll make her a proper coffin if you have to take the planks off the side of the barn, and you'll start it right now, and you won't stop until it's finished, do you understand me?"

George drew back as far as my grip on his shirt would let him. "All right, Maude," he said, and he handed Bud to me and left the room. I pulled the chair up to the bed and sat there with Bud on my lap.

I could hear the sound of sawing and then hammering coming from the barn. The noise didn't matter to Bud, and he fell asleep. After a few hours, George came back. "It's ready, Maude."

I held Bud out to him. "Take him over to Clara and tell her about Lulu. I'll get her ready." George didn't answer me, just lifted the sleeping baby out of my arms and left.

I washed Lulu and combed her hair. I looked through Lulu's dresses and then went to my own room and came back with the embroidered dress I'd worn when I married James and his plaid shirt I'd brought with me from Tennessee. I dressed Lulu in the dress, put her father's shirt around her shoulders, and waited.

After a few minutes, George came back. "Clara wanted to go with us, Maude, but I told her she wasn't well enough yet. The best thing she could do is to look after Bud. Is that all right?"

I nodded. George lifted Lulu and carried her out of the room. I pulled the white quilt Bessie made off of the bed, picked up Lulu's Bible from the table, and followed him down the stairs. The coffin sat on the end of the wagon. Clara waited on the back porch. Bud slept in her arms. Maggie stood by her side, both were sobbing.

George went to lift Lulu's body into the coffin, but I called out, "Wait." George stepped back. I spread out the white quilt in the coffin with the edges folded over the sides and nodded at George. "Go ahead."

He laid Lulu's body in the coffin, folded the quilt over her, put on the lid, and nailed it shut.

George helped me up onto the wagon seat. We made the trip to the cemetery without a word. I waited in the wagon while George found an empty space and dug the grave. He lowered the coffin as gently as he could.

I climbed down from the wagon and stood next to him. I held the Bible in my hand, my mind searching for the right words. Finally, I opened it and leafed through several pages until I found the verses I wanted in First Thessalonians. I read it in a voice so loud, George jumped.

For the Lord himself shall descend from heaven with a shout, with the voice of the archangel, and with the trump of God: and the dead in Christ shall rise first: Then we which are alive and remain shall be caught up together with them in the clouds, to meet the Lord in the air: and so shall we ever be with the Lord.

I closed the Bible and nodded at George. He picked up the shovel and filled the grave. He took a wooden cross from the back of the wagon with the name he'd painted on it, Lulu Connor Foley, and used the hammer to pound it into the dirt.

I said a prayer, and he helped me back onto the wagon. When he climbed up onto the seat, I asked, "Where did you get the wood?"

"I took apart a stall. We only needed one anyway."

I squeezed his hand. "Thank you for that."

He nodded and shook the reins. I gripped the

Bible in my lap so hard, my knuckles were white and, after a while, my hands were numb. We made the return trip the way we came, without speaking.

Chapter 24

I let myself get to where I didn't feel much of anything and slipped into a separate world. The war in Europe officially ended, but I heard the news as something apart from my life. I went about my daily routine in a trance. I cleaned, and I cooked, and I did the laundry. I tended to Bud and saw that he had what he needed. Without his sister and grandmother to pamper him, he clung to me, but instead of finding comfort in the child I still had, I kept my distance. Bud went to George for affection, and George gave it to him. Couldn't anyone say he didn't love his son.

When Bud heard the clip-clop of his father's horse coming home in the evening, he would run to the back porch, yelling, "Daddy, Daddy."

George poured all the love he had into the boy, who was a copy of himself. Bud grew taller and slimmer by the day, his baby fat melting away into the same form as his father's.

George found very little comfort in my arms. There was still no warmth in his touch when he turned to me in the night. Aware of my duty, I submitted. Submission and duty were all I had left to give to him.

Clara tried to get me to come out of my sorrow, but was unable to make a dent in the thick cloud of grief that hung over me. I stopped visiting her and stayed in my own house. I had George bring home what I needed from the stores in town. I'd never missed a Sunday service since the day I was born, but I even stopped going to church. I lived my life on the five acres that were George's property.

Usually up with the first rooster's crow, I took to sleeping late. George didn't say anything. He would fry his bacon and make the coffee for himself. When I put Bud down for his nap, I would lie down myself, and let sleep take me away from my pain until my son woke me.

When Clara came over to see me, I talked in short, sharp answers to Clara's questions. After a few weeks of being hurt by the way I was acting, Clara said, "Maude, I love you but I know you're still grieving. When you need someone, you know where I am."

One morning, about six months after the epidemic was over, it occurred to me that I hadn't the faintest idea how Clara had been getting along. She'd lost her husband, and I didn't even know how she was providing for herself.

I stirred myself and knocked at Clara's back door. She looked so happy to see me there. She threw open the door and grabbed me in a big hug. "Let me pour us some coffee, Maude. I'm so glad to see you."

We sat at the familiar table, and I said, "I feel bad that I haven't been to see you. How have you been getting by without Alfred?"

Clara shrugged. "I hired Billy Simmons and Gregory Hawthorne from the church to help run the store. They're doing all right. I go in and place the orders and do the bookwork once a week."

"Who's going to take care of the man's work around the house for you?"

Clara's place was almost a mirror image of George's, set on the outskirts of town, five acres, a large two-story house and a big barn that housed a cow, two goats, and the horse. Next to the barn was a henhouse.

"I've been doing what I always did. I made a big garden, and I can feed the livestock, but it is a handful, really. It's too much. I'm worn out from all of it. Maggie helps, but I don't want to take away her childhood having her work around here. If something falls apart, I guess I'll hire it done. I've got enough money coming in from the store to pay someone. Alfred was always careful with money. It used to make me mad sometimes when he wouldn't get a new suit or something new for the house, but I guess he knew best. I've been thinking about getting a regular hired hand. He could fix up the shed out back in exchange for a place to live and take care of the livestock for me.

Do you think that would be all right? You know how people are to talk about someone."

"I know better than most how people talk, Clara. It's how I wound up being married to George. I wouldn't give them any shadow of reason to gossip about me if I were you."

"You're right. Maybe I'll ask the pastor what to do."

"Pastor? Did we get a new pastor?"

"About a month ago. We got Brother Aimes to come out from St. Louis. He's young and new to preaching, but he's doing fine."

"What did we do for a preacher before that?"

"We all just met and the men would take turns reading scripture and then we would sing and pray. There's not one family in the church that didn't lose someone, Maude. It was terrible."

I had to look away. "I'm ashamed of myself, Clara. I didn't give a thought to what anyone else was going through. Losing Lulu took the life right out of me. I guess I haven't been a very good Christian, not to think of the others."

"Come back to church, Maude. We all need each other."

"I will. How have you been getting there? Do you walk all the way?"

Clara laughed. "I learned how to hitch up a wagon when I was a little girl. Maggie helps me with it. We've done all right."

"I'll be going with you Sunday."

When the rooster crowed that Sunday morning, I

jumped right up out of the bed. I went downstairs and cooked George's favorite, and only, breakfast and scrambled some eggs for myself and Bud. Then I went back upstairs and shook George's arm. "Get up. Breakfast is ready."

He opened his eyes and looked at me with a curious expression, but got out of the bed without a word. He woke Bud and brought him downstairs, carrying him on one hip. I smiled at him when he sat down. It was the first time he'd seen a smile on my face since that sad funeral.

"I'm going to church this morning, George," I said.

He smiled back at me. "That's good, Maude."

"I want you to go hitch up the wagon. I'll take Clara and Maggie with me. It isn't right for her to have to do that by herself."

George didn't argue. I put a tone in my voice that told him to do what I said. It must have reminded him of his mother, and for some reason, I think he found that comforting.

My fellow church members greeted me so warmly that I was ashamed of myself for staying away this long. The comfort of the church, and the hymns, prayers and the fellowship of others who understood my loss, was exactly what I needed.

Chapter 25

The pain never really goes away. It gets better, and you finally get to a place where you aren't thinking about it every minute of every day. My life settled down again to a pleasant monotony. George ran for re-election, unopposed, and as he always did, he won. Everybody liked George.

Without the old woman to do the bulk of the housework, I had no time for sewing other than mending. I rose early, the way I had before, and gave up afternoon naps. Embarrassed by the dust and cobwebs in the corners that had accumulated while I grieved, I cleaned the house from top to bottom. I pestered George until he tended to the outhouse and was even able to force him to dig a new place for it and move it.

I enjoyed my new authority in the house. George

didn't always do what I wanted right away, but if I asked in the right tone, he would eventually listen. I re-planted gardens out back, mine and George's mother's. It took every minute of sunshine to cook, clean, and take care of the house, the yard, and my son.

Bud was into everything, and I was afraid to take my eyes off him. Left out in the yard, he was likely to pull up half the garden. Left in the kitchen, he would often mix the contents of the sugar and flour and other canisters into a pile in the floor.

He was forever falling down stairs. I saved his life one day by grabbing his shirt just as he was going out of an upstairs window. One afternoon, I was busy baking and didn't hear his footsteps when he awoke. The room that he'd shared with his grandmother was his now. When I went upstairs to get him, he'd gotten into a dirty diaper and spread it all over the room. After that, I had him take his nap on a pallet in the corner of the kitchen.

Late in the summer of 1919, I realized I was in a family way again. There was no morning sickness this time. I could even watch George eat his breakfast. I was strong and well, and didn't have to change my life at all, except I was hungry all the time. I made huge pots of chicken and fluffy dumplings, the way my mother taught me when I was a girl, and ate three times as much as I used to eat. I baked pies and cakes twice a week and ate some every day. Missing a sweet tooth, George ate just enough to keep from hurting my feelings, but Bud adored the pastry and ate almost as much as I did.

By the time I was ready to have my baby in the spring of 1920, I'd put on an awful lot of weight and had only two dresses I could wear. I washed one and wore the other. I waited and waited, but the time I thought the baby would come passed, and still I got bigger. It was all I could do to get up out of a chair, and I went to the outhouse to pass water forty times a day.

I knew the baby was all right. It kicked hard every day, so I didn't worry. I talked to the doctor about it at church one Sunday, and he told me the same thing my hometown doctor told Helen, "It's like an apple on a tree, Maude. It'll fall when it's ready."

I was cooking supper one afternoon when my water broke right in the kitchen. There wasn't any pain, so I just cleaned up the mess, changed my clothes, and went back to my housework. When George came home, and we sat to eat, I told him between bites, "The baby is coming tonight."

"How bad are the pains?"

"I don't have any pains yet, but my water broke a while ago, so it'll be tonight."

"Do you want me to get the doctor?"

"No, I think I'll just have you go get Clara. It's not like it was my first time."

For the first time since we married, George looked at me with something that looked like admiration. "If you say so," he said, and finished his dinner. I was cleaning up the dishes when the first pain started. I stopped my work, held onto the edge of the table until it passed, then went on with what I was doing. I was familiar with the sensation and knew I had

209

plenty of time. After the kitchen was clean, I went over to Clara's house and knocked.

When Clara opened the door, I told her, "My water broke this afternoon, and the baby's coming tonight. I'll have George come get you when it's time."

"I'll come right now," Clara said.

"No need for that. You go on about your chores. There's no telling how long it will be before I need you."

I gathered the linens and pulled up enough buckets of water from the well to heat for the delivery. I checked the fire in the kitchen stove to see that it would bank well enough to keep the water hot but not boil it all away. The spring night was quite chilly, so I told George to build a fire in the parlor fireplace. He kept staring at me and asking if I were all right, but I just waved him away, saying, "I'm fine." I had him take Bud to bed and tuck him in for the night.

George and I went to bed at the usual time. He fell asleep right away. I lay awake in the dark. When the pain reached a point where I knew I needed help, I poked George awake and sent him for Clara. It was after midnight, but Clara came in fully dressed only a few minutes later. She pulled the chair up next to the bed. George went down to the kitchen to make coffee and wait.

I was relieved to see her. "How did you get here so fast? It's the middle of the night."

"I left my dress on and lay down on the divan in the parlor. I didn't want to waste any time when you called me."

Gritting my teeth to ride out a pain, I tried to laugh. "We have time, but not much. It ought to be any minute now. I can feel it."

I sat up and pushed, then relaxed, then in just a minute did it again. After a half-hour of pushing I didn't feel any different. "Clara, take a look and see what's happening down there."

Clara pulled back the covers, and I saw her forehead crease.

"What is it, Clara?"

"I can see a foot sticking out, Maude. It's going to be breech."

"Tell George to go get the doctor, and tell him to hurry."

Clara ran downstairs, and in a few minutes, Clara and I heard Pawnee galloping out of the yard. The pains kept on with Clara watching, hoping for progress. None came. My stomach shifted, and the foot that had been sticking out disappeared back up inside. I felt as if my body were being ripped apart.

It seemed like a long time, but finally, the doctor came. He rushed into the room. Clara told him what had happened so far. He did a fast examination, pressing my stomach here and there and told me, "I'm going to try to turn it around so it can come out the right way, Maude, but it's an awfully big baby. We might have to take it Caesarian." I'd heard of that, but never knew anyone who had a baby that way.

The doctor pushed around on my stomach, pressing hard this way and then the other. After a few minutes, he shook his head, "This isn't going to work."

He pulled the covers all the way off the bed and reached for his bag. Another pain grabbed me, and I couldn't help but push again. "Look," Clara cried. "A foot is sticking out."

The doctor grabbed hold of it and pulled a little. Clara said, "Hold on, Maude, the rest of the leg came out and I can see a little bottom. One leg is out but the other is folded up inside."

The doctor worked to free the baby, and after a little while, he had it out of my body. It was a boy. He rubbed it and slapped its fanny, but it didn't cry. He held it up in the air and slapped it some more. Still no cry. He held it up to his face and tried breathing into its mouth. Nothing. Clara and I were both crying.

He held the baby out to Clara. "Put him somewhere out of the way, Clara. We can't do anything for him. Maude's torn up bad and bleeding, and she needs us to take care of her now."

Clara wrapped a cloth around the baby and laid it on the floor under the bed. The doctor massaged my abdomen and delivered the afterbirth. When he was satisfied the bleeding had stopped, he made the necessary stitches, packed his things and picked up his bag to leave. "I'm sorry, Maude. I wish I could have done better."

Clara cleaned up the bed and cleaned up me, both of us still crying, but now not so hard. Clara leaned over me before she left and kissed my forehead. "We'll bury him tomorrow, Maude. Please try to get some rest for now. You need your strength. I'll tell George. He can sleep in another room for tonight."

I cried for a while and then drifted off to sleep. I don't know how long I had been sleeping when a sound woke me. At first I thought it was one of the cats in the back yard, or that I'd imagined it. Then the night air was split by the scream of a hungry, cold baby. I sat bolt upright in the bed.

I must be sleeping and having a nightmare, I thought, but the screaming continued. I got out of the bed and looked underneath. Squirming and kicking, my baby was demanding attention. I picked him up and wrapped a blanket around him, then got back into the bed. I held him to my breast and looked down at him as he had his first meal. A wave of powerful emotion swept over me. It was a familiar feeling, and I gave thanks to God for it, for the same rush of love that I'd felt the first time I held Lulu.

When George came to see me in the morning, he was speechless. I was sitting up in bed, holding the baby in my arms and singing to it. He had straight, dark-brown hair like mine and my daddy's, and he was the biggest newborn I'd ever seen. His fat cheeks hung down on his chest, and his arms and legs were round and pink.

I smiled up at George. "His name is 'Charles Eugene Foley,' after my daddy," I told him, "and we're going to call him Gene."

George shook his head. "I've not been thinking of any names other than George, Junior, for a boy, but I never said anything to you about it, and I can tell that "Charles Eugene" is a done deal. I guess it's right that you get to name this one."

"Go get Clara for me, George. I can't wait for her to see him."

George fetched Clara, who was thrilled with the news that the baby we thought was lost was doing just fine.

I wouldn't let him out of my sight, so Clara laid him on a towel on the bed and cleaned him up. Clara brought the Bible to me, and I wrote the name under William's.

I was too weak to do much for a few days, so Clara took care of Bud during the day and made our meals, and George did what he could for me at night.

Little Gene was always hungry. When he was a month old, we made our first trip to church, stopping by the feed store on the way home to weigh him on the scale there. At four weeks old, he weighed eighteen pounds.

If Bud was George's boy, Gene was mine. I seldom left a room without taking him with me. I made a sling out of a piece of cloth and carried him around the way the Indians did. Happily, Bud was fond of his little brother, and I saw no signs of jealousy. George gave all his attention to Bud and hardly any to Gene, and that seemed to prevent what sibling rivalry would have normally been expected.

Bud was still the captain of mischief, even though I spanked him and told his father when he misbehaved. George didn't spank, didn't rebuke and, in fact, sometimes laughed at the trouble Bud would get into. That only served to encourage him. He looked for ways to make his father laugh, and he succeeded.

He put my church hats on the cow, stuck string beans up his nose and pretended he was a walrus that he'd read about in school. He chased the rooster around the yard until it turned on him and spurred his back. He tried to ride the goats and only laughed when they threw him off. He tied paper bags on the dogs' feet and laughed at them as they walked. The only animals he never touched were George's horse and the cats. Pawnee was too important to his father. Bud knew that aggravating the horse was a line he dared not cross, and he left the cats alone because cats have claws.

Chapter 26

Woodrow Wilson was still president in 1920 when the amendment giving women the right to vote was passed. An election was coming up soon. Warren G. Harding, a Republican, was running against James Cox, the Democrat, who had Franklin D. Roosevelt as his vice-presidential candidate. I wasn't sure what it was all about, so I decided to investigate. I began reading the newspaper regularly for the first time in my life.

I asked George several times to bring the paper home with him, but he forgot more often than not. On the days I walked into town, I would buy one and put it in with my groceries. At home, when I finished my housework, I would sit in the light from my bedroom window and read it from front to back, then go sit with Clara and talk about what I'd learned.

On Election Day, I dressed the children and

myself in our church clothes. I came downstairs carrying Gene. George was standing at the stove, frying his bacon. Through the screen door, I could see Bud sitting on the porch with the mop laid down the brown dog's back. He was singing and tying the strings around the dog's head to make a wig. The dog wagged his tail and licked at the child's face.

After George's mother died, he took to making his own breakfast every morning, saying that I didn't do it right. When he saw me with my hat on, George looked at me in surprise. "What's the occasion? There a church meeting this morning?"

No, I want you to hitch up the wagon. I'm going to ride into town with you so I can vote."

George stopped poking at the bacon with his fork and shook his head. "You can't do that, Maude," he said in a voice so low I could hardly understand him.

"What do you mean, I can't do that? The new law says I can."

"It isn't fitting for women to try to vote. You won't know what you're doing."

I got so mad my face must have turned purple. I planted my feet and put one hand on my hip. "I suppose you think you DO know what you're doing?"

"Of course, I do. I'm voting for Cox."

"Why?"

"Because he's the best man, that's why."

"Why is he the best man? What does he want to do that's better than what Harding wants to do?"

George's mouth dropped open, and he stammered, "Why—uh…"

217

When he didn't answer me, I tilted my head. "What do you think about the League of Nations? Is it a good thing, or should we just get out of it and mind our own business? What do you think about Prohibition, or letting them teach the children in school that we came from monkeys?"

George had no answers for me. He turned his bacon again and then said, "Who do you expect to vote for, Maude?"

I met his eyes with a steady gaze. "That's none of your business, George."

He stared down at the pan of bacon for a minute, then picked it up and put it on the sideboard. "I guess I've lost my appetite," he said. He went out and headed to the barn. I poured myself a cup of his thick coffee. I'd got used to it over time and could drink it now without loading it with sugar or watering it down. I sat to wait for him to bring the wagon around. A few minutes later, he galloped by on Pawnee.

I took Bud's hand and pulled him behind me as I went to see if Clara had left yet for the store. It was one of the days Clara would normally have gone in to do the books and ordering.

Clara was expecting me. She held the back door open. "I kind of thought you might want a ride into town. Yesterday, I heard the men talking out in the front of the store when they didn't see me in the office. A lot of men are forbidding their wives to vote or telling them who they have to vote for."

I nodded. "It's a good thing it's private. They can just vote for who they want and tell their husbands what they want to hear. I'm not surprised, though. At least George didn't try to forbid me."

"What would you have done if he had?"

I smiled at her. "I guess I'd of had to turn him in to the U.S. Marshall for breaking the law. After all, it's his job to see that we get to vote just like anyone else."

Both of us just about fell down laughing. I went out to the barn with Clara and helped her hitch the horse to the buggy. Clara called to Maggie that she was ready to go, and I got Bud and Gene. The five of us rode into town. We dropped Maggie off at school. It was closed for the election, but the teen-agers had gathered there, and Maggie wanted to wait with her friends.

We went on to the courthouse. George was there to keep order, standing behind a line of men who were jeering at each woman who walked up the steps. I glared at him, then jutted out my jaw in determination. Some of the men turned to George and called out. "Look out, George, next thing you know she'll be wearing your pants and wanting to be a deputy."

George took the ribbing with a smile, but I could tell he wasn't enjoying it much. He let on like it was all right. We marched past the men and into the courthouse, signed the book, and were given slips of paper and pointed to a curtain. Clara and I stood in the line behind three men and another woman. All the time, the men murmured back and forth and scowled at us.

When it was my turn to vote, I handed Gene to Clara, stepped into the cubicle with Bud in tow and pulled the curtain closed behind myself. I made my marks on the paper, folded it over, took it back to the table, and dropped it in the box. Then I took Gene from Clara's arms so Clara could take her turn. Bud could tell that something important was happening, and he stood quietly beside me, well behaved for one of the few times in his life. Clara finished a few minutes later, and we went back outside. The men standing around started up loud complaining about uppity women again. Clara took my elbow. "Let's go home, Maude."

I shook my head. "No, I can walk. I know you have work to do at the store."

"Not today. I told the boys yesterday that the store would be closed for Election Day."

We climbed into the buggy, and Clara slapped the reins on her horse's back. We chatted about different things until we neared the outskirts of town, and I got to thinking about what we'd done and stopped talking. Clara looked over at me and saw that there were tears running down my cheeks. "What's wrong, Maude?"

I shook my head. "Nothing is wrong, Clara. You and I just voted. It's the first time in my life I felt like I mattered, that I had some say about what was going on. Things couldn't be more right."

I was aggravated with George that he tried to forbid me to vote, but later on, I came to appreciate him. I heard that more than one woman in our little town was kept home by force, and some of them were even beaten. George was sometimes slothful, but in all the years we spent together, he never laid a finger on me to harm me.

Chapter 27

In 1923, I got a letter from George's sister Bessie telling me she'd given birth to a fine little girl and named her Maxine. Bessie was beside herself, she was so happy. She'd been wanting a baby all these years and finally had one. That same year, when I was thirty-two years old, I gave birth to another little girl. After having Gene come breech like he did, we'd planned to call the doctor, but the baby came so fast, there was no time. I woke George in the middle of the night, and he ran for Clara. It was an easy delivery. When the baby was cleaned up, and I was taken care of, Clara placed the little bundle in my arms, and I was relieved when the surge of love ran through me, the same way it did when Gene and Lulu were born.

It was his turn, so George named the pretty baby Elizabeth Susan, after his sister, and we agreed not to call her Bessie, but Betty Sue. I'd picked out other names, but since George hadn't objected to me naming Gene after my father, I didn't argue with him. Besides, I loved Bessie, and I had always liked the name Elizabeth. I wrote it in the Bible, Elizabeth Susan Foley. When I'd finished, I blotted the ink and couldn't help but cry a little when I looked at Lulu's name on the top line. She would have loved the boys, but she would have been so happy to have a little sister.

Not long after Betty Sue was born, everyone in the church had a family picture taken. The town's undertaker had traveled to St. Louis and learned how to use a special camera. He set up a little studio in one of the rooms in his house. One of the ladies from the church with a gift for painting had done a mural on the wall as a background.

When Betty Sue was a few months old, we all rode into town and had our picture taken. I sat in a straight-back chair and held Betty Sue in my arms. Gene stood to my right side, leaning against me. George stood next to my chair with his right hand on my shoulder and his left hand holding tight to the squirming Bud. When the picture was ready, I bought a hinged, double frame. I put the family picture on one side with the only picture I had of Lulu on the other. Lulu was eleven when it was taken. She was wearing a white dress and had a wide ribbon in her hair. Her pretty curls fell over one shoulder, down almost to her waist.

When Bud was old enough to go to school, he began riding into town behind his father on Pawnee's back. Bud was a miniature George. He looked just like his father, walked and talked just like him, and shared the same easy way of making people laugh. Everybody liked George, and everybody liked Bud.

At school, he mocked the teacher when her back was turned, and even she laughed at him. At church, he pretended to fall asleep and faked a loud snore until I poked him in the ribs with my elbow. The preacher would smile at him at the door, pat me on the hand, and tell me patience was a virtue. Bud had his father's charm. Everybody liked Bud.

Chapter 28

Life was pleasant enough for me. George didn't ask as often for the painful relations. I enjoyed cooking and cleaning the house. It was a more comfortable place, now that his mother wasn't in it. I'd painted and papered the downstairs rooms without help from George.

Since his mother died, I finally came to think of the place as my home, and I was sometimes able to coax George into spending some of his money for a new piece of furniture. I made curtains for all the downstairs windows and changed the paper and curtains in the old woman's bedroom to make it more of a boy's room for Bud.

Bud grew taller and lankier, and Gene thrived. A happy, sturdy boy, he preferred my company to George's and Bud's, and would sit at the kitchen table and play with his toys, chatting away while I cooked.

Betty Sue got prettier every day, with plump, full features, and dimples on her cheeks, knees and elbows. She was another one who was going to look like her father, with thick black hair that grew quickly and had a soft wave to it. She was a pleasant child, smiling and gurgling as an infant, later, sitting happily, singing and playing on her blanket in the corner of the kitchen. I had my precious children, my home, my best friend, Clara, and my church. My life was happy, and my heart was full.

I realized in March of 1928, at the age of thirty-six, that I was expecting again. I wasn't thrilled with the idea. I was satisfied with the way things were and didn't want them changed. I didn't even tell George for a long time. I'd had what I assumed were miscarriages twice since Betty Sue was born and preferred to keep it to myself, except, of course, for Clara.

I could see George looking at my growing stomach, but it was well into half-way through the time before he finally asked me about it. "Are you in a family way again, Maude?"

"I guess so, George. It'll come in the fall, if I figure right." No more was said about it, and I couldn't tell if George was happy with the news or not.

It was early October and I was changing the sheets on the bed one morning. I picked up the corner of the mattress and a gush of warm water ran down my legs. I cleaned myself from the mess, and made the bed ready for the delivery. When Clara came home from working at the store, I had Bud run over and fetch her.

Clara was there in only a few minutes.

"How is it, Maude? Should I get the doctor?"

"It's not bad yet, Clara, just regular pains. Let's wait and see how it goes. I hate to spend money on a doctor if I don't have to. Betty Sue came so easy I expect this one will do the same."

That's not how it happened. My labor went on and on and got worse all the time. I suffered with it through the night, with Clara sitting by my side. George slept with Bud, undisturbed by the whole process.

In the morning, the pain grew so bad that I didn't think I could stand it any longer. Clara lifted the covers and looked for some sign that the baby was coming, but couldn't see anything. The water was still trickling out, but there was no sign of blood or anything else.

I told her, "You better see if you can get a doctor here, Clara. He may have to cut this one out. I think there's something wrong."

Clara ran downstairs and to tell George to fetch the doctor. He saddled up Pawnee and galloped off. He came back alone an hour later.

"The doc said he'll get here when he can. There was an accident at the mill, and some of the boys were hurt bad. Maude, you'll have to hold on."

I held on all day. If it hadn't been for the children in the house, I would have screamed from the agony. I had Clara tell George to cut me a short piece of the thick rope from the barn, and I clenched it between my teeth so I could be quiet when the pains tore me apart. The doctor finally got there just before sunset. Clara

226

lit several oil lamps to give him light, and he examined me.

After a minute, he stood and huffed out his cheeks, took off his glasses and shook his head. "I'm afraid it's going to be a dry birth, Maude. I'll do the best I can to make it easier for you."

He handed a little glass bottle to Clara. "When the pains come, hold this under her nose, it'll make it better."

It was several more hours before the birth was over. Finally, a screaming boy was delivered. He had his father's black hair and gangly body. When the delivery was over, Clara put the baby in my arms, and I held it to my breast. I looked at it and waited, but the only thing I felt the same as when Bud was born. It about broke my heart, and I asked God to forgive me and help me love this new baby.

Clara was tidying up the room and gathering the bedclothes that needed to be washed. The doctor picked up his bag. "Well, I guess we made it all right, Maude. I'm sorry it couldn't have been it easier for you, but all things considered, we did a pretty good job of it."

I reached out and grabbed his hand. "Can you do something for me so I won't have any more?"

He gasped and stepped back, jerking his hand free of my grip. "Not have any more babies, Maude?"

"That's right, I don't want any more. I've got four to see after now, and I know that I've lost others through the years. Isn't that enough?"

"Babies are a gift from God, *Sister* Foley, and I'll

do nothing to interfere with His will. When you say your prayers tonight, you give thanks you have this family and ask His forgiveness for even thinking about such a thing." He slapped his hat on his head and stormed out.

Clara shut the door behind him. "I've heard about things you can buy so you don't get more babies, Maude, but I haven't the faintest idea how to get them."

"I don't know either, but I do know one thing. I'm not going to have another baby. I'm going to nurse this one as long I can."

Clara giggled. "That'll make it hard for him to go to school."

I shook my head and looked down at the ugly baby. He was so red he was almost purple. His eyes were swollen shut, and he had an angry expression on his little face. "He doesn't look like a college boy to me, anyway," and both of us laughed until we cried.

When the baby finished nursing and fell asleep, Clara called in the rest of the family to see him. Bud stood in the corner, looking embarrassed. Gene poked at it with his finger and talked baby talk to it. Betty Sue looked as if she had been given a new doll and was allowed to sit on the bed and hold it in her arms. George picked him up and rocked him a little in his arms. "We'll call him Paul, after my brother."

I frowned at him. "I didn't know you had a brother."

"He died a long time ago. It's better not to talk about it."

I turned my head to the wall. "Call him what you want, George. Paul Foley is as good a name as any."

The next day, when I took my Bible out of the drawer for my daily reading, I wrote Paul's name on the line under Betty Sue's.

I had a good home, a husband that didn't abuse me, and four healthy children. A woman ought to be satisfied with that, but I seldom fell asleep without thinking about James and what we'd meant to one another. I longed for George to touch me in a tender way, to hold my hand or kiss the back of my neck, like James had every single day we were together, but he never did.

Out of pride, I wouldn't ask him for what I wanted. I suppose, since pride is a sin, I was sinful to keep quiet and ache for something I maybe could have had.

Chapter 29

Outside of my longing for tenderness in my marriage, I was more or less happy with life. I settled back into my routine. I went to church on Sunday, washed laundry twice a week, cleaned and cooked. I said my prayers, giving thanks for the good things in my life, and always making prayer requests for others, not myself, as I'd been taught.

Bud was a rascal, barely a teenager and already drinking. His father was forever getting him out of one scrape or the other. Gene was my precious boy, always obeyed me, eager to help. Betty Sue grew prettier every day. She was the image of her Aunt Bessie, and I wished we could take her to visit so I could see Helen and Faith. George always had some reason we couldn't go. Betty Sue seemed to be growing up faster than the others. I hated the thought that soon she'd be going to school.

One morning in 1929, George and Bud had finished their breakfast and gone out to the barn to get Pawnee ready for the trip to town. Gene liked to walk to school with his friends and had already left. Too big to ride behind his father, Bud should have been gone already, but he never minded being late for classes. I was mixing the dough for bread. I heard a terrible cry from the barn. Afraid that Bud had hurt himself, I ran out. Bud stood with his back pressed against the open barn door, his eyes wide, and a panicked look on his face. George sat on the stall floor, sobbing and wailing, his arms held Pawnee's head. His horse had died during the night.

I froze. I didn't know right away what I could do. Then I took Bud's hand and pulled him away with me, closed the door behind us and left George to grieve in private. I took Bud over to Clara's, and Clara agreed to drop him off at school when she took Maggie, and to tell the deputy that George wouldn't come to the office that day.

I went back to the kitchen. Paul and Betty Sue sat safely where I'd left them. I went about my day, baked the bread and looked out the back window from time to time. It was after noon when I saw George come out of the barn, walk past the house, and head into town. Late that afternoon, a large wagon came with several men on it. One of them knocked at the front door.

When I opened it, he stood there with his hat in his hand, "Good afternoon, Miz Foley. George sent us to fetch Pawnee."

"How's George doing?" I asked.

The man shook his head. "It's real hard on him, Miz Foley. You know how he loved that animal."

"I know. You go do what you have to do, and-- thank you."

He nodded, turned, and put his hat back on. They drove the wagon out back. I didn't look out again until after I heard the wagon drive away.

Bud walked home from school with Gene and Maggie. There was no sign of George. I stayed up later than usual waiting for him, but finally left a lamp burning by the front window and went to bed. When I woke the next morning, the lamp was out of oil, and he wasn't there. I dressed myself and the children. After they were fed I got out the little wagon and set Paul in the back of it, with Betty Sue in front of him. With Bud and Gene walking beside me, we went into town. I stopped at the schoolhouse and left Bud and Gene there, and then I went to the jail.

Deputy Graham sat at the desk. He jumped to his feet. "Good morning, Maude. Did you come to see after George? I was going to wake him when I came in, but then I thought better of it."

"Where is he?"

Doug pointed with his thumb to the back room. "He's sleeping back in the cell. He'll be all right after a while. It's just hard for him. You know."

"Yes, I know." I opened the door to the back of the building. George lay on the bench in the cell. The door was open. He slept soundly. The stale aromas of whiskey and tobacco hung in the room. "I'll leave him be. Thank you, Doug. Say hello to Sarah for me."

"I will, Maude. George will be all right. It'll just take him a while."

I nodded and left. I thought about stopping at the store but changed my mind. I pulled the wagon with Betty Sue and Paul riding in it behind me, and by the time I got home, it was time for their naps. I settled them down and went back to the routine of my afternoon. George didn't come home again that night, but I didn't go look for him the following morning. I figured he would come home when he was able.

After four nights of sleeping alone, I was fixing breakfast when I heard the front door open. I walked into the front hall. George stood there, hat in hand, with a sheepish expression on his face. I just looked at him. "How are you, George?"

He blushed. "I'm all right, I guess. I need a bath and some clean clothes."

I could smell him from where I stood. "There's hot water on the stove."

I went back to my work. After he cleaned up, he came back to the kitchen. "I'm sorry about being gone like that, Maude. I know I worried you."

I hadn't really worried about his welfare all that much. I understood his grieving and knew that the people in town would take care of him. "It's all right, George. I know how much you cared for Pawnee."

He sat at the table and hung his head. "I was always going to stand him to stud, but I thought I had plenty of time."

"There are a lot of his father's stock in town. Maybe you can buy one of them."

George shook his head. "It wouldn't be the same."

"Well, you have to get something."

"I know, I'll think on it."

I didn't say anything else.

George spent time in the barn every night for

weeks. Sometimes, when he came to the house, I could tell by his red face and puffy eyes that he'd been crying. He hadn't grieved that much when his mother died.

For the next few days, George left early to walk to work. Bud went back to his old habit of staying with his father at the jail after school. When they came home, George went out to the barn and stayed there working on something. Sometimes Bud would go out to join him and watch, but he wasn't accustomed to his father being so quiet, and, as often as not, would stay for only a short while.

A few weeks later, I sat at my bedroom window to catch the afternoon light while I sewed. A car drove up to the house and around the back. There'd been more and more automobiles and trucks appearing in town over the years, but they were still scarce enough that I was surprised. I put my sewing aside and rushed down the stairs. The barn doors were both open. Inside, George was climbing down from a Model 'T' Ford. I was dumbfounded. I'd always felt that only wealthy people had cars. George had taken out the boarding that made up the stall and parked the car in the area that used to belong to Pawnee.

He shrugged when he saw me standing there. "Had to have something," he said.

I found my voice. "How are we going to pay for this, George?"

"I bought it off of Doc Hennings. He gets a new one every few years. He gave me a good price on it, two hundred dollars."

"Where are we going to get two hundred dollars?"

"I took it out of the bank."

I stared at him. He'd always been a little tight-fisted, complaining when I spent money on a piece of furniture or when he thought I'd bought a little pricey fabric, but I thought it was because he didn't have money and had to be careful about what he spent. "How much do we have in the bank?"

"Not as much as I did have." He had that grin on his face like he'd told a funny joke and was waiting for me to laugh. "I'll save up more. I like to have something to fall back on. You never know."

"I was wondering. This is a big house. How did your dad get enough money to pay for it?"

"He didn't. My mother had money her father left her from some sort of government settlement with the tribe. When they would fight, she'd remind him he lived in her home, not the other way around."

I wanted to press him for an amount, but decided not to for the time being. It comforted me to know he had something saved. I was well aware of the value of money. "Dinner will be ready in about a half-hour. You're early."

George nodded and waved his hand at the car. "That's all right. I got things to do here."

I went back to the kitchen and my cooking. As I stirred the stew, I realized that after living with him all these years and bearing him four children, there were still too many things I didn't know about this man.

I resented that George wouldn't tell me how

much money he had. That made it his, not ours. I decided I would somehow get more of my own. The question was how to do it. My eyes weren't as good as they once were, and I'd just about given up sewing for friends, only doing the work for a few of them and for my family.

I usually charged things at the stores, and George would pay the bill at the end of the month, so I didn't handle cash. It was ridiculous. I was a grown woman, and except for the small amount still in the bureau drawer that I brought with me from Tennessee, I didn't have money to call my own.

I talked it over with Clara, who had a ready solution. "Sister Thompson down the road quit keeping chickens when her husband passed. She's probably been buying eggs from the store. I bet if you asked her, she'd buy them from you. You've got more than you need for your family. If you explained things to her, she'd keep quiet so George wouldn't need to know about it."

"I don't care if he knows about it or not. He didn't care about my making money from sewing. I think he liked it when I could bring in my own cash."

The next day, I talked to the Thompson widow and made the deal. Then she thought of someone else who would do the same thing. It didn't amount to much, two dozen eggs a week, but those few cents were my money, and it had nothing to do with George. What I made from sewing before mostly went into decorating the house and pretty fabric for clothes for Betty Sue and me. The egg money was different. Every week, I slipped the coins into a pasteboard box and put it under my step-ins in the bottom drawer of the bureau. Every time I added a few cents I felt a warm satisfaction. It wasn't the amount I had so much as it was the fact that I had it, and George didn't know about it.

Chapter 30

There were three dogs on the place when I came, all male. Over the years, when one died, George would grieve for a while but be comforted by the presence of the other two. The lost pet would sooner or later be somehow replaced by a puppy that someone gave George. I liked the dogs, and once in a while, gave one a pat on the head, but they were George's dogs, the same way that Bud was his boy.

After Pawnee died, George didn't bring home any more puppies. I think he'd been hurt too much by losing Pawnee and didn't want to feel that way ever again.

The cats were a necessity and kept the varmints from over-running the barn and house. They were mostly wild. I'd become attached to only one or two over the years. They didn't have to be fed, providing for themselves with mice and snakes. The cats were really George's property, too.

I had the children, but I was lonely. Clara spent more of her time at the store. Except for Mondays, when she stayed home and both of us did our wash and had the afternoon to work together and talk. I was alone all day with the two small children. I had plenty of work to fill my time, but I longed for the companionship of another adult, and George didn't help any. We were like two strangers sharing a house in the daytime. Once in a while, there were a few minutes relations at night that still didn't mean anything to me.

My talks with George were always about practical matters. I didn't talk to him about the things I could talk about with Clara, things like what I read in the paper, my dreams for our lives, and about 'woman' things.

In 1928, I voted for Herbert Hoover. I read about his work as an engineer and how good he'd been working for the government after the war. Partly, I voted for him because I admired his wife's dignity. He turned out to be a sad disappointment to me.

In 1929, I planted my gardens in late April like I always did. I'd kept my flower beds in the original spot I planted the first year I came to Missouri. After George's mother died, I kept the vegetables in the plot of ground that the old woman used. It didn't rain that spring and summer, at least, not enough to water the gardens. For weeks, I carried water from the well to the vegetables, trying to keep the young plants alive.

Some of the neighbors had their wells run dry and had to carry buckets of water from nearby springs to use in their homes. I thanked God we were better off than that. I let the flower beds go dry, even though it grieved me, but kept on drawing enough water for the vegetables.

We had to eat, and as the summer went on, and

the rains still didn't come, prices for food in town went higher and higher. We ate mostly chicken. It was the wrong time of the year for fresh pork. The only thing still left out in the smokehouse were several hams and the slabs of bacon that George loved so much. I wondered if they would last until October, when the hogs would be butchered.

George didn't raise his own hogs, but would buy the meat from the freshly killed and cleaned animals, bring it home, and smoke it himself. He'd never impressed me with any ambitious work, but he seemed to enjoy curing the meat and did a good job of it. He would come home with several dead hogs that had been split down the middle and hang them up on a rack in the back yard, where he cut them into the portions that suited him.

When he butchered the meat, he kept several tubs placed in a circle around him, tossing one kind of bits in one tub, another kind of parts into the next. When he was finished, he would take the large cuts of meat, wrap them in muslin, and carry them into the smokehouse, where he hung them on hooks from the ceiling. He lit the fire in the center of the room and let the smoke do its job.

Outside, the bones were scraped and the rest of the meat ground up in a machine George fastened to the porch rail and cranked by hand. Then, that meat was seasoned with sage and stuffed into the cleaned intestine casings for sausage. He was very particular that it be done just the way he liked, and it was cheaper than buying the meat already smoked.

I'd almost come to appreciate his being frugal. It wasn't over much, and I liked the aroma of hickory that filled the air when the meat was being cured. The bones were boiled, and I used them and the fat to make soap.

The lack of rain went on into the fall. I'd always changed my tub of wash water for the laundry with each load, but I began using the same water over again, washing the whites and light colors first, then the darks. It didn't sit well with my ideas of cleanliness, but I felt it necessary to save as much water as I could.

Each time I drew from the well, I listened for the sound of the bucket hitting the surface of the water as I released the rope. I could tell that it was taking longer than before. I told George about it. He'd always been proud of the sweet, clear water from his well. Now, we both were afraid of what would happen if it went dry. George began taking the little wagon full of buckets and the washtubs down to the spring at the back of his property and drawing water for the animals, the garden, and the wash.

Every Sunday, the preacher would lead the congregation in a prayer for rain that didn't come. I began adding the request to my own daily prayers. It had been a lifelong habit of mine to pray each morning before I began my day, and each evening before I went to bed. Of course, there were what I thought of as emergency prayers in between. I'd been taught that I shouldn't pray for things for myself, so I asked for rain for the town and never mentioned to God the plot of land behind my house, but I still thought about it as I gave thanks for my blessings and recited my requests. I felt guilty that I couldn't keep it out of my mind. When the rain failed to come week after week, I felt that it was somehow my fault.

The harvest from the garden that fall wasn't nearly as much as usual. George said we couldn't expect a better crop to grow from water that had been brought to it instead of real rain. I canned the tomatoes, carrots, beans, okra and corn, but there wasn't enough harvest to fill the shelves of the pantry the way it had in other years.

The peaches, pears and plums from the grove of fruit trees were small, dry-looking little things, but I did the best I could with them. I knew come January, they would still be a treat for my family. I made jams from the little blueberries and strawberries that had survived. As soon as the berries started showing color I'd covered the berry plants and bushes with netting to keep the birds away. It seemed to me that the birds were hungrier this year, their normal abundance of wild fruit having dried up by mid-summer. Once, I watched a bird pluck at the netting over the strawberries until he had it torn away. He pulled at one of the fruits until the plant came right out of the ground. He flew away with the berry in his beak and the whole plant still attached to it.

Rain was still scarce in 1930. When I said my prayers, I gave thanks that the well was still sufficient for our needs. The garden survived with the same efforts as the year before, but there was a smaller crop than the bad year before.

There was even less rain in 1931 and 1932. I read in the paper that wells were drying up all over the state, and I was thankful that ours was still holding out. I made even more changes to our routine to save water. My family wore their clothes longer, took fewer baths, and used the bath and laundry water to water the garden

The farmers that came to town for supplies were desperate. Their crops had been thirsty for four years in a row. Most of them had borrowed money from the bank to get by, and now the bank was foreclosing on their property. I didn't see the sense in it. If they took the farms away from the people who worked them, and no one else had the money to buy the land from the bank, what good did it do the bank?

There wasn't rain, so there was dust. Great clouds of it would get kicked up by the least little wind, and there were times you couldn't see across the road. I kept the windows shut tight most of the time but it was impossible to keep it out of the house.

Our home was on the outskirts of Kennett, and from time to time, families I knew from church would stop to say goodbye on their way out of town. Some were moving west, as far as California, where the land was still growing good crops. Some headed north to Chicago or Detroit or other cities in hopes of getting manufacturing jobs in the factories.

In 1934 we got a letter from Bessie and John.

Dear George and Maude,

Things are really bad here. Almost everyone in town has left to look for work somewhere else. I don't know if Helen wrote you about it, but the general store had to close down because hardly anyone could pay their bill and Tommy and Helen couldn't buy more merchandise to sell. They kept the doors open until everything was gone and then just locked up and went home. Helen says they have enough money saved to tide them over, but we never saved much ourselves.

I just wanted to let you know that we're moving to Detroit. John has a brother there who can get him a job at the Buick factory, and we can stay with them until we get a place of our own. I don't know yet what our address will be, but I will send it to you as soon as possible.

Take care of yourselves and write me. We love you. Kiss those babies for me. I wish I'd had a chance to know them. We always intended to come visit. If things there don't get better, you know you will always be welcome anywhere we have a roof over our heads.

Love,

Bessie and John and Maxine

I was grief-stricken over the thought of Bessie and her family moving to Detroit. Even though I hadn't seen them for years, it comforted me to know we had family only a few days away and doing well enough. Now Bessie would be a distance from us I couldn't even imagine.

I worried about Helen and Tommy and Faith. What would they do if things didn't pick up before their money ran out? I was angry that Helen hadn't even written me about their problems, but I realized that neither one of us was much of a letter-writer, and Helen certainly wasn't one to share bad news.

I wondered how Clara was doing. Clara wasn't one to share bad news either. I knew that things at the store had grown worse, but Clara managed to keep the doors open with just one helper to do the heavy lifting. How much longer could the business survive?

I didn't buy the newspaper any more, but when I went into town I'd stand in front of the counter and look over the main articles. They were calling this *The Great Depression* and saying things were just as bad in the cities as they were in the farm areas. I thought about Bessie and John. I hoped they weren't going from the frying pan into the fire by moving to Detroit. It was only a few days later that George came home upset about something. I waited for him to tell me, but when he hadn't said a word by suppertime, I finally asked him, "What is it, George? You've been unhappy ever since you got home."

George shook his head. "The mayor told me that I'd have to let Doug Graham go. There isn't any real crime in town anyway, and the council can't see its way clear to keep on paying two salaries. I don't know how I'm going to tell him. They've got three youngsters to feed. Where's he going to get work?"

"That's terrible, George. Poor Sarah, I just don't know where it's going to end. The drought has to be over soon. If they can just hang on, maybe next year things will be better. I'll pray for them."

George looked at me. "You do that. If things don't get better, you might want to say a prayer for us too."

"Do we have enough money in the bank to last us for a while if they let you go, too?"

George shook his head. "Depends on how long this mess lasts, Maude."

When time came around for the next election, in 1936, for the first time in years, George didn't run unopposed. Doug Graham registered to run against him. Doug visited the jail and apologized to George but explained that he had to think about his family first, and he couldn't make it anymore. He'd taken out a mortgage on his home when he was laid off, and now that money was almost gone, and he had payments to make. He could only get day-labor jobs, and those were scarce. He had to do something, and being a deputy was the only other work he'd ever done.

George didn't think he had to worry about losing. Everyone liked him. He thought he would win this time, just as he'd always done.

When the results came in, George lost the election. He explained it to me. "Things have been so bad that people just want a change, want to see if there's something else that can be done. The mayor lost, and every one of the council members too."

I was suddenly scared in a way I'd never been before. "How much money do we have in the bank, George?"

"A little," he said.

I wasn't satisfied with that for an answer. "Do we have enough money in the bank to get by for very long, George?"

"For a while."

It made me want to wring his neck, but I let it go. It was his job to provide for us, and he always had.

He must have had quite a bit saved up. Even with him out of work except for a day at labor now and then, the money lasted for another year. There was still no rain and no steady work to be had. It was true that everyone liked George, but the men who might have hired him were well aware of his fondness for resting up. They smiled at him and clapped him on the back. For the most part, they told him, "Nothing today, George."

George took out a loan on the house. He couldn't get as much money as he'd hoped, but things were bad for the bank, too. He planned that the money would make the payments on the loan, pay our expenses, and last us until things picked up.

I scrimped on things as best I could. None of us had new clothes for a long time. Gene wore Bud's hand-me-downs, Paul wore Gene's, and I made over some of Lulu's and my own things and used flour sacks to make clothes for Betty Sue.

Shoes were different. The children could go barefoot in the summer, but they had to have shoes for the winter. A box was set by the wall in the front of the church, and people put their children's outgrown shoes in it. If a family was lucky, they might find a pair in the box that would fit one of their children. Most of them had holes in the bottom, but I became an expert at stitching on scraps of leather to cover the soles. I used an upholstery needle and a pair of pliers to poke the heavy needle in and out of the leather.

To save on oil, the lamps weren't lit unless we had to have the light. I'd always been proud of the quality of my meals and the abundance on the table, but now the children didn't dare put more on their plate than they could eat. I gave thanks to God my children had never been hungry. I knew well that others in the town had not been so blessed.

One morning that fall, Clara and I were hanging our laundry on the line the way we always did. Clara was unusually quiet, and I let it go without saying anything until we were finished with the work. Then I poured some cold tea and we sat on the porch and rocked. When Clara didn't explain her mood, I asked, "Well?"

"I'm getting married, Maude."

I couldn't believe it. Clara hadn't said a single word that she was even interested in anyone. I just sat there with my mouth wide open.

After a moment, Clara went on, "I borrowed money against the store to keep it going, and when that ran out, I borrowed money against the house, and now I can't pay that either. I'm going to lose both of them." She started sobbing. "I've made a terrible mess of things. I should have closed the store before all this happened. I tried to sell it, but there aren't any buyers anywhere. Everyone in town is in the same boat."

I finally found my voice. "Who are you going to marry, Clara?"

"Brother Humphreys has been coming around to the store for quite some time. He's been asking me and asking me, and up to now I've been pretending I wasn't interested, but now there's nothing else I can do. I can't get work. How can we live without money? I don't have any family of my own to fall back on. Maggie's going to St. Louis to live with her daddy's sister and go to the secretarial school there."

I jumped up and stamped my foot. "You can't do it, Clara. I won't let you. Brother Humphreys is nice enough but he's thirty years older than you are and ugly as a moose. You deserve someone you can love. You've already been married to someone like him."

"I appreciate your concern, Maude, really, but what else can I do? He's well off compared to most of us, and he can keep Maggie in school and pay her keep. Her aunt has a spare room, but she's not in a position to support her."

When it came time for Maggie to leave, I helped Clara and Maggie pack her things and went to the train station with Clara to see Maggie off for St. Louis. School was starting, and Maggie couldn't stay for her mother's wedding. She had to be in St. Louis for the start of the semester. I got the feeling that Maggie was glad she would miss the ceremony.

Both of us sobbing, we watched the train grow small in the distance. I wished that Lulu could have been on that train with her best friend.

One week later Clara and Brother Humphreys

were married after the Sunday service. There was punch and cake after the ceremony, but no one seemed to be celebrating except the bridegroom. Everyone looked at Clara with sympathy in their eyes.

Chapter 31

With his father no longer the sheriff, Bud's hijinks weren't tolerated as well as they had been. When he and another boy from the town got drunk and drove the boy's car into the front of a vacant store, the judge suggested they might be better off in the army. I was glad he went easy on them, but I knew it was partly because of George's popularity and partly because the town didn't have funds to keep them in jail.

So, in 1937, Bud joined the army and left town. It's sad to say, but I was relieved to get him out of my hair. He wasn't any more energetic than his father and was considerably more worry for me. It was an embarrassment to have a child that got into one scrape after another and wouldn't attend church. We all drove with Bud to the bus stop and waved as he left. When I returned home, I felt as if a burden had been lifted from me.

George spent the afternoon puttering around the barn. When he came in for dinner, his eyes were red and puffy. I didn't say anything. I knew Bud was the apple of his eye.

Gene was seventeen that spring and growing taller by the minute. He'd already passed six feet. Once my sturdy baby, he'd thinned out, and I worried about him not having enough meat on his bones. I urged him to eat more and fussed over him in a way I didn't with any of the other children. I'm afraid it was plain to see by everyone who knew us that Gene was my favorite. He sat next to me at church. In public I might brush his hair off his face or straighten the collar of his shirt. As he grew older, it embarrassed him, but he didn't complain about my attentions. He was as devoted to me as I was to him, drawing the water from the well for me, milking the cow, feeding the chickens, doing everything he could to lighten my workload. He looked like my daddy, who he was named after, with the same shade of brown hair and dark eyes.

He'd graduated from school and looked for work, but there was none to be had, even for a young man who'd shown considerably more ambition than his father or older brother ever had.

The Civilian Conservation Corps, the CCC, was set up in 1933 to give work to young men who were unemployed and whose families were having a hard time of it. President Roosevelt had just changed the age minimum for the Corps and Gene joined up to go off on what he expected to be a great adventure, rebuilding the roads, bridges, and forests of America.

I hated to let him go, but I realized it was the only opportunity open to him. I examined the clothes he would wear to make sure the buttons were all attached and there weren't any rips on them. I packed one extra outfit, his best. The Corps would provide him with two new sets of work clothes, so he didn't need to take more than that. I made him a big box lunch to eat on the bus for St. Louis.

We drove him to the bus stop and waited with him. I hugged him goodbye without a tear and waved cheerfully as the bus pulled away. Betty Sue and Paul hung on to me and cried. George stood behind them, his face not showing his pain.

I kept quiet on the drive home, and when we got to the house, I went up to the bedroom and shut the door. George said he could hear me crying for a long time. He left me to my grief, giving Betty Sue two pennies to take Paul for a walk to the store in town and buy some candy. He said he sat on the back porch and talked to the dogs, his own way of dealing with the absence of both his boys.

To me, the only good thing about it was that I knew Gene would always have a place to sleep and a good meal, and he would be paid one dollar a day.

Part of Roosevelt's New Deal, the CCC hired over two million young men from 1933 to 1942 and put them to work planting forests, building dams, and protecting America's natural resources. Roosevelt was a hero to me. I never voted Republican again.

The house seemed empty without Gene in it. I

asked God to provide an angel to keep him safe while he was away from me. I didn't give much thought to Bud, but my heart ached with missing Gene. I comforted myself with knowing that what he was doing was good for the country and good for himself. I thought of him every day, prayed for him every night, and missed him every minute. It felt to me as if a part of who I was had left.

Almost ten, Paul went to school but didn't do well. He pretended to be sick more often than not, and George pampered him and let him stay home. He told his father the other children picked on him. Like Bud, he was the image of his father, already tall and lanky, but he didn't have his father's charm. He claimed the teachers didn't like him, and I think he was right. I don't think anyone liked him. He was rude and lazy and made no effort to be nice to anyone.

George worked a day here and there as a laborer and made no attempt to help with the chores, even when he didn't have work. He spent his time puttering around the house and barn, whistling a tuneless song. It irritated me more and more, and I found that as time went on, I sometimes wanted to smack him.

Betty Sue was my comfort. She was usually sweet and helpful, but every now and then, showed a temper that would surprise me. It came out of nowhere. Betty Sue would play with a doll for hours, and then, vexed over some imagined bad behavior, whirl the doll over her head and smash it into the wall. At those times I swore I could see George's mother in my little girl. I learned early on that only rag dolls were good playmates for my quick-tempered daughter. I prayed about it at night, asking God to look after her.

Early in the summer of 1938…the money was gone.

Chapter 32

George came home from town one day and sat me down at the kitchen table. I could tell by the look on his face he was about to give me bad news, and I braced myself. George had never been much of a talker when the subject was serious, and I could see he was searching for the right words. Finally, he cleared his throat and said, "Maude, I went to the bank today, and it was closed. They say it just ran out of money and shut the doors. They don't know when it will open again, or if it ever will. Even if it does open, there's no guarantee that our money will still be there."

My heart raced with panic. I'd given up hope of George finding a real job. Men who'd shown a lifetime of ambition were out of work. No one would hire George. They all liked him and smiled when they saw him coming, but he wasn't what they were looking for in a worker.

"What are we going to do, George?"

"I've been thinking that the only thing we can do is sell out here and go stay with Bessie and John in Detroit. John writes that I can get plenty of work there."

I just nodded, but my heart filled with a black heaviness. The thought of leaving my home was frightening. Detroit was frightening. Caruthersville was the largest town I'd ever seen. How could I survive in a city that had buildings like the Penobscot office building I'd read about, 47 stories high. It must reach to the clouds.

"What about the house? Are we just going to leave it?"

"I don't know what else we can do. There's no one to buy it. I can't pay the taxes. Even if the bank never asks for it, the government will take it. If we stay here, we could starve to death. We don't have any choice, Maude."

I crossed my arms and jutted out my chin. "I'm not leaving my home."

George threw his hands in the air and slumped back in his chair. "All right, Maude. We're not leaving. How are we going to live?"

"I'll take in sewing and laundry, like I did when James died. I made my way for almost ten years all on my own before you came along."

"Maude, for one thing, you didn't make it on your own. You lived on Mrs. Connor's property, and you didn't pay rent. You ate at her house as often as you ate at your own, and you only had Lulu to think about. You must know there's not one person in this town who can afford to hire you. Didn't you hear what I said? The bank is closed. We lost a few hundred dollars. Some folks lost thousands, everything they saved over a lifetime."

Tears welled up in my eyes. What he said was true. There wasn't anyone now who could afford to hire me to do the kind of work they could do themselves.

I thought about the long drive to Detroit. "How are we going to get the money to get there? Are we going to sell the car and take the train? Are we going to try to drive?"

"We have to drive, Maude. We'll need a car."

"How much money do we have, George?"

"I have about twenty dollars, but I can raise more."

"How can you raise more?"

"I'll sell as many of our things as I can. We won't get anything near what they're worth with everyone broke, but it'll raise enough money to buy our gas and oil and feed us on the trip. If we get some extra, maybe we can stay in one of those motor lodges. That would be better than sleeping in the car. We have to take only what we need, Maude--our clothes, maybe a few household things, whatever we can fit in the car and still have room for the children to sit."

"When do you want to leave, George?"

"Next Wednesday, I guess. We can have the sale Monday and Tuesday, then get going early the next morning. What we don't sell, we'll just leave here."

I wrote to Gene and Bud and gave them Bessie's address so they'd know how to reach us, and then wrote to my sister Helen, and told her about our plan. I promised we'd stop to visit. George wrote to Bessie and told her when we would leave Kennett.

Sunday morning, I told the preacher of our plan. At the end of the service he called me and the children forward and the members came, shaking my hand in the last gesture of fellowship. It was a ceremony the dwindling church had performed often in the last few years. Afterwards, Clara clutched both my hands in hers, and the two of us talked with tears running down our faces, promising we would see one another again someday. George drove off from the church with me twisted around in the seat, looking back after Clara until she was out of sight.

George put up posters around town advertising a two-part sale. We sold most of the furniture and household things the first day, leaving the mattresses, the kitchen stove, and the table and chairs. George sold them, but with the understanding that they'd be picked up the morning of the day we left.

I took the clothes out of the bureaus and packed them in cardboard boxes, labeling them neatly so I could find what I wanted when we got to where we were going. The parlor and the dining room were emptied.

Fourteen-year-old Betty Sue clutched my arm and cried when they carried out the things from her bedroom. She couldn't believe what was happening. I tried to comfort her, telling her that when we got to our new home she would have all new furniture. Paul was nearly ten. He watched like he didn't care, studying us the whole time as if we were strange beings. More than once, I'd overheard someone say, "That boy ain't right."

The second day, men came to look over the things in the barn. One of them gave George ten dollars for the wagon that had brought me and Lulu to Missouri from Tennessee. Various tools brought a nickel or a dime. George put the chickens into pens that he'd nailed together with wood and wire from the fence, and sold them by the half-dozen. He joked and laughed with his customers the way he'd always done. I watched from the upstairs window, and I hated him for it, for being able to make jokes as if our lives weren't falling apart.

Late in the afternoon, the people were all gone but one. George walked with him to the door of the barn and waved goodbye. The man left carrying Pawnee's saddle and tack, the stirrups hooked over the saddle horn. George had kept it clean and oiled all this time, and the leather glistened in the setting sun.

George watched as it was carried down the path and thrown on the back of a truck. He turned his back to the house and propped himself against the barn door. I could see his shoulders shaking, and my heart softened toward him. I hadn't thought of his grief at all, only my own. I realized he was leaving the home his grandfather and mother had given him and everything and everyone he'd ever known.

He didn't come back to the house for supper. I was only dozing when he finally came to bed. He slipped under the covers as quietly as he could.

I asked, "How much money do we have now, George?"

"I think it will be enough."

"How much, George?"

He turned his back to me and sighed. "Almost two hundred dollars. I got the best price for the saddle." His voice choked when he said it, and I didn't ask anything else. I hoped the two of us could get some sleep. Tomorrow would not be an easy day.

I'd almost drifted off when he said, "I made a mess of everything. Being sheriff was the best job in town. People looked up to me, and I lost it. This house has been in my family for three generations, and I've lost it, too. I always had in the back of my mind that I'd buy one of Pawnee's kin and I would get to use that saddle again, and now, it's gone too." His voice broke and I could tell he was crying again. "Now, I don't even have that to remember him by."

I put my hand on his arm, hoping he would turn to me for comfort, but he lay as he was. I needed comforting, too, but my pride wouldn't let me ask for it. I didn't get much sleep, and I don't think George did either. I heard him crying off and on during the night.

Early in the morning, George and I loaded up the car, tying the boxes to the roof and covering them with a canvas tarp to keep any rain from soaking them. He put some of the smaller things on the center of the back seat, leaving just enough room for Betty Sue and Paul

261

to sit. I put my sewing box on the floor by my feet, next to the box of food and water I'd fixed for the trip.

There wasn't enough room for everything, and George carried some of the boxes of household things back to the kitchen, saying that maybe we could send for them later. I was just getting in the car when Paul started screaming, pointing to the little wagon on the back porch. George went and got it and tied it to the back of the car. Paul quieted down and sat staring out the car window.

We drove past the house and onto the road. Neither one of us looked back as we headed out of town, but my thoughts were behind me with the place where I'd borne four of my children, the curtains I'd sewn, and the wallpaper Clara and I put up. I knew George must be thinking about his father's home, and his mother, and Pawnee.

When we passed the cemetery, my eyes searched for the little headstone on Lulu's grave, but I couldn't catch sight of it, and we didn't stop. We crossed the Mississippi River at the same place we had before. The old raft had been replaced by a new, larger one.

George agreed to stop by my hometown so we could say goodbye to my sister Helen. We'd always intended to visit one another, but circumstances hadn't allowed. Helen made us supper, and we spent the night. George and I slept on the bed that was Faith's before she married and moved to Memphis. Betty Sue and Paul slept on pallets on the floor next to us.

Helen's house had been wired for electricity, and I marveled at it. There were white pipes that held the wires running across the ceiling and down the walls leading from the fixtures to the switches. She could flip the switch, and the whole room lit up. Tommy had running water installed and the well covered. An electric pump ran the motor, and all Helen had to do was turn a faucet. Tommy put a bathtub in the wash room and a toilet right in the house. To me, next to the toilet, the best thing was the water heater. Helen ran me a tub full of hot water, and I had my first rich-woman's bath. I couldn't believe it.

I bragged on all of it to Helen. I couldn't help but think how I would have loved to have had all that for my own home. I'd asked George about getting electricity and running water many times, and he'd told me we would get around to it someday. Now we didn't even have a home.

In the morning, we set out again with a full picnic basket that Helen packed for us. There were tearful goodbyes and promises to write more often. As we drove away, I realized that, as much as I loved my sister, I was much closer to Clara now than I had ever been to Helen. I wondered if I'd ever see either one of them again.

George kept the car moving at an even pace, about 30 to 35 miles an hour when the road allowed. We headed to Nashville and reached the outskirts just as the sun was going down. George found a motor lodge, and we paid $3 for a room big enough for the four of us. There were four bunk beds, two on each side. George and I took the lower beds and the children slept on the top. We ate our supper on picnic tables set out under the trees, visited the community bathroom that was at the end of the row of cabins, and went to bed.

We slept sound, and when we came out in the morning, the boxes that had been tied to the roof of our car were gone. For a moment I panicked, trying to remember what had been in them, my bedding, the quilts I'd stitched so carefully, and some of our clothes. The little wagon was still there. It was so old it hadn't been worth stealing. George checked the car. The thieves hadn't taken the trouble to break in, and the thing that was most important to me, my sewing box, was untouched. Among the items in it were the little purse with my secret money, the nightgown I'd worn on my wedding night to James, and the family pictures. The other things could be replaced.

We loaded up again and headed for downtown Nashville. George had been there before, but the children and I were amazed at the size of the city. In the back seat, Betty Sue and Paul kept their noses pressed against the windows and o-o-oh-ed and a-h-h-ed over what they saw. I could scarcely believe it when George told me that Detroit was larger than Nashville. We drove through the city and turned north toward Kentucky. It was beautiful, but the hills were steeper than the soft rolling hills of home, and it took two days to get to Cincinnati. North of there, the road flattened out, and we made better time for a while.

We were about twenty miles from the city when I heard loud popping noises, and George had to struggle to keep control of the car. He managed to get it over to the side of the road safely. He got out of the car and walked around it, looking for the problem. Both tires on the passenger side were flat. They were sliced right open. George looked back in the road and saw a scrap of metal. He'd driven right over it. He put the spare on the front wheel, then jacked up the back of the car and took off the wheel. He leaned in the window to tell me, "I have to go buy another tire. We passed a service station a few miles back. Stay with the car. I'll be back as soon as I can."

He picked up the wheel, crossed the road, and started walking back in the direction we'd come, stopping and sticking out his thumb whenever a car went by.

After a while, a truck pulled up and George jumped down and took the new tire off the back.

"Thanks, Bobby," he yelled, and he waved after the driver as the truck made a U-turn and roared off down the highway. He put the wheel on the car and we were on our way again. George stopped a few miles down the road and got a new tire for the spare, just in case. It took twenty dollars from our purse to pay for the tires.

We stopped at another motor lodge for the night, but when we did, we took everything out of the car and in the room with us. What things we still had were too important to risk losing.

Our money was running out on us fast. Gasoline for the car, two new tires, and food for four people were all expensive. When the box of food I'd packed and the picnic basket from Helen were empty, I had

265

George stop at a service station with a grocery, and I bought a loaf of sliced bread and a jar of peanut butter. It would feed us for the day. We refilled our bottles with water from the sink in the rest room. Betty Sue and Paul complained about the sandwiches but we all ate them, and drank enough water to wash them down. The next day I bought another loaf of bread and another jar of peanut butter and two apples for the children.

Settled in my bed at night, I gave thanks to God for each day's safety, each day's progress, and each day's food.

We slept in the car the next night, a few miles south of Toledo. I saw George spread out what money he had left and count it. It didn't look like very much.

"Are we going to have enough, George?"

"We'll be all right, Maude, as long as nothing else happens to the car, and we don't take a liking to steak dinners."

I could see the worry making furrows on his forehead. "How much longer is it going to take us to get there, George?"

"Maybe tomorrow night, maybe another day after that. Bessie lives on the east side of the city, so we have to go all the way across it."

In the morning, George filled the car with gasoline, and we set out on what I hoped would be the last day of this terrible trip.

Chapter 33

We passed open fields of corn just north of Toledo. The car made a loud grinding noise and lurched to a stop. George got out and pushed it off to the side of the road, knelt down on one knee and looked under. I waited, wondering how bad it was. When George straightened up, I could tell by the look on his face it was worse than I imagined. He opened the door and sat beside me. "The transmission's dropped right off, Maude."

"Is that expensive to get fixed?"

"Too expensive for us, even if we were close to a garage that had the parts."

"What are we going to do, George?"

He looked down the road in the direction of Detroit. "Whatever it is we *have* to do, Maude."

I told Betty Sue and Paul to sit still, and we got out of the car.

"It's a good thing Paul cried after that wagon," George said, untying it. He loaded on what he could and tied it down with the tarp over it. Then he pushed the car further off the road and stood looking at it for a minute. He welled up and choked, "Pawnee would never have let us down like that."

We began what I hoped would be the last day of our trip, me carrying my sewing basket over one arm Betty Sue and I walked in front. George came behind us, pulling the wagon, and Paul walked beside him. From time to time, an open truck would pass, and George would stick out his thumb, but no one stopped. We walked until dark, stopping by clumps of bushes to relieve ourselves. We paid a farmer a dollar to let us sleep in his barn. When I said my prayer that night, I thanked God for the barn and asked Him to watch over Gene, wherever he was, and keep him safe from harm. I'm ashamed to say, I didn't pray often for Bud. Maybe I felt he had the U.S. Army to take care of him.

I hoped the farmer would offer us breakfast, but he woke us early when he came to milk the cows, and except for a gruff, "Good morning," said nothing. We gathered our things and started out again, our stomachs already growling.

We walked some more, then from behind me, George called, "Wait a minute, Maude." Betty Sue and I waited for him and Paul to catch up to us. He said, "Paul's crying for something to eat, and there's no telling when we'll find a store."

I wondered why he wanted to stop. He said, "I never stole anything in my life, but I'm going to now."

He looked around to see if there was anyone in sight, then jumped across a ditch to the edge of a field of corn. He plucked two small ears off a stalk and hurried back to us. "Keep walking," he told us. We set out again and he stripped the husks and silk from the corn as he walked and gave one to Paul and one to Betty Sue. They gnawed them down to the bare cobs.

I asked, "What about us?"

"If anyone saw us, I figure they'd have mercy on us if we only fed the children. You and I can wait."

After a while, we came to a service station. George bought a bag of peanuts so we could use the restrooms. I filled our water bottles from the tap. We walked what I figured was a few miles longer and then sat under the shade of an oak tree and ate the peanuts.

Detroit didn't seem any closer than it had in the morning. We had to go at a pace the children could keep up. Sometimes, people would pass us, usually a man walking alone, but a few times, a man and woman, once a family with children. We would nod at one another and keep going without talking, like we had to save our strength for the trip.

About eight hours into the day's trip, we could see a small cluster of buildings that looked like it might be a town. I heard a soft clucking just off the side of the road. I knew what it was. I handed my sewing basket to Betty Sue and followed the sound. In a clump of high grass I found a stray hen sitting on a nest full of eggs. I almost shouted. I made a fold in my skirt and gathered the eggs into it. I went to George and showed him the treasure.

"How are we going to cook them, Maude? We left the pans back in Missouri."

"We aren't going to cook them, George. We're going to trade them."

We walked the rest of the distance to the town, and at the service station with a store, I traded my eggs for a loaf of bread. George counted out his coins for a can of Vienna sausages. It would do. Unless my children were hungry, and George had spent his last cent, I had no intention of letting him know I had money hidden away.

"How much farther is it to Detroit?" George asked the man behind the counter.

He shrugged. "It's about forty miles to downtown."

I wondered how long it would take us to walk that far. I had no idea. We used the restrooms and then sat on a bench outside the store while we ate. When we finished, George picked up the handle of the wagon and we set out again. We walked until dark. We only had a few dollars left, so there was no money for a cabin, even if there had been one nearby. We settled down for the night under a big tree. George took the tarp off the wagon and spread it out for a blanket, and we huddled together. In my prayer that night, I gave thanks that it wasn't raining and that our shoes didn't have holes in them. I asked God to provide food for the children and George.

In the morning, we set out again, hoping it would be the last day. I was disgusted by how long it had been since we had a bath. I'd always been clean about myself and the children, and grateful that George had always been clean about himself. It was awful to me that I hadn't had a bath or changed my clothes for such a long time, especially since we were walking in the dust and the dirt of the roadside.

We stopped by a little stream to relieve ourselves, and I pulled the big hairpins out of my hair. It fell loose and unrolled down to my knees. It had never been cut, and I brushed it one hundred strokes each morning. Like all of the married women of my church, I would wind it into a bun at the back of my neck and fasten it with the big U-shaped pins. I took my brush out of a box and tried to smooth out the snarls. It was awful. It made me half wild.

I hated this trip. I hated the Depression. I hated George for letting this happen. I hated the Detroit I hadn't even seen yet, and now, I hated my hair. I took the scissors out of my sewing basket, gathered my hair into my fist, and cut it off right at the back of my neck. Betty Sue screamed, and Paul started crying.

I threw the hank in the stream, turned, and gave George a glare. His jaw dropped open, but he didn't say a word. I guess I had a look on my face that he'd seen on his mother, and I was standing there with the scissors still in my hand.

We started back walking north. As we plodded along, I mourned my spurt of temper. My neck felt naked and somehow exposed to the point of indecency.

We stopped by a stream to eat the last of the bread. The Vienna sausages were long gone. George took a string and a hook from the wagon, tied it together, and stuck a piece of the bread crust on the line. He threw it into the stream and stood there watching it.

Another couple came along, saw us, and stopped for a minute. The women looked like she was craving to talk to another woman. She told me her name was Imogene Rich and her husband was Wesley. She said, "We left Oklahoma two weeks ago and took the bus as far as Toledo. We didn't have enough money to go all the way to Detroit. When we looked at it on the map, it didn't seem like it was so far away."

I asked her, "Do you have family in Detroit?"

"No. Everyone we knew was going to California, so we thought we might do better if we went somewhere else. Now, we're broke. I don't know what we're going to do when we get there."

"How long is it since you ate?"

"Yesterday."

I looked around me. The roadside was dotted with yellow flowers. I said, "I used to hear my mom talk about eating dandelion greens for a salad. She never made it at home, so I don't know how they taste, but they don't cost anything."

About that time, George let out a whoop and pulled in a fish. It wasn't very big, about the size of my hand. He told Wesley, "See if you can get a fire started."

He put another little piece of bread on the line and dropped it back in the water. Wesley gathered up some twigs and dried grass and got a little fire going. While George angled for another fish, Wesley cleaned the one we had.

Imogene and I gathered some of the dandelions and washed them downstream. After a while, George caught two more and cleaned them. He stuck the pieces on a green stick of wood and held them over the fire for a few minutes. When they were about to fall apart, he took them out of the flame and we all shared what we had.

Back on the road, the Riches said goodbye. I thought about them not having any family and told her, "If things get bad, I heard you could always get help at a Salvation Army."

She hugged me, and they went on ahead. They could walk faster than we could. I hadn't seen anyone walking south. I said to George, "It looks as if whoever came this far must have found work. There isn't anyone walking south."

He looked at a car driving past and said, "Some of them may still have their cars. We'll see."

After a while, the children stopped complaining. We were too tired to do anything but put one foot in front of the other and keep going. We spent another night sleeping in a field. In the morning, I was so hungry, I would have spent my hidden money for a meal for my children, but no store came in sight. After a while, I saw scrub apples hanging on a tree a ways off the road. George went and picked a dozen or so. "These are the best of them," he said. I could see they were wormy. I wiped them off as best I could, and George cut them into pieces with his pocket knife. We ate what we could without bothering the worms and kept walking. We came to a service station, and George bought a candy bar, broke it in half, and gave it to the children. We drank water from the tap in the rest room and filled the bottles we kept with us.

Finally, we could see Detroit in the distance. The buildings were closer together now. The children complained that they wanted to stop, and I felt as if I couldn't go on myself. I wanted to just sit down in the middle of the road and wait until someone ran over me, but George prodded us on, and shortly before we reached the Detroit area, a truck stopped and picked us up. George sat in front next to the driver, and the children and I piled in the open back, next to some wooden crates.

Through the window, I could see George talking to the man. In only a minute, he had the driver laughing in the same way he always did the men back in Kennett. Then George took a paper out of his shirt pocket and held it out in front of the driver, who nodded his head. George folded the paper and put it back in his pocket.

We reached the city, and drove, and drove, and drove. It was amazing how large it was. We passed factories on the west side. Huge columns of gray smoke billowed up to the sky, joined one another, and flattened out in an overhead blanket so thick and wide it blocked out the sun. Black pieces of soot, too large to be dust, fell like snow and settled on me and the children. As soon as we brushed them off, more took their place. It seemed as if we crossed a railroad track every few feet. I could see the skyscrapers, and I pointed out the one I thought was the Penobscot Building to Betty Sue and Paul. Then the tallest buildings were behind us, and we still kept driving. After a while, we were on a wide street called Jefferson Avenue.

Up front, I could see George talking and waving his hands, and the driver throwing his head back and laughing. It was the first time I'd ever been grateful for George being so social. The longer he could charm the driver, I thought, the closer he would take us to where we needed to go.

As it turned out, he took us all the way to Bessie's house.

Chapter 34

It was late afternoon when the truck pulled up in front of a large, square, two-story house. George helped me and the children down from the back and unloaded our things. He and the driver shook hands and slapped each other on the back. George shook his head and smiled. "You sure were kind to bring us all the way here, Dave. I don't know how to thank you."

The driver grinned at him. "My pleasure. It was the best trip I had all year, George." He climbed back in his seat and waved out the window at George until he'd driven out of sight.

We were gathering up our things when Bessie and John came running out of the house, followed by a tall blonde girl that I thought must be Maxine. John pumped George's hand while Bessie grabbed me and hugged me, then Betty Sue, then Paul, and finally, her brother. She took Betty Sue by the shoulders. "Lord, Almighty, just look at you. It's like looking back into my childhood."

It was true. With the same build, height, black hair, dimples, and round faces, Bessie and Betty Sue were mirror images of one another with only the years to separate them.

John shook his head. "We been ready to send out a posse to look for you, George. We were afraid that something bad had happened."

"The transmission fell out of the car near Toledo. We didn't have the money to fix it, so we had to push it off the road and leave it."

"How did you get here, then?"

"We walked mostly, almost to the city limits, then a truck picked us up and brought us the rest of the way."

"Well, let's get these things inside and get some dinner. Bessie was just putting it on the table. She's been cooking enough for an army for the last three days."

I told Bessie, "The only thing we had to eat today were some wormy apples we found on a tree, but I can't eat anything until I wash off some of this road dirt." I held out my arm and turned it palm up. "Look at it."

The dirt was sunk into the pores of my skin. It filled the creases on my wrists and the back of my fingers, and my fingernails were lined with it. I couldn't help it, I started crying. "I've never been this dirty in my life, even when I was a little girl and helped

Daddy at the stable. Most of our clothes were stolen, and what we have left is filthy from being worn for so long."

Bessie said, "I know you're all starving. Wash up to your elbows and then we'll eat. You can all have a nice bath after dinner and wear some of our things until you can get more for yourself."

So that's what we did. After washing our hands and faces, we sat at the table, joined hands while John said the blessing, and then had our meal.

Bessie had outdone herself. There was a platter piled so high with fried chicken that I guessed three or four birds had given their lives for us. She'd made a huge bowl filled with fluffy mashed potatoes with butter melted around the curves in the top. We emptied the gravy bowl filled with golden gravy, but Bessie said there was more staying hot on the stove if we needed it. One dish held green beans that had been cooked all day with bacon drippings. Another had a pile of corn on the cob and next to it a bowl of melted butter with a little mop in it. There were white cornbread johnnycakes, fried in a skillet, and a pile of biscuits, light as a feather. It had been a long, long time since we'd seen a meal like that!

We ate until we couldn't hold any more. Then the men, followed by Paul, went out to sit on the front porch and smoke while Betty Sue and I took turns getting a bath. I scrubbed every inch of me until there wasn't any more dirt and washed my hair. It felt so good when I could finally get the brush through it. When I looked at myself in the bathroom mirror, I wanted to cry. My hair jutted out in wild, uneven clumps.

Bessie gave me clean clothes to wear, and Maxine found some for Betty Sue. The girls went up to Maxine's room. I told Bessie about the trip, how our things got stolen on the very first night, and about the tires going flat and the transmission falling out. She cried with me when I got to the part about not being able to brush my hair and cutting it off.

While Bessie and I talked, George and Paul got cleaned up. Paul made us all laugh when he came out of the bathroom in clothes John gave him, a shirt that hung down to his knees and pants rolled up about ten times.

When we were finished with the talking, Bessie showed me the room George and I would sleep in. She'd made up a pallet by the wall for Paul. Maxine had a bed in her room for Betty Sue.

We were all saying good night when John asked me, "Maude, when did you cut your hair?"

I started giggling and couldn't stop. "A few days back. I threw it in a stream somewhere outside of Toledo." Bessie and I laughed wildly. Looking back on it now, I think the laughing did more to feed my soul where I was hungry than the food did.

It was late when we finally went to bed. I stretched out on the mattress and sighed. I had to fight to stay awake long enough for my nightly talk with God.

"Thank you, Lord for taking care of us and getting us to a safe place, and thank you again for that wonderful meal and for the family that prepared it for us, and thank you for sending your angel, dressed like a truck driver, to bring us the rest of the way. Bless Gene in his camp, and Bud at Fort Knox, and Bessie and John and Maxine, and keep your angels watching over Gene and Betty Sue and the other boys. Amen."

Chapter 35

At breakfast the next morning John said he wanted to take George to the factory with him so he could apply for a job, but George said he was still tired from the trip and would go tomorrow. His sister gave him a knowing look but kept quiet. When he made an excuse the following day, Bessie walked over to the stove and picked up the big steel coffee pot with its scalding hot coffee. She held it over his lap and said, "George" in a way that immediately got the attention of everyone at the table. "Get ready and go to work with John. You got a wife and two kids to support, and that Kennett, Missouri, glad-handing you've been doing for the last thirty years won't go over here."

George didn't say a word, just stood, put on his hat and walked to the screen door to wait for John. I looked down at the table and kept quiet, but I had to hold back a little smile. I'd actually seen a look of fear on the faces of both John and George. It gave me a little thrill.

After they left, Bessie poured us both a cup of coffee and sat with me to talk. She laughed. "I know how lazy George is. He could get away with it at home. He thinks he's like the lilies of the field, not that he thinks he's beautiful, but that if he keeps everyone laughing, that's enough in the line of helping out. That won't work here."

I knew she was right, and I was grateful she was strong enough to make George get up and get to a job. Sometimes, I wished I had the same gift. My life would have been a lot easier if I'd just been able to make George behave the way he should have, but I guess I simply didn't have it in my nature to boss people around. George was actually afraid of Bessie. Nobody in my whole life was ever afraid of me.

When George didn't come back for three hours, I told Bessie, "I hope his being gone means he got the job."

She gave me a smile. "Don't worry about it. John's a foreman now, and they think right highly of him. They'll hire George on his say-so, and I'll explain to George that I expect him to work hard enough that John isn't embarrassed about it."

Betty Sue went to school with Maxine. She was all excited about it, and I felt relieved to see her smiling again. I kept Paul home with me for the first day. Even at ten years old, he hung onto my arm like he was afraid of everything. Bessie and I went down to Jefferson to a store called Goodwill. It sold used

282

clothes and furniture. She said to get enough clothes to tide us over for a while and she would pay for it. George could pay her back out of his first check. She said, "Betty Sue would probably rather pick out her own things. She can wear Maxine's clothes for a while. Maxine has enough for five or six girls."

I picked out a stack of clothes for myself, George, and Paul. They even had underwear that looked almost new. Those two used dresses I took looked more expensive than any new ones I'd ever made for myself. They had a lot of fancy seams and nice buttons. Bessie said a lot of rich people gave their things to the Goodwill when they got tired of them. It was hard for me to imagine that. All my life, I only had new clothes when I'd outgrown the old ones or they were too worn and frayed to be respectable.

After that, I kept my sewing kit for mending, but I never made another dress. It was cheaper to get one at Goodwill than to buy fabric and make one.

George came home with John at the end of the day, and even though I waited for him to talk about it, he didn't say anything about the work he'd been doing.

The evening passed pleasantly enough. Bessie and John had a big Motorola radio in the front room, and we all sat around and stared at it while we listened to Jack Benny. I loved it. I'd heard radios before, at Clara's and at the homes of some of my other friends from church, but since George would never do anything about getting electric power for our home, we never had one. It was just like having Jack Benny in the living room.

On Sunday morning we dressed for church and went with Bessie, John, and Maxine to their new church home. Even George went without a fight. He knew Bessie expected it.

The church met in a rented storefront on Jefferson Avenue. The windows had been covered with ivory-colored drapes, and instead of the long pews that all the churches at home had, there were old seats that looked strange to me. Bessie said they came from an old movie house. They were arranged in a 'v' pattern. At the front was a lectern sitting on a table.

I'd never been in a church that didn't have its own building. They didn't use the name, *Holiness*, either, but called themselves the *Pentecostal Church*. Once the service got going, I saw that it was the same as my church at home, and it filled my heart.

Having a meeting in a storefront was a curiosity to me, but the members were welcoming, and in only a few minutes I relaxed and felt at home.

George worked at the factory for two weeks before he told me how he felt about it. He lay on his back in the bed and sighed. I could tell he was wanting to tell me something, so I just said, "What?"

"I hate working at the factory. It's dirty and noisy, and you have to punch a time card. I want to do something else."

Oh, Lord. What will we do if he quits this job the way Bud used to quit all the jobs he got when he was home? "You should be grateful that God sent you a job. Don't you know how many men are still looking for work? If you weren't related to John, they never would have taken you on. How's it going to look for him if you up and quit? You might never find another place. Besides, how would Bessie like it?"

That ended the discussion. When George brought home his first paycheck, we rented the house next door to Bessie. It was just like hers, only reversed, a two-story house with small porches on the front and back, and a narrow driveway on one side that went to a garage that bordered the alley out back. The two houses were like all the others on the block, so close together that if you reached out of the window of one house, you could touch someone reaching out of the other. Bessie told me it was a good deal because it had four bedrooms, and the landlord would pay for the water, and George would only have to pay for the electricity and gas. I'd never thought about paying for water.

It was as if I'd stepped into another world. Certainly, it was an easier life for me. I loved the bathroom, the running water, the flush toilet, with the box on the wall over it and the pull chain that washed the bowl. It was like a miracle. I didn't have to go outside and draw water from the well at the end of the porch to carry inside for cooking and laundry and for baths, then empty the tubs when they were used. The bathtub was so big, I could lie in it with my legs stuck almost straight out.

Bessie and I had a good laugh at the idea that we would need to buy an alarm clock, since we weren't allowed to keep a rooster inside the city limits.

There was an icebox in the kitchen, and Bessie

said that she would tell the iceman the next time he came to add us to his route, so there was no more going to a root cellar for things that needed to be kept cool in the summer.

The gas stove was a wonderful thing to me. No more watching out for snakes in the woodpile when I needed to build up the fire in the kitchen stove, and no more going outside when it was freezing cold to get wood.

In the basement was a huge coal-burning furnace. Bessie told me that in the winter a truck came and dropped the coal through a small trap-door into the little coal room. From there it was shuttled into the furnace by a large corkscrew-looking thing called a hopper. George certainly liked the sound of that. No more cutting firewood for him. I worried about all these new expenses that we had never had before-- rent, electricity, coal, and ice. The depression was easing its grip on the national economy, but we would still have to be very careful.

We moved our few things next door and John drove George around in his truck to places where they could get used furniture. Bessie loaned us her extra mattresses for a few days, and Paul slept on a pallet until George found enough mattresses for us. When he brought them home, I took a lamp and inspected them, front and back, before I let him bring them into the house. I knew enough to make sure there weren't any bedbugs. George said he'd expected as much and examined them before he paid the man, but I double-checked anyway.

I don't know if having running water made the laundry any easier for me. I didn't have to pump from a well anymore, but even with a tap and sink in the basement, I had to carry clothes downstairs, wash them on the board, rinse them, wring them out, and then take the wet clothes to the back yard to hang them in the sun. It wore me out. I tried to get Paul to help me, but he would run off and hide until I was finished and George wouldn't make him do any kind of work at all.

The second week we were in the house, George found a nice table and four chairs that were only ten dollars second hand. George and John brought something home with them every week until the house was furnished well enough to get by. The best thing was the radio, not a big console that sat right on the floor like Bessie and John had, but one that looked like a church steeple and sat on the table. We gathered around it at night and listened to Fred Allen, Fibber McGee and Molly, and best of all, on Saturdays we listened to the Grand Ole Opry. It was sponsored by The National Life and Accident Insurance Company and Prince Albert Tobacco. When a salesman from National Life knocked on my door one day, out of my appreciation for the Opry, I bought a thousand dollar policy on George. The nice young man came by every week to collect the dime payments and to mark in the little passbook he had given me that my premiums were up to date. A lot of the men who worked in the factories got killed on the job and I worried about what would happen to me and the children if I lost George.

I was pretty sure I couldn't make enough money sewing and doing laundry to support us.

My favorites on the Opry were Roy Acuff and the Smoky Mountain Boys, especially when Roy sang *Great Speckled Bird*, and Bill Monroe and the Bluegrass Boys. Some nights we also heard Red Foley. George claimed he was a cousin, but I didn't believe him. I asked Bessie about it one day, and Bessie said it was the first she'd heard of it.

We all had our favorite shows, the Opry for me, and Jack Benny for George, which I thought was no co-incidence, him being so stingy and all. Paul was hypnotized by *The Shadow*, and Betty Sue loved when the big stars like Bette Davis or Katherine Hepburn did a drama on *The Lux Radio Theatre*. We all gathered around the radio after dinner each night. I sat and rocked in the perfectly good rocking chair George found in an alley. I'd scrubbed it down on the back porch, just in case, and then placed it next to a small lamp table in the living room.

I bought a small radio for the kitchen. While I cooked and cleaned during the day I listened to *Stella Dallas* and *My Gal Sunday*. It felt like walking into another world, into someone else's life more complicated than my own, and I found that comforting.

Chapter 36

In spite of all the luxuries we had in Detroit compared to Missouri, I still didn't feel quite at home. I bought sheets and made proper curtains for all the rooms and crocheted pineapple pattern doilies to go on the backs and arms of the upholstered pieces. It made me feel more as if it were my home, even if it was rented.

I gave thanks to God for the life we lived. We had plenty to eat, a church home, and a decent house. I enjoyed keeping it clean and decorating it, even if it weren't mine. I asked God to forgive me for the resentment I felt toward George and for my sometimes un-Christian attitude. It seemed to me that as I grew older, it was more and more difficult to forgive others. I'd been taught that it wasn't right to ask God for forgiveness for my own sins if I couldn't do the same for someone else.

When I could afford it, I bought red and white checked fabric and made a tablecloth and curtains for the kitchen. The cloth cost an outrageous price, ten cents a yard, but I told myself that it would cheer things up. I still put a few cents in my savings when I could. It didn't come from selling eggs, but I took it out of what George gave me for the groceries. If I found something on sale, I put the difference from what I would normally have paid in my sewing box and, after a while, it seemed like my money. Every now and then I would take a dollar's worth of change and get myself a one-dollar bill for it.

There wasn't much area for a garden, but I cleared a patch in the back yard and planted tomatoes and green beans. My gardening skills stood me in good stead, and the next fall I had a nice little crop with enough to trade some of my harvest with Bessie, who'd planted her own garden with turnips, green peppers, and cabbage.

Even though we'd been separated for a long time, Bessie and I picked up our old friendship right off. It was comforting to me to have a woman friend who understood my situation and to share my life. I admired Bessie's strength and the way the men obeyed her.

Chapter 37

By 1940, I was forty-eight years old and, for the most part, pretty much contented with my life. Betty Sue quickly made friends in school. George worked steadily, if not happily. I suspected it was more out of fear of Bessie than anything else. He managed to get his job at the Buick factory changed from the assembly line to that of custodian. When he first told me about it, I asked him, "What is a custodian?"

"A janitor. I clean up and look after things. I like it better than the line."

I just shook my head. If George preferred it, it must be easier work.

Paul still missed school most of the time. George was always telling me to let him stay home because he wasn't learning anything anyway, and it seemed to be true. At twelve years old, he could read and write only a few words. His teachers suggested sending him to a special school for slow learners, but George refused to even hear about it.

One day they sent Paul home with a note from his teacher, Miss Spence. It asked for a parent to come in and talk to the teacher at the end of school on the next Monday. I went in like they asked, but I was nervous, scared a little by the size of the school building, Bellevue Elementary. It was a great difference from the one-room school where I'd studied. With the help of a student, I found the right room. A pretty young woman and an older man were waiting for me.

They both smiled at me warmly and waved me to a seat at one of the desks. I clutched my handbag on my lap and waited for them to say whatever it was they had on their minds.

The woman began. "Mrs. Foley, Paul hasn't made any progress at all in his classes, and we think we may be able to help him. There's a special school he could go to, one with a medical staff, that could see if he has a physical problem and maybe correct it."

I frowned. "Where is this school?"

The man leaned towards me. "I'm Dr. Goodwin. I'm the supervisor at the school. It's in Oxford, about thirty miles north of here."

"Thirty miles north? How would I get him there every day? We don't even have a car."

"He would live at the school for a while, until we could give him some tests and see if his learning difficulty is physical or disciplinary."

I shook my head. "I don't know if his father

would allow that. I'll have to talk to him."

Dr. Goodwin stood and held out his hand. "Fine, I'd like to talk to him myself if he would agree to come in for a meeting. I'll be here with Miss Spencer, next Monday, at the same time."

I shook his hand. "Thank you, I'll let you know what he says."

That night I waited until we were in bed before I brought up the subject. When I explained about the special school, George sat up in bed and shook his head. "No! I'm not letting them take my boy and experiment on him. Tell them to forget it."

"But George, he can barely read and write. Maybe they can help him."

"I said no, and that's the last I want to hear of it!"

I let the subject drop. The next Monday, I went to the school and told them what George said, and added, "I gave up arguing with my husband about it a long time ago. Maybe if you come to the house and talked to him, he'd see that he isn't doing the boy any good."

Doctor Goodwin shook his head angrily. "If he won't let us help him at my school, there's nothing else I can do."

Miss Spencer looked like she felt sorry for me. "Can't you get Mr. Foley to at least come to school and talk to us?"

"I'm afraid not. He'd have to miss work, and we can't afford it." The truth was that George wouldn't mind at all to miss work, but I knew he'd never change his mind, and we would just wind up losing a day's pay.

I walked home thinking about the situation. Paul wasn't right, anyone could see that. I wished George would let the doctors take a look at him, but I knew it was hopeless.

Chapter 38

All the time Gene was away at the CCC, George and I received regular letters from him describing the important work he was doing for the country and how much he enjoyed the life of a ranger. He was paid thirty dollars a month, and twenty-five dollars was sent home to his family. Gene told us that he didn't need much money anyway. His meals were provided, and he'd never taken up tobacco. The only real expense he had was when he could get into town to see a movie. He loved the movies, especially the character actors, he said. He didn't go to see Roy Rogers, but rather to see Gabby Hayes, and wouldn't miss anything with Ward Bond, Victor McLaghlen, or Edward Everett Horton, who he thought was the funniest man in Hollywood.

Bud only wrote home once or twice a year,

usually when he was in the stockade for some trouble he was in. After three years in the army, he had been busted for bad behavior so many times that he was still a private.

Early one afternoon in the fall of 1940, there was a knock at the door. I wasn't expecting anyone, and it wasn't Tuesday, the day the insurance man came to collect his dime. I turned down the gas under the meal I was cooking and went to the door, wiping my hands on my apron and growing irritated. It had better not be a salesman, like the Fuller Brush man who came by from time to time. I'd already told him I wasn't interested.

I jerked the door open and nearly fainted when I saw the tall, handsome young man standing there. He'd grown another two or three inches and put on at least forty pounds since I'd last seen him. He was deeply tanned, a reddish brown, and stood there with a look of expectation and a big grin on his face.

It was my precious boy, my Gene. He grabbed me in a big hug, lifting me right off the floor and rocking me right and left. Tears ran down my face and his. When he finally let me down, I wiped my cheeks on my apron. "What are you doing here? Are you all right? You didn't quit the CCC, did you?"

"Let's sit down, Mom, and I'll tell you what happened."

This scared me, but there he stood, looking perfectly fine. So, whatever it was, it didn't matter. If he'd gotten fired or was in some sort of trouble like his brother, I didn't care, as long as he was all right.

I took his hand and led him to the kitchen. "Let me fix you something to eat," I said, in the language of mothers, "and we can talk about it."

I poured him a cup of the strong coffee that always sat on the stove, and took some cold fried chicken and potato salad out of the icebox and sliced a big tomato on a plate in front of him. I got a cup of coffee for myself and sat across from him so I could watch his face.

"Tell me about it," I said, holding on for what I knew would be news I didn't want to hear.

He nodded. "I'll just start out that I'm going to be just fine. The doctor said all I have to do is rest up a few days, and I can start to look for work."

My heart lurched at the word, *doctor*. "What happened?'

"Well, I was helping some of the other boys to put a new roof on the barracks, and I fell off. I landed on my back on top of some of the bundles of shingles. Doc said I'd be all right, Mom. Don't worry so." He reached out and patted my hand, then picked up another piece of chicken. It eased me some to see that he had a good appetite.

"If you're going to be all right, why did they send you home?"

"Now, don't go getting all upset, but he said that I hurt both of my kidneys, falling on that stuff. I had blood when I passed my water. That made me disabled, so I had to come home. I'll be just fine for regular work."

"How much blood?" I felt faint at the thought of

his pain, but I went to the stove and kept my eyes on the pot of stew I was stirring and steeled myself so my worry didn't show.

"Quite a of blood bit for the first few days. Then it kind of tapered off, and when there wasn't any more, they put me on a train and sent me home."

I felt the need to pray about this later. I didn't want to bother Gene with my worrying over him, so I changed the subject and asked about the work he'd been doing. We talked for the rest of the afternoon. I went back to my cooking and listened, asking a question now and then, while Gene sat in his chair, telling me all about what his life had been like for the last two years. We laughed and talked, and I pressed more food on him, making him eat two pieces of my special apple pie. It didn't take a lot of pushing to get him to take the second piece.

When Betty Sue and Paul came home from school and saw who was there, they whooped all around the kitchen. Betty Sue flung her arms around her brother and then held his hand and made him tell some of his stories again. After a quick hug, Paul stood in the corner of the kitchen and listened, but didn't have anything to say.

When we heard John's truck pull into the garage next door, Gene hid behind the door. George came in, carrying his lunch bucket.

"Some man is here to see you, George," I said.

His brow wrinkled, but when he heard Betty Sue giggle, he caught on. "Really? It wasn't a special messenger from President Roosevelt, was it? He's been after me to come to Washington and help out."

"It's Gene," Paul blurted out. "He's hiding right behind the door."

George turned his head and caught sight of his middle son. He grabbed him in a bear hug. I was surprised to see George moved to tears by the homecoming.

We took Gene next door to show him off to Bessie, John, and Maxine, who'd never met him.

I was so proud of my tall, handsome boy. He looked like a movie star in the *Silver Screen* magazines that Betty Sue was always reading. We all talked for a while and then went home for supper only to talk more after we ate. Gene put away another big meal. It made me happy to see his appetite.

My prayers that night had many thanks for Gene's safe return, and I begged God for his health to be restored. I lay awake in my bed until George's breathing told me he was fast asleep, and then I crept down the hall to Gene's room, carrying a quilt. He was sleeping on several blankets that had been folded on the floor in the empty fourth bedroom. I watched him for a long time, taking pleasure in the regular rise and fall of his chest. Then I spread the quilt out over him and walked as softly as I could back to my own bed.

There was peacefulness to my sleep that night that I hadn't felt since the day he left. I knew that my precious boy was safe. I knew where he was, and what he was doing.

Chapter 39

In Detroit, a boy on a bicycle brought me the *Detroit News* every day. It was a wonderful treat, another one of the miracles of big city life.

I read in the paper about the wars in Europe and Asia. It was horrible, so many being killed. I remembered the young men coming home from the last war, with limbs missing and hearts broken. I also remembered the awful flu they brought home with them that took my little girl away from me.

I was glad America wasn't fighting. I gave thanks that it had nothing to do with me and my family, and I asked God to bring it to an end and put Hitler out of business. I didn't pray for him to die, that wouldn't be Christian, but that he would somehow be stopped. It didn't seem that my prayers were having much effect.

Every day the news grew worse.

The government put out a lot of orders for goods, and Gene had no trouble finding work. He was hired on at a small factory the first day he went looking. George had met the foreman through John and wrote Gene a note of recommendation. When the foreman read that Gene was George's son, he slapped him on the back and put him to work. Just like in Missouri, everyone liked George, and as time went on, I realized that Gene had inherited his father's charm. Everyone seemed to like Gene, too. I was glad that he had his father's way with people, but not Bud's wild streak. I felt proud he'd inherited my own habit of hard work. A favorite saying in my family was that the Lord loves a working man. I often wondered how the Lord felt about George.

Gene brought home his first week's pay envelope, counted out the bills at the kitchen table, and handed half to me. When I didn't reach out to take it, he pressed it in my hand. He said, "I'm a grown man, Mom, almost twenty years old. I have to pay my own way."

I felt my throat close up, and a tear ran down my cheek. We'd just barely been getting by on George's pay and what money came home from Gene's pay in the CCC. Some weeks we ate a lot of beans.

"I didn't expect you to do this," I said.

"I know you didn't, but I eat more than anyone, and I use the lights, and you do my clothes. I'm just giving you what I owe you. What else am I going to do with it?"

"Go down to the bank and open a savings account. Put a little aside every week. You never know when you'll need some money."

"That's a good idea. I wanted to save up for something special anyway. I guess the banks will be all right now. I haven't heard about one going under for a long time."

"What are you saving for, Gene?"

"You'll see," he smiled.

He went to the bank the next day. They gave him a little passbook, and every week he made a deposit. He liked watching the teller write in the amount, total it up, and stamp the line in the book.

I thought about the box in the bottom of my sewing box where I was still saving what money I could and wondered if I should start my own account. George wasn't one to snoop, but Paul was into everything. What if he found my money and told George about it? I went to the bank and opened my own account and hid my passbook inside my Bible. That was the one place where I could be sure Paul wouldn't bother it.

On my forty-ninth birthday, in 1941, I found out what he was saving up to buy. No one had made much of a fuss of my birthday since James died.

Bessie baked me a special cake, and they lit the candles and everyone sang to me. Maxine gave me a blue headscarf. Betty Sue used baby-sitting money and bought me a pretty housecoat. Even Paul made me a card. George ate two pieces of the cake and gave me a smile and a wish for a happy day. Then they all looked at Gene, who smiled at me and nodded his head at John. They both went out of the house. I didn't know if I should be upset or curious.

A minute later, John's truck backed up the driveway all the way to the back porch, and he and Gene lifted off an electric washing machine and carried it down to the basement.

They put a chair where I could sit and watch while they hooked it up and gave me a demonstration. It was amazing. They ran hot water through a hose into it. It had come with a box of powdered soap. No more cutting up a bar of Fels-Naptha. They measured out the soap, poured it in, and added some clothes. When they turned it on, a shaft in the center of the tub churned back and forth for a while, then they turned it off, took the clothes out one at a time and ran them through a wringer on the top. Gene waggled a finger at me and warned me, "Now, you've got to be careful when you do the wringing so you don't stick your fingers right through the rollers and mash them all up."

The clean, wrung-out clothes came out the other side of the rollers and fell into the wash sink, which Gene had filled with cold water for the rinse. He swished them around with his hand and then ran them back through the wringer. "Ta-da, all ready for the clothesline."

Then he showed me how to empty the machine. It was the most beautiful thing I'd ever seen. Bessie already had one that I was too proud to ask to use. I'd been secretly looking at the electric washers at Sears Roebuck. I even thought about spending my little secret savings if I ever got that much built up, but didn't dare dream I might have a washing machine so soon.

I sat and cried. I'd washed clothes on a washboard since I was eight years old, sometimes for six people. I hauled the water from the well to fill the tubs, and when I was finished, hauled the water out in the yard to pour on the plants in the garden to kill the bugs and water the crop. Gene had a tear in his own eye. I could see that he understood how much this meant to me.

I gave special thanks for him that night, for the best son any woman had ever been blessed to have.

I hadn't been so happy since before James died. My children were happy. For all his nonsense, Bud liked being in the army. Gene had a good job, seemed to have recovered from his fall, and his kidneys gave him no trouble. Betty Sue loved her friends and was doing well in school. George and Gene were working steady and bringing home enough money between them to pay the bills and buy all the groceries we needed. I loved my modern home, with running water, an inside toilet, a gas stove, and now, an electric washing machine.

The only worries I had were for Paul. He was a moody boy who refused to go to school and sat and stared out the window for hours at a time. He didn't have a single friend. Whenever I tried to force him to go to church or to school, George would just tell me to leave him be, and I mostly did.

Gene worked first shift at his factory, getting up

at five in the morning and coming home at three in the afternoon, the same time Betty Sue got home from school. I would make them a snack to tide them over until supper, and they would sit in the kitchen and talk about their day. Except for her occasional temper tantrums that always made me think about her grandmother, Betty Sue was a happy girl with her own share of her father's charm, making friends easily, excited about school and her lessons.

Chapter 40

In the summer of 1941, President Roosevelt brought back the draft. At the prime age of twenty, Gene hadn't been called. I held my breath when the first rounds of numbers came out. Several of the neighbors' sons had to report. The thought of my precious boy going into the army was awful to me. Bud was already serving, and I felt that was enough.

I read about the war in Europe every day. The President was sending all kinds of help to Britain and he loaned them a billion dollars. I couldn't even imagine how much money that was, but they were supposed to pay it back when the war was over. I loved President Roosevelt and knew he had to be doing the right thing. Wasn't it better to help fight Hitler this way than to send our boys over there like we did before?

I hoped the money and supplies America sent

overseas would be enough. If Gene had to go away from home again, I thought, it would upset my whole life. What I didn't know then, was that the thing I had to fear the most wasn't across the ocean at all.

Gene came home from work one day and sat at the table while I cut some slices off a ham to make him a sandwich. Sixteen-year-old Betty Sue came bouncing into the room, followed by the most beautiful human being I'd ever seen. She was prettier than any of the movie stars in those books Betty Sue was always reading. Betty Sue grabbed the girl's hand and pulled her into the kitchen. "Mom, this is my friend, Evelyn, she's in my class at school. Evelyn, this is my mom and my brother Gene."

"Hi," the girl said, smiling almost shyly, with her head down.

"Hello, Evelyn," I said. "Can I make you something to eat?"

"No, thank you, Mrs. Foley, I'm fine. I can only stay for a minute. I have to get home and help my mother with the other kids."

I realized I was staring. Evelyn looked to be about five-feet-four inches tall and was large busted for a girl so slim. She had slightly rounded hips, and a tiny waist. Her chestnut hair had deep red lights where the sun hit it, and it curled almost down to her waist in the back. Her eyes were the deepest blue I'd ever seen, and her lashes were long and thick. She had an oval face, with a small, full-lipped mouth and a perfectly shaped nose. I had to force myself to look away, and when I did, I saw something that scared me.

Gene stared at Evelyn with a look on his face like he'd gone into some kind of a trance.

Chapter 41

After that, Betty Sue brought Evelyn home with her once or twice a week, and Gene hung around her like a puppy. He tried to talk, but could barely put two words together. I could tell it was hard for him to hide his feelings. By the end of a month, he was hopelessly in love.

As the months went by and Gene fell more and more in love, I made sure they were never alone for a minute, keeping them in the kitchen or on the porch. Maybe I was jealous. I told myself that they were both too young.

The only hope I had was that Evelyn didn't seem to see how he felt. She came to our house to spend time with Betty Sue, to read their movie star magazines or sit on the porch and laugh and whisper teen-age gibberish to one another. Gene would hang around as much as he could without Betty Sue complaining that she never had any privacy. Paul was in love with her, too, and would stand at the kitchen window, staring at the girls outside on the porch.

Sometimes Evelyn would stay in Betty Sue's room with her, experimenting with different hairstyles. Neither girl was allowed to wear makeup yet, but they would pin up each other's hair, like Joan Crawford or Merle Oberon, and come downstairs to the kitchen to show it off for me. I would tell them they were as beautiful as the stars, and Evelyn really was. No one in Hollywood was more beautiful, and without so much as a bit of lipstick.

When the girls were upstairs, Gene would sit on the porch and wait for them. I found small comfort in the fact that Evelyn was only sixteen, the same as Betty Sue, and that she must get a lot of attention from boys. I hoped one of them would draw her away from Gene. After a while, one of them did.

Evelyn began dating a senior at the high school where she and Betty Sue were in the eleventh grade, and she didn't spend so much time at our house. Gene sat at the table with a disappointed look on his face every day. It had been few weeks since Evelyn had been to the house before he finally brought up the subject with his sister. "Why don't you bring Evelyn home with you anymore?"

Betty Sue finished chewing a bite of her sandwich before she answered him. "She's been meeting Bobby Hudson at the sweet shop almost every day. They're an item."

I could see that Gene was heartbroken. Even though I hated his pain, I couldn't help but feel my own heart leap with relief. Maybe the girl was out of our lives. I continued my cooking without comment. Gene left the sandwich I'd made for him, stood and went out to the back porch.

Through the window, I could see him sitting in the swing, absolutely still, staring out into space. Paul guffawed loudly, spitting pieces of his food out onto the table. "He thought he had plenty of time, now he's out in the cold."

I stared at him. Maybe the boy was smarter than I thought.

George didn't come home from work until almost six in the evening and had never met Evelyn. He was totally unaware that his second son had lost his heart, but after a few days of Gene moping around the house, even George noticed that something was wrong. He waited until we'd gone to bed one night before he asked me about it.

"What's wrong with Gene? He's been dragging around here for weeks, and he won't even talk to me about it."

"He's in love with some girl, and she's going out with someone else."

"What girl? I never heard him say one word about any girl."

"Evelyn Mayse, that friend of Betty Sue's."

"I never met her. If she's a friend of Betty Sue's, why don't I know her?"

"She only stayed here for a little while after

school when she came over. She always said she had to go home and help her mother with the other children in the house. She was always gone before you came home."

"Well, if she's seeing someone else, he'll just have to get over it. There's plenty of fish in the sea. He's smart and good-looking and he's got a good job. How long could it take?"

I rolled over and turned my back to him. "I don't know, George, I don't know."

Chapter 42

I remember every second of the afternoon of December 7th, 1941, a Sunday. Bessie and I were in the living room, making plans for Christmas. Betty Sue and Maxine were upstairs in Betty Sue's room with a new *Silver Screen* magazine. George and Paul were napping. Gene was reading in his room.

I heard the sound of voices shouting outside. Bessie and I went out to the porch. People were gathered in clusters on the sidewalk and in the street, talking loudly, waving their arms, men shaking their fists in the air. Some of the women were crying.

Bessie went over to a group and asked what had happened. When she came back, her face was white, and she was shaking. I was afraid to hear the news. She grabbed my arm. "Maude, the Japanese bombed the fleet at Pearl Harbor."

"Where is Pearl Harbor?" Betty Sue asked.

Bessie said, "It's in Hawaii."

"What does that mean? What's going to happen now?" Maxine asked.

I looked at her, then at Bessie. I didn't have any idea.

Bessie frowned. "I don't know, but we'll find out soon. Let's go inside."

We turned on the radio and listened to the news.

I had only one thing on my mind, Gene.

The news was repeated often, and we listened to it on several stations. After an hour or so, George, Gene and John joined the men out on the street. By late evening, we all finally went to bed. I think Paul was the only one who slept well that night. I lay awake wondering what the future would bring. George worried about Bud, already in uniform. I worried about Gene, whose health seemed to be fully restored. He would be a prime candidate for the draft.

It would be days before the final tragic toll would be realized, but almost the entire Pacific fleet of the United States had been in port at Pearl Harbor when a Japanese force estimated at 360 planes had started bombing just before eight o'clock that morning. They targeted the ships in port, the American planes sitting on the airstrips, and ground troops stationed on Oahu. Eighteen ships were sunk or greatly damaged, and American forces suffered 3,700 casualties.

The next day, the President addressed Congress, and it declared war on Japan. On December 11, Germany and Italy, who were war partners with Japan, declared war on the United States.

It was all anyone talked about. Even in church the next Sunday, the pastor preached a sermon on how it was up to Christians to fight against evil. The male members sat there shouting, "Amen!" The women nodded their heads in agreement. I felt the grip of terror in my heart. We'd all thought that sooner or later, we would have to fight Hitler. Most of us didn't worry about Japan until that awful day.

The next morning, Gene didn't come downstairs at the regular time to get the breakfast I had ready for him. I hoped he was just oversleeping, but in my heart I had a pretty good idea why he wasn't at the table. I went upstairs and tapped on his door. "You're going to be late for work, Gene. Better get up."

The door opened and Gene, dressed in his church suit and tie, and holding his hat in his hand, stepped out in the hall. "I'm not going to work today, Mom. I'm going down with some of the other men to enlist."

I froze, wanting to grab him and hold him but not able to move. I just stood there and stared at him. He wrapped his arms around me and held me close. "I'll be all right, Mom. We'll get into this and in a few months it'll be over. Who did they think they were messing with? Didn't they know this would be the end of them?"

I opened my mouth to speak but couldn't force any sound from my throat. I just nodded and turned to go to the kitchen. Gene followed me downstairs, and I finally found my voice. "Come eat before you go. No telling how long it will take. I hear that every able-bodied man in the country is lining up to enlist."

Gene took a seat and buttered a biscuit while I slid his eggs and ham off the plate and back into the frying pan to warm them. Then I put them back on the dish and set it down in front of him. He ate as if he didn't have a care in the world while I made myself busy around the kitchen. I tried to sound normal when I asked, "What kind of work do you think they'll have you doing, Gene?"

He pursed his lips and thought it over. "Well, I heard that men with CCC experience would probably go into the Corps of Engineers, building bridges, roads, that sort of thing."

Somehow, this eased my fear a little. If he were building bridges, maybe he wouldn't have people shooting at him. I sighed and turned to look at him. "Gene, Bud is already in the Army. He'll have to go. Can't you stay here?"

He looked shocked. "Mom, how could I stay here? I have to go, or I'd never be able to show my face. Any man my age with no family has a duty to do."

I nodded. "I already made your lunch. You may as well take it with you. You may be gone all day, and I don't know if they'll have anything there for you to eat."

He stood, hugged me again, and kissed my cheek. "I'll come straight home as soon as they're through with me. Don't worry. I'll be fine."

He grabbed the lunch pail and hurried out the back door. I stood there looking after him. "Don't worry," he'd said.

A few minutes later, George came into the kitchen and started cooking his bacon. "Gene's gone down to sign up," I said.

George yawned. "I know. He told me last night that he thought it was the right thing to do."

I was speechless. George had known this since last night and hadn't said a word to me, hadn't made any effort to prepare me? He didn't even take the trouble to come downstairs and say goodbye to his son.

I stared at the handle of the cast-iron skillet where the thick slices of bacon hissed as the grease cooked out of them. I wanted to pick it up and hammer George's head with it. For a moment I hated him, really hated him.

Then shame filled me. I seemed to fail more and more every day in my search for a state of grace. I would have to pray twice as hard for God to forgive me and to help me to be the Christian woman I wanted to be.

Gene came home with a sad expression on his face. He was 4F. His injury at the CCC was too severe for him to serve. I couldn't control my emotions. I was relieved he wouldn't be in the army, but at the same time, I felt sorry for him. He'd been rejected and felt bad about it. I felt guilt that inside I was celebrating his rejection, but I was filled again with fear for his health. He'd been hurt so much that even in a time of war, he couldn't serve his country.

Bud came home on leave with the news that he

wouldn't be shipped overseas right away. He had too much experience and was needed here to help train the hundreds of thousands of men who had joined up since the attack at Pearl Harbor. He would be transferred to Fort Knox, Kentucky, for his new assignment.

Bud was home for two weeks. He went out drinking almost every night. After the first night, I locked him out. When he came home late, he pounded on the door and woke the whole house. George started to get up and to let him in. I grabbed his arm. "Get back in bed, George. I won't have a drunk sleeping under my roof. If he wants to stay here, he better get sober and stay that way."

"You can't turn him out, Maude. If he goes overseas, he could be killed. Then how would you feel?"

"He isn't likely to get killed in Kentucky unless he starts up drinking too much of that homemade moonshine they make there. He can sleep in the garage, but when he's drunk, he can't sleep inside my house."

George got out of bed and stood there in his long underwear. "I don't care what you say. I'm not going to let my son sleep in the garage in the middle of winter."

I stood, too. "Tell him to sleep inside John's truck. He's got enough alcohol inside him to keep him warm."

George shook his head. "I can't do that, Maude. This is my boy, and I'm the one that pays the rent here, not you. I'm not letting him sleep outside, but I'll tell him if he wants to sleep inside after tonight, he has to stay sober."

If George told him to stay sober, it didn't do any good. Bud came home drunk every night until the last day of his leave and then finally sobered up for his trip to Kentucky. George and John drove him to the train station to see him off. I didn't go with them, and I didn't pack him a lunch to take for his trip. I was glad he was gone. That night I asked God to help me deal with my feelings, or lack of them, for my oldest son and to help me fight hating George for making me feel so helpless. It was as if I had no say over what went on in my own house.

Gene and Betty Sue had never given me an ounce of grief. Bud and Paul had given me nothing but grief.

Chapter 43

One afternoon in April of 1942, Betty Sue came in with Evelyn following quietly behind her. I hadn't seen Evelyn in months. The girls said a polite hello to me and went up to Betty Sue's room. I was irritated to have Evelyn back in our home. Gene had just come home from work and gone to take his bath. He would be downstairs soon for his sandwich. I hoped that with the passing of time, and the war and all, he'd gotten over her. I was afraid that seeing Evelyn again would just stir up his old feelings. He hadn't mentioned another girl since she'd stopped visiting.

I put the sandwiches on the table, including an extra one for Evelyn, but no one came to get them except Paul. After a few more minutes I walked to the hallway and started to call up the stairs. I put my hand on the banister and opened my mouth, but what I saw made me stop.

Gene was standing outside Betty Sue's door, leaning close to it so he could hear what was being said inside. I stood and watched him. I could hear the sound of the girls' voices but couldn't make out what they were saying. After a minute Gene tapped on the door. Betty Sue opened it and he went in. I didn't move. I heard Evelyn crying, then more talking.

When the door finally opened, I hurried back to the kitchen and stirred the pot of chicken and dumplings I was making for supper. Betty Sue came into the kitchen, followed by Gene holding Evelyn's hand. Evelyn kept her eyes on the floor. I knew it was going to be bad news and braced myself.

Gene smiled at me as if he were afraid of me. "Evelyn and I are getting married, Mom. We're going down to city hall tomorrow."

I looked from him to Evelyn, who still kept her eyes down. I knew as sure as I knew anything that it wouldn't do me any good to fight with him about it. "All right," I said, and turned my back to them. I was filled with anger, filled with fear for my boy, and fear for myself, but there was nothing I could do to stop it. Gene was determined to marry this girl.

When I was a child, my mother had tucked me in every night and at first said prayers for me. Then as I grew old enough, she listened to me say my own. After my mother died, I'd said them on my own every night of my life. When I got ready to pray that night, I stopped myself and put it off until another day. For the first time, I went to sleep without talking to God. I knew now I would never attain the sinless state of grace I sought. I felt a seed of hatred growing in my heart for this beautiful girl my precious son loved so much. I knew without a doubt that Evelyn would bring grief into our lives.

They were married Friday at city hall and the next day Evelyn's parents brought her clothes and things over to our house. I could see where Evelyn got her looks. Her father was handsome, tall, and well-built. He had black hair, brown eyes, and chiseled features that told of his part-Cherokee family. Evelyn's beautiful mother was much younger looking than I was. She had golden-brown hair and deep blue eyes, with a rounded figure that must have once been the same as Evelyn's, but that time and childbearing had filled out to a pleasant, matronly look.

George welcomed them and he and Gene tried to make them feel comfortable. After they carried Evelyn's things upstairs to Gene's room, George asked them to sit down and offered them coffee. They sat in the kitchen and talked a little about their families.

The men hit it off, George's charm working as it always did. Evelyn's father was named Smith, his wife, Ola.

Smith poured some of the steaming hot coffee into the saucer to cool and sipped it with little slurps. I thought that undignified but ignored it. George told him about our trip to Detroit and Smith nodded his head. "We came from Silver Point, Tennessee, over on the east side of the state. I had a little farm and we kept it going as long as we could, but we never had good bottom land. Some of our fields were so steep it was hard not to fall out of them."

The men laughed over the joke and when Smith swayed and almost fell out of his chair, I realized Evelyn's father had been drinking. I was outraged. It wasn't even noon.

Smith went on with his story. "We were just getting by with what crops would grow in such a little bit of rain. We finally gave up when the cow died. There were too many children to be without milk and we didn't have money to buy another cow. I made a little from the still, but the government men found that and smashed it. I didn't have money to build another one. We had to come here. A friend got me in at the United Rubber Company."

I couldn't help myself. I burst out, "You ran a still?"

Smith could tell how I felt and he shrugged. "We came from the hill country. A man did what he had to do to feed his family. If the crops failed, he sold whiskey. I got my first still when I was twelve. It meant I was a man. I was finished with school and worked the farm full-time, just like my daddy. He taught me how to plow a hillside, how to tend to the livestock, and how to make corn liquor. Every farmer around had a still. You prayed you wouldn't need to use it, but when you did, you gave thanks that you didn't see your children go without eating." He had no apology or embarrassment in his voice.

I didn't have an answer to that. I'd had no idea that such things went on, children quitting school to make moonshine. It certainly wouldn't have been allowed in my home town. Eastern Tennessee must be an entirely different world from the west side of the state.

The room became uncomfortable for everyone in it. Smith pushed his cup and saucer away and stood. "Thank you for everything." He looked directly at Gene, who stood with his arm around Evelyn's waist, and nodded. "We appreciate it."

Gene nodded back at him, blushing at the meaning of his words.

I knew the Mayses were relieved that Evelyn had married, even under these circumstances. It was no small thing in 1942 for a young woman to be in a family way and not married. She would have been said to have "gotten herself in trouble," and the whole family would be looked down on.

I couldn't even force myself to go beyond not being outright rude. I couldn't help thinking if they had properly watched over their daughter, this wouldn't have happened.

The whole situation was uncomfortable. I was relieved when they left. I stayed in the kitchen while George, Gene, and Evelyn walked them out to their car. George kept talking to Smith until the car finally drove away. When Gene and Evelyn went up to what was now their room, George turned angrily to me. "Maude, what in the world is the matter with you? You could at least be polite."

I gritted my teeth and frowned. I almost shouted, "You know how I feel about this whole situation. It's bad enough as it is, and then he comes here drinking."

"Keep your voice down. Do you want Evelyn to hear you?"

"I don't care if she does hear me. She needs to tell that father of hers if he ever comes here again he better be sober."

"He wasn't drunk. He's only had one or two. It's not easy for him, this happening, besides, I have a beer or two myself, from time to time."

"I don't think he was drinking beer, and I know very much that you drink, George, and that you always have, and you know what? I've about had enough of that, too, but at least you have the consideration that you don't drink so much that you show it."

George opened his mouth to say something else, then just put his palms up in front of him in surrender, turned, and left the house.

Chapter 44

Evelyn ate as much as any of the men. She grew bigger every day. Gene doted on her, bringing little gifts home with him the way he used to do for me, and buying her special candy. If they were in the same room he was always touching her, his hand on her arm, his arm around her waist, or holding her hand. I could clearly see that she didn't return his affection. For so many years, I'd longed for George to touch me that way. It made me want to smack her to see that she didn't appreciate it at all.

Every man in my house loved Evelyn, including Paul. She and George formed a bond almost immediately, laughing together, leaning in to whisper to one another.

Her mother and father pretty much stayed away from our place. When George asked about them, she told him that her mother had her hands full with so many children. There were six still at home, including a toddler. It was a full time job to see after them, even if Freda, the oldest after Evelyn, did a lot to help.

Once Evelyn was living with us, her friendship with Betty Sue cooled off. I understood that. Betty Sue was crowded out of her place with her father the same way I was crowded out of Gene's time. Sometimes, when Gene or George was making a fuss over Evelyn, how pretty she was, or something like that, Betty Sue would stomp up the stairs and slam her door. I could hear her up there, crashing around her room. A few times, she and Evelyn exchanged sharp words and I saw Betty Sue clench up her fist. I knew that if she weren't afraid of what Gene might do, she would have punched Evelyn right in the nose.

Paul followed Evelyn around like a puppy. He was fourteen and would do anything to get her attention, making faces like a six-year-old, standing on his head in the corner, telling stupid jokes to make her laugh.

By the end of August, Evelyn weighed almost two hundred pounds. She turned eighteen on August 28th.

On the 17th of the September, her water broke, and Gene went next door to Bessie's to call the doctor. We Foleys were still scrimping to pay the bills and a car of our own and a telephone were still luxuries to us.

Gene was told to take her to Cottage Hospital in Grosse Pointe Farms, several miles down Jefferson

Avenue. There were closer hospitals, but many were flooded with American soldiers and sailors recovering from the battles going on in the Pacific and Africa.

They took her bag and left. Gene was gone all night. When he came home the next day, he told me all about it. Evelyn was admitted to the hospital. They put her on a gurney and left it at the end of a line of gurneys placed in the hall. There weren't any rooms available at the time, but they promised her she would get a room as soon as possible. Gene said he stood next to her and held her hand. After several hours, a kind nurse brought him a chair and put it against the wall so he could sit.

Evelyn went into labor that night and still, no regular beds became available.

Evelyn labored all day on the 19th and the baby still hadn't been born. Gene came home for a few minutes to tell us what was happening, take a bath, and change clothes, then went back to the hospital.

I had five babies born at home with no drugs and not much help. I wondered, how bad could it be to give birth in a hospital?

Gene said he sat on his chair, still in the hospital corridor, for another long night while Evelyn suffered even more than she had the day and night before. From time to time one doctor or another would come by, lift the sheet and do a quick examination. He would pat her hand and say, "Don't worry, it won't be long now," and go his way.

They explained to Gene that drugs were in short supply and childbearing was the most natural thing in the world, not something to waste painkillers on when boys were dying all over the world. When Gene told us how she was suffering, even I felt sorry for her.

It was early on the morning of Sunday, September 20th, that the pains got the worst. Still, Evelyn wasn't offered any medicine to help her. Her crying and moaning became screams, and the doctor called several nurses who rolled out curtained partitions and placed them around her gurney to give her a little privacy. Gene was sent to the waiting room where he paced and prayed and worried. He called Bessie's again to tell us that the baby was finally on its way into the world.

Shortly after that, the nurse came and informed him that Evelyn had a healthy baby girl, nine pounds, fourteen ounces, and that the baby was doing just fine, but the mother had lost a lot of blood, and her hip had been dislocated. They finally put Evelyn in a ward that had eight beds crowded in a room built for four.

Gene was led to her and stayed there with her for several more hours. When the nurse came in carrying the baby for Evelyn to breast-feed, he was sent out of the room. After a half-hour, the nurse came out carrying the baby, and he followed her down to the nursery. He was told to go stand in front of the window, and he could see his baby. She laid it in a little bed next to the side wall of the nursery. When the nurse saw him craning his neck to look at it, she rolled the bed over to the window so he could get a better view.

Evelyn stayed in the hospital for three more days in a ward so packed there was barely room for the nurse to walk between the beds. Gene went back to work on Monday, but was at the hospital that night until they chased him out.

He went on and on about that baby, like there'd never been another baby born in the world. He visited with Evelyn for a while each afternoon and spent the rest of the time staring at the pink bundle in the nursery.

Gene borrowed an extra bed from Bessie and put it in the dining room so Evelyn wouldn't have to walk up and down stairs for a while.

On Wednesday, the doctor decided Evelyn had recovered enough, and she and the baby were sent home in an ambulance. I met them in front of the house. Gene handed the baby to me, and he and George locked hands, lifted Evelyn out of the ambulance, and carried her in the house.

I pulled the blanket away from the baby's face, expecting to see a miniature Evelyn. What I saw about knocked me out. I was holding a copy of my Lulu. The baby's head was perfectly round, her skin pink. She opened deep blue eyes and looked up at me, then closed them and went back to sleep. Her head was covered in soft, blonde fuzz. She looked, for all the world exactly the way Lulu looked when she was first put in my arms so many years before.

I made no move to go inside. I stood for several minutes on the sidewalk and finally went up the steps. I sat in the rocker on the front porch, rocking and staring at the child I'd expected to resent, but who already filled my heart to overflowing with love. Her plump, pink cheeks and blonde head seemed all too familiar to me, taking me back so many years to another baby girl. I knew this baby wasn't my blood, but my heart stirred all the same.

I didn't know how much time passed when Gene came out to get me. He reached out his hands for the baby. "The doctor told Evelyn she had to nurse her every three hours, even if she had to wake her up, and it's way past that now."

I made no move to hand her over. I just rocked and stared at that baby's face. Gene said, "Mom, I have to take her inside."

I stood and held the baby even closer to my chest. I started toward the door, and Gene held it open for me. I carried her to the dining room that had been made into a temporary bedroom for Evelyn, and stopped several feet from the bed. Evelyn held out her arms expectantly, but I couldn't give her the precious bundle. Evelyn frowned, "Give me the baby, Mrs. Foley. I have to feed her now."

Still, I clutched the baby to myself. It woke and started crying. I still made no move to give that little girl to her mother. Gene put his hand on my elbow, "Mom, give Donna to Evelyn."

The sound of the name woke me. "Donna? Is that her name? Donna?'

Evelyn smiled, "Donna Lee, after Donna Reed, the movie star."

"What about Lee? Is that one of your friends?"

"No, I just thought it sounded right, Donna Lee Foley," Evelyn said, still holding out her arms for the baby, who began crying even louder.

I looked down at that little face again and finally handed her to Gene, who gave her to Evelyn. I turned and left the room.

I went back out to the porch and Gene came out and took the chair next to me. We sat without speaking for a while, looking out at the passing cars.

Gene put his hand on mine and told me what went on at the hospital, "I don't know what happened to me, Mom. When I saw that baby it was like a whole part of me that I didn't even know existed woke. My mind hasn't been off her for a split second ever since. I thought that I could never love anyone the way I love Evelyn, but that baby has changed my mind. I don't care if she does belong to someone else, she's mine. Does that make any sense at all?"

I rocked and nodded. "It's a funny thing, that feeling. It doesn't always come when it's supposed to, and sometimes it happens when you weren't even looking for it."

"Is that the way you felt when we were born?"

I didn't answer right away. I looked out at the street and kept my face turned away from my son. I would never lie to him.

"Mom?"

"Like I said, it doesn't always come when it's supposed to."

Now there were two females in the house that got all the men's attention. Even Betty Sue and Paul took to the baby. We all wanted to hold her when Evelyn wasn't feeding her. Gene and George would come in from work and go straight to Donna, cooing and talking to her until it was time for her to get her bath and go to sleep.

In a few weeks, Evelyn was strong enough to move her bed back upstairs to Gene's room. She lost the extra baby-weight right off, and in only six months was as slim as ever.

My own body had thickened a little with each birth, and I couldn't help but resent how fast Evelyn got her figure back. I was happy to tend to the baby when Evelyn wanted Gene to take her to the movies or anywhere else.

Betty Sue helped when she could, but she was still in school. I shopped for groceries, cooked all the meals, washed, folded and ironed for the seven of us, and did all the cleaning, including Gene and Evelyn's room. Evelyn slept late, fed the baby, and read movie star magazines.

I was sorry my eyes had begun to fail and I couldn't sew and embroider the little dresses for Donna that I made for my other girls. I doted on that baby all the same. Whenever I shopped, I always found enough extra money to buy her something, even if only a pair of knit booties with little balls on the strings.

The child thrived, surrounded by smiling, adoring adults. By the time she was a few months old, Paul was carrying her around the house perched on one hip so much George teased him that he'd be lop-sided for the rest of his life. It even softened my heart for the boy. If Paul could love this child the same as the rest of us loved her, maybe he wasn't as hopeless a case as I'd feared.

Chapter 45

A little banner with a blue star on it representing a family member in the armed forces hung in the window of our front door. Early one Saturday afternoon in the spring of 1944, it shook when someone knocked.

There stood my oldest son, Bud. His job was training new recruits. His commanding officer must have really liked him, because he didn't set a very good example for the men. He spent most of his leave time drunk in the stockade, so we hadn't seen him for over two years. He gave me and Paul a quick hug, then grabbed his sister Betty Sue and lifted her off the floor, twirling her around. When he set her down, he turned his attention to his father, hugging him first and then shaking his hand as if he would never let it go.

After Gene came to see what was going on, Bud

grabbed his hand, pumping it up and down. "I hear you're an old married man now, with a baby to boot. Let's meet the old ball and chain."

Gene smiled sheepishly. "Okay. I'll call her."

He went to the bottom of the stairs and called up, "Evelyn, come on down here. I've got someone I want you to meet."

Evelyn stuck her head out of the bedroom door, "Just a minute, Gene, I'm…" her voice trailed off when she saw the tall, handsome man in uniform standing next to Gene. She came bouncing down the stairs with a flirtatious smile. I saw the look on Bud's face, and I couldn't help but snicker. He was already just as hypnotized by her as the rest of the men in the house.

Gene wrapped his arm around her waist, claiming her as his own. "Evelyn, this is my big brother, Bud. Bud, this is my wife, Evelyn."

Bud never took his eyes off Evelyn. After a moment, he was jarred out of his trance, realizing he needed to say something. He slapped Gene on the shoulder. "How did an ugly mug like you ever catch this beauty?"

There was an awkward silence, and then George said, "We just locked her up in the kitchen and wouldn't let her leave until she married one of us. Since I'm taken, and Paul was too young, she got stuck with Gene."

Bud held Evelyn's hand. "Well, I'm sorry you didn't keep her locked up till I got here. I would have kept her for myself."

Gene tightened his grip on Evelyn, pulling her against him. "Well, she's all mine. You missed the boat on that one."

Bud shook his head. "Too bad. That's what I get for not getting shipped out sooner."

George's face turned white. "What do you mean, shipped out? I thought they would keep you here to train the new recruits."

"All good things must come to an end. Just about every unit at Ft. Knox is shipping out. The war won't last much longer. I've got two weeks leave, and then I'm getting my unit ready to go overseas."

George's voice thickened. "Where are they sending you?"

"Who knows? Everything's a secret nowadays. You know what they say, *loose lips sink ships*."

I patted Bud on the arm. "You'll be safe. I'll pray for you every night. Right now, I'll make you a special dinner, anything you want."

"Anything?"

I smiled. "What would you like?"

"I'll take about ten pieces of that fried chicken and some of those float-on-air biscuits and mashed potatoes and the gravy so thick it won't even pour."

"Good as done. I don't even have to go to the store."

George wrapped his arm around Bud's shoulder. "I'm going to take all three of my boys out for a beer, Maude. We'll be back in no time."

My heart sank. I knew if Bud started drinking, he wouldn't stop. "Why don't you just stay home and let

Bud tell you about what he's been doing? I know Paul would like to hear his adventures."

"Paul can go with us," said George. "He can have a Coke-cola. I want to show my boy off a little. He looks so good in that uniform, and he's going off to serve his country. I'm proud of him. Look at his sleeve. He's got his sergeant's stripes back again."

George walked next to Bud with his arm still draped over his shoulder. They were the same height and build, and had the same gait. From the back, only the uniform and a little gray in George's hair told them apart. Gene walked behind, and Paul ran in circles around them

I called after them, "Dinner will be on the table at six."

I had dinner on the table at six sharp. I walked to the front door every ten minutes and peered down the street, but there was still no sign of them. Finally, at seven, Evelyn began to complain. "I'm hungry, let's eat."

Betty Sue joined in, "Let them eat when they get in, Mom."

So we three women had our dinner. Usually a healthy eater, I just pushed my food around. After dinner, Evelyn took Donna back upstairs to bathe her and tuck her in for the night. Betty Sue and I took the plates to the kitchen and threw a cloth over the food on the table. The men could eat it cold when they came home, whenever that would be. I heard the radio in Gene's room come on. I knew I wouldn't see Evelyn again that night. It was no loss to me. Every minute spent alone with her was tiresome. I had nothing to say to the girl.

Gene and Paul came in around nine o'clock. I met them at the door, "Where are your father and Bud?" I asked. I leaned close enough to Gene that I could smell his breath. There was no trace of beer.

"They're still down at the beer garden," Gene said. "The two of them are telling jokes and stories, and they've got everyone laughing at them. You know how they are."

"Yes, I know how they are. I'm glad you had the good sense to come home sober." Gene was always the one I could depend upon, always my good boy.

"Paul and I did have one Dr Pepper too many. Didn't we Paul?" Gene elbowed Paul in the ribs.

Paul smiled. "Yeah, but we won't have a hangover in the morning, will we?"

"That's right," Gene answered.

I prodded Paul toward the stairs. "Get to bed or there's no way I can get you up for church in the morning."

Paul sulked and hung his head. "I don't want to go to church."

"I don't care what you want. Get upstairs this minute."

Paul turned and, grumbling to himself, went to his room.

Gene gave me a quick hug. "I better get upstairs myself or Evelyn will be chewing me out."

I watched him with a frown as he went up. Before he married, he never missed a Sunday service, but I wouldn't call him to get up early in the morning. Evelyn's mother was a Baptist, and the girl refused to go to church with me, but didn't make any effort to go with her mother, either. Since Evelyn didn't go, Gene stopped going. He preferred to spend every possible minute with his beautiful wife and daughter.

I felt it was George's fault that members of my family showed disrespect to church attendance. He'd set the example. I didn't even try to stifle the resentment gnawing at me.

I went to bed, but lay awake in the dark and listened for George and Bud to come home. It was after midnight when I heard the sound of voices singing loudly and George and Bud stumbling up the front steps. I almost ran to meet them.

I planted myself in front of them as they came in the door. They held one another up, and both of them ignored me. They reeked of beer and cigarettes. Bud practically fell on the sofa and went right to sleep. George took Bud's shoes off and covered him with a blanket. I went back to bed.

I got up early the next morning and dressed for church. Paul refused to get out of bed, kicking at my hand when I pulled on his foot to wake him. I finally gave it up, and Betty Sue and I went next door and rode with Bessie and her family. I was grateful Bessie had the good sense not to ask about them. I knew she had to have heard the men come home.

George had to work the next day, so Bud went out alone Sunday night.

Monday afternoon, when George came home

from work in John's truck, he brought a full size set of bedding with him. He'd bought it second-hand from one of the men he worked with at the factory.

I asked, "What's that for, George?"

"I'm putting it in the basement for Bud. I don't want him to have to sleep on that sofa. It's too short for him."

"He's only going to be here for two weeks, and he'll be drunk most of that time. What are we going to do with it then?"

George lowered his head and glared at me. "He's going off to war, Maude. If he's scared and feels the need to ease that a little by drinking before he goes, then that's all right with me. I'm scared myself. Once he leaves, we may never see our boy again, and I'm going to treat him right while I still have him."

I threw my hands in the air and went back to the kitchen.

George and Bud went out together that night. George came home early by himself and came to bed without his supper. I lay with my back to him and said nothing. Sometime early in the morning, I woke when I heard Bud come staggering in and going to the basement. I guessed George explained the arrangement to him.

Bud came home drunk every night. George went out and drank with him on Fridays and Saturdays.

The two weeks leave came and went, and Bud made no move to pack up and re-join his company.

I asked him, "Won't you get in trouble?"

"Nah. Me and the Old Man are buddies. I saved

his life one time."

"How did you do that?'

"I had a bunch of new recruits out on the firing range when the Old Man came to check us out. One of the greenhorns went a little nuts. He pointed his rifle at the Old Man and said he was going to kill him. I got between them and said he'd have to shoot me first."

"Oh, Bud! That was so brave of you!"

"Not really. I knew the boy was just scared of going off to war. I talked to him until I could see he was calming down. He finally put down the rifle, and they took him off to the infirmary. We never saw him again. Since then, the Old Man goes out of his way to make my life easier. That's why I got my stripes back."

One afternoon at the end of the third week, two MPs came to the door looking for Bud. He was still sleeping, and when I called down to him, he came and greeted the MPs like old friends. The three of them slapped one another on the back and joked like long-lost brothers. I couldn't believe it. Like his father, Bud certainly could charm the birds out of the trees.

The next thing I knew, the three of them had gone off somewhere. They didn't come back until early morning. I found one sleeping on the sofa and Bud on the floor. The other one slept in Bud's bed. They went out drinking together the next night and the next.

Two more MPs came to the door, and Bud greeted them as heartily as he had the first pair. I couldn't help but wonder if he'd made friends with every MP in his camp. As often as he'd lost his stripes over the years, I figured he probably was on a first-name basis with each and every one of them. This new pair must have had had stricter orders than the last and refused the offer of a beer. Bud finally gathered up his things and the five of them left after Bud gave hugs and handshakes all around. He promised to write home.

George stood on the porch and watched them drive away with his oldest son, carrying him back to Kentucky and then to the war. He didn't come inside for a long time, and when he did, he went straight to the basement.

He didn't come up until he had to get ready for work Monday morning. I went about my business. I knew I couldn't comfort him, but I promised myself I would remember Bud in my prayers every night as much for George's sake as for Bud's.

Chapter 46

One day a few weeks after Bud went back to Fort Knox, I was getting ready to go to the grocery store. I put on my hat, and Paul grabbed the canvas bags we used to carry what we bought.

"Tell your father I'm ready," I said. Paul ran to the door. George was in John and Bessie's garage, watching John as he worked on the truck.

I stepped out to the porch just as a car with a seal on the door pulled up in front of the house. I stopped in my tracks. Two men wearing Army uniforms got out. One of them, an officer, had an envelope in his hand. He looked at it and then up at the house. When his eyes met mine, my knees went weak, and I leaned against the door jamb for support.

"Run get your father," I told Paul.

"Why? I thought we were going to the store."

I squeezed his shoulder hard. "I told you to go get your father right now." I clenched my teeth. "I mean it!"

Paul's eyes got big. He ran between the houses.

The two men came up the walk and stopped at the stairs. I waited silently.

George came walking around from the side of the house. "What's wrong, Maude? Paul said I had to come out here right away. I was just telling a good story to John--" He stopped talking when he saw the uniforms. He walked up the steps and put his arm around my waist. It felt like he was doing it more to support himself than to support me. It was the first time he'd touched me since Bud left.

Both soldiers removed their hats, and the officer stepped forward. "Mr. and Mrs. Foley?"

George leaned against me. "Yes, we're the Foleys. Maybe you should come inside."

Right then, John came around the side of the house carrying a wrench in his hand. His mouth was opened to say something, but he snapped it shut when he saw the car and the men. He ran to his house. I knew he would bring Bessie. We would need her.

George's voice rasped. "Why don't we go inside," he said again. He stepped back and held open the door for me and the soldiers.

We all went in the living room. Paul was the only one who didn't know what was happening. I took off my hat, "Please, sit down. Can I get you something to drink?"

"Thank you, ma'am. We're all right."

The two men sat on the sofa. I sat on the edge of the seat of the easy chair and George stood next to me. I could feel him shaking. Bessie and John came in the door without saying anything. Bessie gripped my hand.

One of the men cleared his throat. "I'm sorry to inform you that your son, William James Foley, was killed in the line of duty."

George made a choking sound and sobbed, "How did it happen?"

"They were on their way to ship out overseas. He was on his way to the railroad station, riding in a convoy with other GIs. His truck went over a big pothole, and he fell off the back. He was run over by the next truck in the line. You should still be proud of him. He may not have died in battle, but he died in the service of his country, just the same as if he'd been killed in action."

I didn't ask, but I wondered if Bud had been drinking. Of course, they wouldn't tell me that, even if it were true.

They filled in a few more details, like when the body would arrive home and what the government would provide. Then they stood, the officer handed me an envelope, and took their leave. George walked them to their car. I could see him through the window, shaking both their hands. He stood for a moment, watching the car drive away, before he came back in the house.

Bessie and Paul were crying. John and George held in their emotions. I sat in the chair and stared into space, and when Bessie tried to comfort me, I waved her away.

John patted George on the shoulder. "I'm sorry, George. I know how you loved Bud." George just nodded, unable to talk.

John and Bessie went home, and George and Paul went down to the basement. I sat in the chair and felt sinful.

My oldest son was gone, and what I felt wasn't so much grief as it was guilt. Guilt, because when George's mother first put him in my arms I hadn't felt any love for him. Guilt, because for his whole life I hadn't really loved him the way a mother should love her child. Guilt that I hadn't tried harder, hadn't done more. Why didn't I feel the love I should for my son? Was it because George's mother took him away from me for that first day and a half after he was born?

I was still sitting there when Gene came in, carrying Donna. Evelyn had gone over to see her mother that morning, and he'd stopped on his way home from work to bring them home. As soon as Gene saw me, he knew something was wrong.

"What happened, Mom?" He knelt down on one knee in front of my chair.

I handed him the letter, and he put Donna on my lap and opened it. Donna seemed to pick up on his distress. She leaned back against my breast and watched her daddy while he read. As he took in the words, he groaned and tears came to his eyes.

"What's the matter?" Evelyn asked.

Gene handed her the letter and asked me,

"Where's Dad?"

"He's downstairs with Paul," I said.

Gene left me holding Donna and went to be with his father and brother in the basement. I could hear them sobbing. I wished I could have the same release, but it didn't come to me.

I took Donna to the kitchen and put her in the high chair. Donna watched me, never making a sound. I made a meal out of leftovers. There would be no happy dinner.

When the food was ready, I called down to the basement. Paul and Gene came up and sat at the table. I didn't ask where George was. I understood too well. They ate quietly, and then Gene picked up Donna. "I think I'll go on back to the Mayse's and tell them," he said. "They'll want to know."

I nodded.

That night George slept in the basement on the bed he'd made for Bud. He didn't go to work for a week, went out drinking every night, and came home late. At almost any other point in history, he would have been fired, but his job was secure. I suppose during wartime, no employer would have been unsympathetic to a man who'd sacrificed his son.

On Sunday, I rode home from church with Bessie. She always knew what was happening in her brother's house, and she asked me, "Is George showing any sign of sobering up yet?"

"Not that I can tell," I answered.

"I'll talk to him," Bessie said.

When we got home, I went to the kitchen and

Bessie went down to the basement. I opened the door and leaned over a little so I could hear what was being said.

Bessie's voice was loud, "George, wake up!"

George mumbled something. Bessie raised her voice and said, "Wake up. I have something to tell you."

George said, "--lost my son, don't care about anything..."

"You had a week, and that's enough." Bessie told him. "Drinking your life away won't bring Bud back. Now, you get yourself sobered up and get back to work in the morning--"

He mumbled something and then her voice changed to one I'd heard before, the one that made the men's faces go white. "Or else!"

Bessie came back upstairs and gave me a hug. "He'll be all right now," she said.

George stayed in the basement all day and night Sunday. On Monday morning, he came upstairs, cooked his breakfast, and went back to work. Nothing was said about Bud.

I think now, I was grieving as much for the way things should have been as I was for losing a son, but I had to hold it all inside. I wanted us to put our arms around one another and find comfort. That didn't happen. I wished George would talk about it, but when I brought it up, he went down to the basement.

I talked to Bessie, but that wasn't enough. I shared this loss with George, and even though it didn't mean the same to both of us, I felt the need to discuss it with him. I didn't have the slightest idea how to bring up the subject in a way that would break through his silence.

We replaced the blue star on the banner with a gold one to signify our loss. It was a while before Bud's body came home. The funeral director set up a platform in the living room to hold the coffin. It was plain wood, covered with a flag. Chairs were set up in rows. Neighbors and church members brought food and paid their respects. Brother Els, the pastor from my church led a service, and then they took him out to Forest Lawn Cemetery for the burial. Soldiers fired guns in the air. Then it was over, and we came home.

Chapter 47

We thought the war would end soon, but it went on and on. There was a big invasion of Europe on June 6, 1944, they called D-Day. I guess they were planning that for a long time, and it must have been the reason they were sending Bud overseas, to help. The papers said it was a great success, but I wondered how many mothers and fathers lost their boys.

Everyone on the home front did what they could to help the war effort. In my house, there was nothing new about the slogan, "use it up, wear it out, make it do." We'd always been frugal. I considered waste a sin, but even I tried harder not to waste anything. Everyone I knew did what they could to support the war effort.

When Paul's shoe soles wore out, I couldn't find leather pieces to mend them, so I cut a stack of cardboard in the shape of the insoles and padded them so they would last longer. He changed the liners every night. I wore heavy cotton stockings instead of nylon, and when the elastic garters wore out I learned to stick my finger in the top of the hose, twist it several times and tuck it in the binding to make it stay up. I wore them until the toes and heels were completely gone and I had blisters on my feet. It wasn't long until every one of the women in my house was wearing white anklets. They lasted better than stockings.

I held the milk carton over Paul's cereal bowl until the very last drop drained out, and when I broke an egg for breakfast, I took my fingertip and wiped out every bit of egg white from the shell. George tried to tease me about it. I didn't care. Mostly, I felt his tomfoolery was just a way of covering up his laziness. After a while, he let it rest.

George had his own streak of patriotism. He cut back on his beer and smoking. He stopped buying cigarettes in a package and went back to rolling his own the way he did in Missouri.

Betty Sue graduated from high school in late June. I made a special dinner, borrowing ration stamps from Bessie to get enough sugar to bake a cake, and held a little party for her with just the two families.

The friendship between Betty Sue and Evelyn was completely over, but Evelyn smiled and congratulated her. I couldn't help but see the sorrow in Evelyn's eyes and knew she was thinking about what she'd missed. For once, I felt sorry for her.

The week after Betty Sue's graduation, she got a job making Jeeps on the assembly line at the Willys plant. We went shopping for two pair of slacks for her to wear to work. Betty Sue had never worn a pair of pants in her life, but she wouldn't be allowed to help make an automobile wearing a dress.

We found some trousers that fit, in dark colors that wouldn't show the wear and the dirt. They had pleats on the front and zipped up the side.

Betty Sue reported to work the next Monday with her long black hair tied up in a scarf. She came home bubbling over with stories about her job installing the little windshield in each Jeep as it rolled by her station. I envied her. Betty Sue would have a life I'd never dreamed possible, working alongside men and women in the outside world.

By the fall of 1944, Donna was running all over the house. She ran to meet her daddy when he came home from work each day. Gene would scoop her up in his arms and hold her close to him.

He would sit down at the kitchen table and play "This Little Piggy" with her toes, and she would squeal with laughter when he got to the end of the song and wiggled her little toe. They would sing "Itsy Bitsy Spider" and play "Pat-a-Cake." I watched them play and it made my heart glad. Gene was happy with his family, and bowled over by his love for Evelyn and Donna. Maybe I was wrong to be afraid that Evelyn would bring grief to all of us.

Betty Sue began dating a young man she met at the factory. Ellis Marshall was from Kentucky, tall, well-built, and good looking. He had wavy blond hair that fell over his forehead. He had a gentle way about him. He had a bit of a limp, but he seemed in good health otherwise. I asked why he wasn't in the service. Betty Sue explained he'd been in the Army, but wounded in the knee and sent home for good.

That made me wonder if other people looked at Gene and thought he was a draft dodger. You couldn't tell by looking at him that he was 4-F.

Betty Sue came home from work one day with a tear in her blouse and scratches on her arm.

I dabbed mercurochrome on her and asked, "What happened?"

"We were in the lunch room. That witchy Maris Tavers was rubbing herself all over Ellis. When I told her to stop, she shoved me and told me to mind my own business, so I punched her in the nose. She hit me back, and the next thing you know, we were rolling around on the floor, and Mitch, the foreman, had to pull me off her. When I stood up, I had a fistful of her mangy hair in my hand."

"Are you going to be in trouble?"

"No, everyone in the room told how she started it. When Mitch asked me if I wanted her fired, I said no. I was over being mad by them. I wouldn't have minded pulling out all her hair, but I didn't want to be responsible for the girl losing her job."

Why didn't you punch Ellis?"

"He didn't do anything wrong. He was trying to push her off him."

I'd seen Betty Sue's outbursts of temper ever since she was a baby. This Maris person was lucky she got out of it with only a handful of hair missing.

Chapter 48

The war dragged on. When it started, everyone around us had been convinced that once the Americans got involved, it would be over in only a few months. By 1944, we could see it was going to be a long, hard fight.

Chapter 49

The one war I couldn't win was the one being carried on in my own household. Evelyn complained about everything.

She couldn't have new clothes. Donna was too much work. Gene was gone too much, working as many overtime hours as he could get and leaving her alone with his family. Gene gave me too much money and didn't give her enough. She didn't like my cooking, but didn't offer to help with the meals. She thought I was too fussy about keeping the house clean.

I had a few complaints of my own. She left a trail of empty glasses and magazines wherever she went. Her jackets were left hanging on the backs of chairs. There were sometimes so many of her clothes on the doorknob to their room she couldn't close the door.

I bit my tongue. I gave up trying to be friends

with the girl and simply tried to stay away from her as much as possible. I wanted to have it out with her, but I didn't dare. I didn't want to know what would happen if Gene had to choose between her and me.

I knew Gene was still so taken by Evelyn that he would take her side. That was the way it was supposed to be, wasn't it? She was his wife. I loved the baby something awful, all of us Foleys did, even Paul, but I couldn't help wishing that none of us had ever laid eyes on her beautiful, pouting mother.

One morning I came out of my room just as Evelyn started downstairs. I was several steps behind her, and a cold, hard feeling came over me. It was all I could do to keep myself from giving her the same push that George's mother had given me all those years ago. I didn't have it in me. The realization that I hated someone so much I would wish them dead made me sick to my stomach. I went back to my room to ask God for forgiveness.

I'd been praying about the situation daily ever since Gene married Evelyn, and it was only getting worse. What was the use of praying, if prayers did nothing to help? But I kept on praying about it anyway.

I was carrying a laundry basket full of clothes from the back yard one day when I heard arguing coming from Gene's room. I stopped at the top of the stairs and listened. It was Gene and Evelyn. The girl's voice was demanding. I could picture her, pouting, with her bottom lip stuck out. She yelled, "Your mother takes almost all your money, and I can't even have a new dress. You ought to tell her that you're cutting back on what you pay her."

Gene tried to reason with her. "Mom doesn't take my money. I give it to her. If we're going to live in her house, we ought to pay our way. There's food, electricity, gas for the stove, and lots of other things that have to be paid for. Besides, she's out in the back now taking *our* laundry in from the line."

"Well, if we're such a burden, we ought to get a place of our own. I hate living here. She looks at me like she hates me. Even Betty Sue won't talk to me anymore."

"Nobody hates you, Evelyn. Maybe if you did more to help out around the house, they would warm up to you."

"I've got a baby to take care of, and you expect me to clean up after them? Your mother is a fanatic anyway! Clean, clean, clean. She won't even leave a glass in the sink overnight."

"That's part of her religion, Evelyn. She's always believed that cleanliness is next to Godliness."

"Well, my mother is just as religious as she is, and you won't see her spending her life scrubbing and cleaning."

There was a pause in the argument, and I could picture Gene holding his tongue. Mrs. Mayse was far from a good housekeeper. The few times I'd been to her house, it was a mess. When we went over there, Ola was usually sitting of the front porch of the Mayse house on St. Paul, chatting with a neighbor.

The first time she invited us to come inside, her housekeeping shocked me. Jackets and coats were thrown one on top of another on the dining room chairs. Schoolbooks were strewn on the table. The table, sink and drain boards were piled high with dishes. I could see where Evelyn got her habits. It was just as well Gene didn't say anything about Ola's housekeeping during his argument with Evelyn.

I turned away from Gene's door and went to my own room. I didn't want to hear any more. I had the feeling Evelyn wouldn't be happy until she talked Gene into moving out.

Chapter 50

I read about the war in every day's paper and listened to it on the radio news every night. I never missed one of President Roosevelt's "Fireside Chats." I found it comforting that the President of the United States came into my living room from time to time. It was almost as if he were talking right to me and my family.

I kept on praying for the troops, asking God to put a guardian angel in charge of each and every one of them.

I encouraged every member of my house to do what they could for the war effort. George hadn't bought another car but was still bumming rides from John to get to and from work. I gave some of my food rationing stamps to Bessie to help with the expenses. I stretched my groceries to the limit, skimping on butter and flour and other things to make them last as long as possible. I planned to plant another small victory garden in the summer, even though our patch of backyard was so small it wouldn't yield much of a crop. I kept a can in the icebox for extra grease, and when it was full, I had George take it to the collection center and turn it in. Our tin cans were flattened and set out by the curb for pick-up. I can honestly say we did our best.

Chapter 51

Paul was crazy about Evelyn and hung around her every minute he could. He joked and clowned, trying to make her laugh. He would stuff a raw egg all the way into his mouth, sing silly songs, make faces, anything to get her attention. One morning, Evelyn was in the kitchen and got up to take the milk out of the icebox. When she went back to the table, Paul bowed and made a big show of being a gentleman. He pulled out her chair for her, grinned real big, and held it. When she went to sit down, he jerked it out from under her. Evelyn fell to the floor with a plop and sat there with her feet sticking straight out in front of her and her mouth open.

I could see Paul was waiting for her laugh, and when it didn't come, realized that he'd made a huge mistake. "I'm sorry, I'm sorry," he sobbed. I hurried over and helped Evelyn to her feet.

"Paul didn't mean anything by it, Evelyn. He would never try to hurt you. He was just clowning."

Evelyn didn't answer, just turned, glared at me, and went upstairs. Paul went into the living room and sat on the chair by the window, staring out at the traffic. When Gene came in from work a few minutes later he could sense something was wrong. He picked Donna up out of her high chair, nuzzled her, then looked at me. "Where's Evelyn?" he asked.

I sighed but didn't turn around. "She's upstairs."

Gene hurried upstairs and didn't come back down until I called to them that I had dinner on the table. While they were eating, he put his hand over Evelyn's and made his announcement.

"Evelyn and I have decided to get our own place. It's just too hard to have two families under one roof."

I looked down at my plate, expecting George to make some sort of protest. He didn't. He just kept on eating. "If that's what you think best," he said nonchalantly. "John will help. We can use his truck."

I fought the urge to pick up the bowl of mashed potatoes and dump it on George's head. How would we get by without the money Gene gave us each week? Knowing that nothing I had to say would make a difference, I remained silent while we ate.

Washing up later in the kitchen, I hoped that having Evelyn out of the house would remove some of the un-Christian feelings I had toward the girl. Maybe it would all work out for the best.

Gene found a little apartment for them a few

363

miles farther out Jefferson Avenue. It was closer to his work, but farther from his family. They moved in with the furniture from Gene's bedroom and some things that Ola and Smith Mayse gave them. Evelyn was all excited about having her own home. She looked so happy that I felt a little better about losing my boy, who was now 23 years old. Maybe if she were satisfied he would be satisfied, and that's all any mother really wants.

Gene brought the baby over for several hours every weekend, giving Evelyn some time to herself. He caught the bus a block from his apartment, and it was only a fifteen minute ride to our place. Evelyn never came with him, and that was fine with me. We would take turns playing with Donna, and I would fix a special meal. It was my one perfect day. I had Gene, Donna, and Betty Sue all with me at one time.

When Gene left he would slip me some folded bills. At first I didn't want to take them, but he insisted. He knew I was having a hard time making ends meet since he moved out. George was not one to volunteer for overtime. I wondered if Evelyn knew he was still giving me money. I figured not. If Evelyn had known, she would have put a stop to it, one way or another.

On April 12th, 1945, President Roosevelt, passed away, and Harry Truman was sworn in as President. I prayed for him. I didn't know a lot about him but had read that his language was sometimes salty. I didn't like that, but decided I would wait and see how he did before I made any judgment about him.

On May 9th, the Germans officially surrendered

and the war in Europe was over.

On August 6th, the atomic bomb was dropped on Hiroshima. It was horrible, and to me it was what I envisioned as the wrath of God.

Still, the Japanese would not surrender, and on August 9th, another bomb was dropped, this time on Nagasaki.

On September 2nd, the Japanese gave up the struggle, and the world was finally at peace. The men would be coming home soon.

On September 20^{th,} little Donna turned three.

Chapter 52

Gene showed up at my house one Friday evening right before dinner. I'd always been proud of how he took care of himself, but he was a different person that night. His hair wasn't combed, he had stubble, and his clothes looked like he'd been sleeping in them. When he walked in the kitchen, I nearly fainted at the sight of him.

"What's happened? Is Donna all right?"

"I don't know. Evelyn had Smith come get her. They took her and her clothes and the baby. She's left me, Mom."

"When?"

"Tuesday night. I kept thinking she would change her mind and come home. Tonight, I went over to the Mayse house and tried to talk to her, but she sent one of her sisters out to the porch to tell me it was too late.

She wouldn't even come out and talk to me."

"What did you fight over, Gene?"

"That's just it. We didn't have any big fight, or anything like that. We were all right one day, and the next she wouldn't have anything to do with me." His face twisted, and I thought he was going to start crying. "I thought if I gave her what she wanted she would come to love me like I love her, but it never happened. Now, I guess she's just glad to be rid of me."

He slumped down in a chair at the kitchen table and sobbed. A rush of anger ran all over me. If Evelyn had been in the room, I would have choked the life out of her. This was exactly what I'd feared the first time Evelyn came to my house, and Gene had that love-struck look on his face.

I patted Gene's shoulder, but I couldn't speak until I made an effort to control my rage. How dare anyone hurt a man as good as Gene! How could she be so ungrateful? Gene rescued Evelyn when she was desperate, pregnant, and alone. He had been a good husband to her. He had loved her, had adored her, in fact. To see him hurting so, I wished for a minute that I *had* pushed her down the stairs that day.

"You didn't fight at all before she left?"

"We argued about the money I gave you. She had my pay stub and she knew that I didn't spend it all on rent and the things she wanted. She's been after me about it all along."

My heart was breaking at the sight of my boy's pain and the thought that I may have been part of it. "I'll go talk to her tomorrow. Maybe I can get her to change her mind."

He shook his head. "It's no use. She's not coming back."

The next morning I walked the few blocks to the Mayse house on St. Paul Street. Ola answered the door. When she saw me, she looked sympathetic.

I tried to smile but wasn't very successful. "Ola, I'd like to talk to Evelyn, please."

"Come on in. I tried to talk to her last night but it didn't do any good. She's got her mind made up."

She held open the door and waved toward the sofa. "Sit down. I'll get her." I moved a pile of clothes over enough to sit.

Ola called upstairs, "Evelyn, Mrs. Foley is here. She wants to talk to you."

"I don't want to talk to her."

Ola's big bosom heaved in a long sigh. "Get on down here and listen to what she has to say! That's the least you can do."

I heard Evelyn stomping her feet as she came down the stairs. She came in and stood across the room from me, her arms crossed and her head tilted to one side. She gave me a stubborn look and jutted out her bottom lip in a pout as she did so often.

I didn't know where to begin but plunged in. "Evelyn, please come back to Gene. He loves you so much. He's miserable with you and the baby gone."

"I'm not coming home. I'm getting a divorce."

A divorce? *She was already thinking about a divorce?* "Isn't there anything we can do to change your mind? Gene said you were upset that he gave me money. I promise, I'll never let him give me another penny."

"I don't care, it's too late now."

"But how will you make a living?"

"Daddy already got me a job working with him at the Rubber Company. I'll start Monday."

Working full time? "But what about Donna?"

"You don't have to worry about her. Mama will take care of her for me."

I realized it was hopeless. Evelyn must have been planning this all along. Jobs at the Rubber Company weren't that easy to come by, especially now with the men coming home from the war. I thought again about the time I'd fought the impulse to shove Evelyn down the stairs. For the second time in one day, I regretted doing it.

I asked, "You'll still let us see the baby, won't you?"

Evelyn tilted her head as she thought it over. "Sure, anytime you want."

I rose to leave. "I hope you'll change your mind someday, Evelyn. There won't ever be a man who loves you more than Gene."

Evelyn didn't say anything, only smirked, so I said goodbye to Ola and left.

When I got home, Gene waited at the front door. He must have been watching for me out the window.

"What did she say? Will she come back?"

I shook my head. "She's determined, Gene. I don't think she'll be back."

"What about the baby? Can I still see her?"

"I already asked that. She said you could see her anytime you wanted. At least we have that. I hope she doesn't change her mind about it."

"I'll see her every minute I can."

The next day, Gene gave up his apartment and moved back into his room at our place. He said the landlord wasn't sorry to see him go since the men were coming home, and since the demand for housing was at an all-time high, he could raise the rent considerably.

Gene was back in the family as if Evelyn had never come into his life. The only difference was he could still see his little girl. He was ordered to pay child support, and I never once heard him complain about it. In fact, he went way above that. He bought all Donna's clothes and shoes as well.

He stopped by the Mayse's every Friday afternoon on his way back from work and brought Donna home with him. He returned her on Monday mornings on his way to the factory.

Even after the divorce was final, he never lost hope that Evelyn would agree to come back to him. From time to time, she would let him take her to the movies and out to dinner.

He pinned his hopes for the future on the day she would come back.

Chapter 53

About a year after the divorce, I was sweeping the walk out in front of the house one day when I looked up and saw Gene walking home from the bus stop. He stopped a few doors down to chat with a neighbor, Henry Wills. Henry knew both the Mayse and our families.

Gene talked to him and smiled until Henry said something that caused Gene to step back so fast he almost tripped. His whole appearance changed. He said a hurried goodbye and ran the rest of the way home.

He grabbed my arm. There were tears in his eyes. "Mom, Evelyn's gotten married again. Now I'll never get her back."

My heart broke for him all over again. I wondered if he would get over loving Evelyn. I hugged him. "I'm sorry, Gene. Maybe it's all for the best."

He pressed his lips together and nodded. "I guess." Then he had a horrified look. "Oh, God! What if they take Donna to live with them? They may not let us see her anymore."

I almost started crying myself. I couldn't think of any words to comfort him. The thought of not being able to spend time with the little girl we loved so much was terrible. If that was what Evelyn wanted, I knew there might be nothing we could do about it. The courts always gave children to the mother.

We needn't have worried. Evelyn didn't take Donna with her when she moved out of her mother's house into a flat with her new husband. It seemed to me Donna was the last thing on her mind.

Chapter 54

With Evelyn mostly out of our lives, my house was considerably more peaceful for the last years of the 1940s. Bessie and John bought a house near Jefferson Avenue and St. Jean. We all missed them, so we rented a house nearby.

Gene and George worked full time, and Gene took what overtime came his way. We had enough money to pay the bills without scrimping.

On weekends, Donna was with us on a regular basis. She kept clothes at both grandmothers' homes and went back and forth between the two houses. Everyone in my house adored her. I wondered how much attention she got at Ola's, what with one boy only three years older than Donna and the next one five years older. From what I'd seen of them, Ola had her hands full.

When she was with us, she climbed in her daddy's bed and the two of them would read, propped up on pillows, until Donna fell asleep. I would often find them in the morning, sometimes with the light still on, their books and magazines piled up between them.

Almost every weekend, they were off on some sort of adventure. Gene took Donna to the Michigan State Fair every September, and she came home with stories about a cow made of butter, chickens that looked like they were wearing feather pants and French fries that were as long as a ruler. They went to the movies almost every week, usually at the neighborhood Cinderella Theatre, but at times they rode the bus all the way downtown to see something special. After the movie they would eat at the Kresge lunch counter in the store's basement.

It was at the United Artists Theatre on Cadillac Square where Donna first saw *Gone With The Wind* when she was eight or nine. She was so excited about it, Gene had to take her back the next weekend to see it again. She talked about it for weeks.

Sometimes Gene took her to a live stage show. They went to see Betty Grable and Harry James and later, Dean Martin and Jerry Lewis at the Fox Theatre on Woodward Avenue. When they went to see Duke Ellington and Ella Fitzgerald, Gene told me he was sure she was the youngest person in the audience.

Chapter 55

Betty Sue still dated Ellis Marshall, the young man she'd met at the factory. She'd been seeing him off and on since the war began. One evening, she came home all excited. He'd finally asked her to marry him.

I wasn't happy about it. "Are you sure he's the right one for you? You shouldn't rush into this."

"Rush into it?" Betty Sue said. "We've been seeing each other for seven years."

"He smells of beer sometimes when he comes over here. Is that what you want for a husband?"

She stuck out her chin. "Daddy smells of beer, too."

"That's what I mean."

"I'm doing it, Mom. I'm going to marry him. I'm twenty-eight years old, and no other man has even shown an interest in me. I don't want to be an old maid."

"Maybe no one else has had a chance. You're always with him."

Betty Sue set her jaw, and a flash of Bessie's expression came on her face. "I'm going to do it, Mom."

I surrendered. "All right, I guess I can't stop you. You know you can't be married at the church.. Brother Graham won't marry a saved member to a lost person."

"I don't care. We'll get married at City Hall. Ellis doesn't want a big wedding anyway."

Betty Sue ran off next door to tell Bessie and Maxine. I sat at the kitchen table when George came in. I nodded my head toward the chair at the other end of the table. "Sit down, George. Betty Sue was just here. She and Ellis are getting married."

He picked up an apple from the fruit bowl on the table and took a bite of it. "About time. He's been seeing her for years now."

"Don't you think you ought to have a talk with him before they do it?"

"Talk about what?"

"You know very well *what*. He's got a right to know about her temper."

George laughed. "He's six inches taller than her. I think he can handle himself. Besides, I haven't seen her get really mad for a long time."

"Things have been going her way for a long time."

George stood and patted me on the head as if I

were a child. "You worry too much. Maybe she's not as much like Mom as you think." He laughed and left the room. I didn't care about Ellis one little bit, but I didn't want to see my girl get in trouble if she hurt him.

George, Gene, and I went down to City Hall with Betty Sue and Ellis and I watched while my little girl became someone's wife. I was sure he'd make her miserable.

They moved Betty Sue's things out of the house and to a little basement apartment only a few houses down from us. The fact that my girl lived one minute's walk from me didn't do much to fill the empty spot in my house. I knew it was unreasonable, but I wished I could have kept Betty Sue home a few more years.

Chapter 56

Donna helped me stop worrying about Betty Sue, at least on the weekends. From the time she was three, she stood on a chair and helped me cook just the way I'd done with my mother and Betty Sue did with me. Now, she didn't need a chair, she was tall enough to cook standing next to me.

I let the girl experiment, baking cakes and rolling out piecrust with no advice from me unless she asked.

Donna wasn't allowed to cook at Ola's house, but she was given free rein at mine. Not that there was any mention of a competition between the two grandmothers. At our house, she went to bed when she wanted, got up when she liked, and wore whatever clothes she picked out. In the summers, when she was with us for weeks on end, she could take a bath right in the middle of the week and play in the tub as long as she wanted. In my house Donna wasn't a child to be seen and not heard. We showed her the same respect as an adult.

The older Donna got, the more she resembled my Lulu…her blonde hair and blue eyes, the way she would watch the adults' behavior. I felt almost as if I had regained my lost treasure.

Chapter 57

I was hanging up clothes in the back yard one afternoon when Betty Sue came up behind me and grabbed me in a hug. "Guess what? You're going to be a grandmother again."

I dropped the shirt I held back in the basket and hugged her back. Betty Sue looked so happy that I was happy too. It would be nice to have a baby in the house again.

"When are you due?"

"In November, I think. I had my last period in March. I haven't been to the doctor yet, but I know I'm having a baby. Won't it be wonderful? I was starting to worry that maybe something was wrong with me." Betty Sue picked up the shirt and some pins and fastened it to the line.

"I'm sure you're just fine. Sometimes it takes a

while to get things started. Are you going to get a bigger place?" I hoped they wouldn't move too far away. I liked being within walking distance.

"The second-floor apartment is going to be empty next month. It's only ten dollars more a week, and it has two bedrooms. I told the landlord we would take it."

Relieved, I hugged her again. "We'll start shopping now. If we get something for the baby every week, it won't be a big outlay all at one time. How long will Willys let you work?"

"I'm not going to tell them until I have to. They make you leave at the sixth month."

"Are you sure that's all right? The work isn't too heavy, is it?"

"I'm strong. I don't think it will be any problem. Plenty of girls work while they're carrying a baby."

I was already making plans. "We should buy the layette in yellow, green, and white, so it won't matter if it's a girl or a boy. Then, after it comes, you can fill it in with pink or blue. I wish I could still knit and sew like I used to. I made you such pretty little dresses. If I'd thought of it, I would have saved some of them." I thought about Lulu but didn't mention her. "What do you want, a girl or a boy?"

"I want a girl, but Ellis is sure it's going to be a boy."

I laughed. "All men are like that. If they had their way, there wouldn't be any little girls born at all. They never think about what that would mean down the road. They all want some other man to have the daughters for their sons to marry."

Betty Sue smiled and got all dreamy-eyed. "Well, I don't really care that much. A little boy would be fine with me. We can have a girl the next time."

The two of us kept on hanging clothes until the basket was empty, then went in the house and sat at the kitchen table with pencil and paper, writing a list of things the baby would need. Before we went to the grocery store that week, we stopped at Sears and Betty Sue bought a little white nightgown. I bought her a dozen Birdseye diapers. Each week when we shopped, we bought more. Betty Sue would buy something pretty, and I would buy something useful and let her have the pleasure of picking out the fancier items.

As we bought things, we crossed them off the list. When it was almost time for her to stop working, near the end of August, we were halfway through, leaving only the more expensive things, like a crib and high chair.

I regretted now that I hadn't taught Betty Sue how to sew when she was a girl, but she'd never had any interest. I thought I'd have plenty of time to show her. By the time Betty Sue got pregnant, my eyes were too weak.

She gained quite a bit of weight, but not nearly as much as Evelyn had. She felt fine and planned to keep working until her seventh month, which was the end of September.

It was still August when a loud pounding on the door woke the whole family. Gene jumped out of bed, pulled on his pants, and went downstairs. I stood waiting at the top of the stairs, my robe clutched around me. Paul came running out of his room and stood next to me. George came up from the basement, wearing his long underwear. Gene opened the door.

It was Ellis. He looked up the stairs at me. "Mom, Betty Sue's bleeding and she's having terrible pain. I think the baby's coming."

I gripped the banister. It was much too early.

"Tell her we'll be right there. Gene, go wake Bessie and tell John to get the truck so he can take Betty Sue to the hospital."

Ellis ran back to his apartment. Gene went to get Bessie and John, and George and I dressed. I went to Gene's room and grabbed him a shirt and his shoes and socks. In only a few minutes we were all at Betty Sue's place. She lay on the bed rolled up in a ball and holding her knees. My heart almost stopped beating. I was scared by the amount of blood on the bed.

"John, you men get her into the truck and take her to Receiving Hospital. Gene, you and Ellis, go with them. The rest of us will walk up to Jefferson and catch a cab. It will be faster than calling for one."

Ellis and Gene joined hands in a chair-lift under Betty Sue and carried her out to the truck. They got her in the seat and then Ellis and Gene ran around to the back and jumped in. I handed Gene his things so he could finish dressing on the way, and John started the truck and headed for Jefferson Avenue.

The rest of us, including Bessie and Maxine, were left standing on the sidewalk. I was almost in shock. I didn't think I could live if I lost my girl.

Bessie took charge. "Maude, you and George go ahead to the hospital. Paul, you come stay the rest of the night at my house."

I nodded. I went back to the house and got my purse. George and I walked the one city block to Jefferson. It was only a minute or two before a cab came along. There was very little traffic, and we were at the hospital on Saint Antoine Street in ten minutes. It was the first time in my life I rode in a taxi.

Ellis sat in the waiting room looking like a scared little boy. I hadn't realized it before, but he really did love Betty Sue. I sat next to him and patted him on the shoulder. He fell against me, sobbing. "I can't lose her, Mom. She's all I have in the world."

My dislike for him evaporated. I hadn't even seen how much he cared for Betty Sue.

The hours passed, and we sat and waited. From time to time, Gene would get up and question the nurse at the desk, but she never had news for us. The sun was beginning to show through the glass in the doors when a doctor finally came out and asked for Mr. Marshall.

Ellis jumped up and introduced everyone. Gene and George also stood but I had no strength in my legs. I sat and looked up at the doctor, my fears probably written on my face.

The doctor patted Ellis on the shoulder, but looked directly in my eyes. "She's going to be just fine. She lost a lot of blood, and we had to give her some transfusions, but in a few days she'll be good as new."

I closed my eyes and gave silent thanks to God. Ellis gripped the doctor's hand. "What about the baby?"

The doctor shook his head. "I'm sorry, Mr. Marshall, but we couldn't save the baby. The placenta was delivered first, and by the time your wife got here, there was nothing we could do."

Ellis groaned, "It's my fault. We should have called the ambulance."

The doctor took hold of both of Ellis's shoulders. "It's not your fault. Who knows how long it would have taken for the ambulance to get there, and who knows what they could have done for her? Things like this happen sometimes, but she's fine, and she can have more babies."

Ellis looked up at the doctor. "Was it a boy or a girl?"

"It was a boy."

Ellis groaned and fell into the chair, his head in his hands.

"Can we see her now?" I asked.

"She's sleeping, and she really needs her rest. Why don't you all go on home, and I'll have the nurse call you when she's up to having visitors."

I gave him Bessie's telephone number, and we all left.

On the trip home, Gene and Ellis rode in the truck with John, while George and I waited for a bus.

It was after noon before Bessie came to tell me that the hospital called and said Betty Sue could have visitors. The men had gone to work, so I went to tell Ellis, and we walked to Jefferson and caught a bus downtown.

Ellis went in the room first and after a half hour of waiting in the hallway, I went in. Betty Sue sat in bed but looked pale and weak. I wanted to cry, but held back my tears.

When Betty Sue saw me, her face twisted up, and she reached out both her arms for me the way she used to when she was a little girl and had hurt herself. I sat on the edge of the bed and held and rocked my daughter as we both grieved for that lost baby.

Chapter 58

Two years after Evelyn married Herschell, she was divorced again. Gene heard the news from a co-worker and came rushing home to tell me. He was all excited. "Mom, Buddy down at work told me that Evelyn got a divorce."

He sounded so hopeful. "Did Buddy say why?"

"No, he didn't know. The men were kind of joking about them only being married such a short time. All I care about is that now I have a chance. She works an early shift at the Rubber Company. She ought to be getting home soon. I'm going to go over to her place and ask if she'll see me."

"How do you know where she lives?"

Gene's face turned red. "I asked one of her little brothers a while back. I walked by the Mayse house, and he was in the yard. Evelyn's place is right down the street from them."

I gave him a quick hug and brushed back a lock of hair from his face, "I guess you have to do whatever makes you happy."

He hugged me back and left. The whole time he was gone I was torn up with mixed emotions. If Evelyn could bring him happiness, I would do everything I could to stay out of their lives. But deep inside, I knew he would only wind up being hurt again.

When he came home a few hours later, he was grinning from ear to ear. "She's going to the movies with me Saturday, Mom."

Though he looked so happy, I was afraid for him. I didn't know what would be worse for him, getting Evelyn back, or losing her again.

As time passed, I could tell by the expression on Gene's face how the renewed courtship was going. If he had a date with Evelyn on the weekend, he smiled all week, looking forward to it. She was dating other men besides Gene, and when she was out with one of them, he was miserable.

A few months later, she stopped seeing Gene altogether and she married a man named Delmous Newland, Junior from Tennessee.

I saw Mrs. Mayse on the street one day, and she told me about them and showed me a picture. I had to admit, he and Evelyn made a good-looking couple. He was as handsome as she was beautiful. They had a flat a few blocks from her mother's, and she told me they even had Donna over once in a while for a visit. As far as I knew, she didn't do that a single time when she was married to Herschell.

Delmous drove a truck and delivered lumber for the Sibley Lumber Company. His friends called him Junior. Unlike Herschell, who couldn't abide being in the same room with the child, Mrs. Mayse said that Junior was always friendly to Donna, and she got along with him on the few occasions they were together, but Evelyn never mentioned Donna coming to live with them, and that was a relief to Gene.

The only time he cheered up was when he was with Donna. They went to movies or shopping for clothes. The time he had with her almost kept his mind off Evelyn. He hoped she wouldn't be any happier with Junior than she had been with Herschell, and that when the marriage was over he would again have another chance to win her back.

A few years later, Evelyn became pregnant, but she miscarried in her fourth month. Donna was looking forward to having a baby sister and was so disappointed she cried. They didn't explain what a miscarriage was to her.

I learned about it when she was at our house that weekend. Donna wasn't her usual bubbly self. I sat on the sofa next to her and wrapped my arm around my granddaughter. "Are you all right, baby?"

Donna stuck out her lip in a pout that was like her mother's. "My mother was going to get me a baby sister, and now she changed her mind."

I knew Evelyn was expecting and guessed that she'd had a miscarriage. People who knew both families were only too happy to pass along any gossip.

"When did she tell you that?"

"Mama Mayse told me."

"Honey, Evelyn didn't change her mind. The baby she had inside her got sick and died. She'll have one for you someday."

"Why didn't she just tell me that?"

"Sometimes people don't think children are old enough to understand. She was just trying to make it easy for you."

"I understand a lot more than they think I do."

I was shocked by the girl's remark, but realized the truth of it. I'd never seen a child who studied adults the way this one did.

A few months later Donna was at the house when Betty Sue suffered her second miscarriage. She watched as they carried her aunt out on a stretcher to a waiting ambulance. Betty Sue was only four months along this time, so it wasn't as hard on her as the first time had been. Scared by the blood and the upset of the adults, Donna put her arms around me and leaned her head against my side. "Is she going to be all right?"

I patted her on the back, reassuring the girl as much as I was myself, "She'll be fine. The doctors will fix her up, and she'll be good as new."

Chapter 59

The next few years seemed to go by in a blur. Betty Sue had a miscarriage about every six months, but the doctors kept insisting there was nothing wrong with her.

Donna did well in school and we saw her regularly. At our house, she spent a good part of her time with George. They played checkers or poker with matchsticks as money. He taught her how to roll a cigarette, but I'm sure he never let her try one. Even George wasn't that crazy. When he came upstairs to listen to the radio at night, she would sit between George and Gene, holding on to one and then the other. She never called me Grandma, the way you would have thought, but, since everyone else except George called me "Mom," she did too. It was all right with me. It must have been the same at her other grandmother's, because she called her Mama."

When Donna was around eleven, Evelyn and Junior moved to a flat on Fairview, only a few blocks from our home. Donna was still splitting her time between her two grandmothers.

The Mayses sold their house on St. Paul and bought a wonderful, big house on Van Dyke. Donna lived with the Mayse family during school, and mostly at our flat on St. Jean on weekends and during school vacations.

She didn't sleep with her daddy any more, but since she was six or so, shared my room. As she climbed in the first time, she told me she liked my bed. It was soft, warm and comfortable, with a feather ticking on top of the mattress. I got in bed next to her and started to turn out the light. Donna was wide awake. She lay there for a few minutes, then sighed. "I'm not sleepy. I'm used to reading. Can you tell me something about how things were when you were my age?"

I thought about it for a minute. "All right, I'll tell you about when I was a little girl."

I talked for a long time. At one point I turned on the light and showed Donna the keepsakes in the bottom drawer of my dresser. I picked up the nightgown I'd made for my wedding night to James. I hadn't held it in my hands for a long time and the sweet memories that came rushing back brought tears to my eyes. It was wrapped in yellowed tissue paper and tied with a ribbon. I untied the bow and unwrapped the papers so Donna could see it.

She ran her fingertips over the soft fabric. "It's so pretty. Aunt Dorothy helps me with my sewing. I hope I can make something like this someday."

Gene had bought Donna a little red and white Singer sewing machine that was powered by turning a wheel. The only interest she had in dolls from that time on was in making them little dresses. I liked to think that she got that from me, because her grandmother Ola didn't sew at all. Dorothy, Evelyn's youngest sister, sewed very well. I had seen some of her work, and it was lovely. I was glad that Donna had someone to teach her, now that my eyes were too weak.

Another night, I told her about Lulu. I wasn't going to tell her how awful it had been the way she died, but her curiosity wouldn't let up and I finally had to tell her everything. I showed her the picture of my first little girl. Donna gasped, "Mom, she looks just like me!"

It was true. Donna bore a great resemblance to Lulu. She cried along with me when I told her about burying Lulu.

Most of the stories took a long time to tell. I think sometimes I kept talking for a long time after she fell asleep. It felt good, to tell someone about my life.

Chapter 60

Inflation made it harder and harder for me to keep the bills paid. Even though it was less than half of his forty-hour pay at the plant, George took his Social Security pension and quit his job as soon as he was sixty-five. One of my friends from church told me that she took in boarders to help her get by. That seemed like a good idea. I was already cooking and cleaning for four or five. What difference would two more make?

We rented a larger house and moved a few blocks away. The two extra bedrooms were rented out to young men who had come north to work in the factories. I made their breakfast, a sack lunch to carry to work, and dinner on weekdays. On Saturday and Sunday, they were on their own. I laundered their sheets once a week.

Although he was a grown man by then, there was no help coming from Paul. He found and rapidly lost a number of jobs. Employment was easy to find, but a boss expected some sort of work to be done. Paul would go in to work for two or three days and then come home saying the boss didn't like him, or the work was too hard, or he couldn't read and write well enough to do what was expected of him.

George told him that if he didn't want to work, he didn't have to work. We argued over it time and again. I wondered what would happen to him when George and I were gone.

Chapter 61

In 1954, when Donna was twelve, I heard Evelyn was carrying another baby. This time, she passed the sixth month with no problems.

One day, Donna surprised us with a weekday visit. The front door of our home was never locked during the daytime. She came directly there after school and came in the kitchen. She knew I would have a snack ready at that time of day. Gene, Paul, and I were at the table when she walked in. She kissed her daddy and me.

Gene hugged her. "How did you get here? Did someone drive you?'

"I walked. I'm going to be living with my mother on Fairview. I can walk here any time I want. Isn't that great?"

Gene's forehead creased, "Living with your

mother? Who decided that?"

"I guess she did. She's going to have the baby in February, and she needs me to help her. I hope it's a girl."

"Are you happy about living with her, Donna?" he asked.

"I guess, as long as I get to be with the baby."

Gene opened his mouth to say something else but then thought better of it.

Later that day, when Donna was down in the basement playing checkers with George, Gene talked to me about it. "Mom, what do you think about this, Donna living with Evelyn? She hardly knows her."

I shook my head, "If that's what Evelyn wants, there's not much we can say about it, unless she tries to keep her away from us. Then we could go to court or something. Donna seems to be happy about it. Most little girls love to have a baby to play with."

"What about him? How do I know he's going to act right?"

"She's old enough to tell us if he doesn't."

As it turned out, Donna was at our house after school almost every day until the baby came.

Donna came over all excited to tell us that, just as she wanted, Evelyn had a beautiful, healthy little girl. She named her Nancy. She was the image of her father, thick black hair, a round face, and deep pink complexion. Junior had his own Indian ancestors just like Gene did, and that showed up in the baby. Donna said Evelyn called Nancy her little Papoose. As soon as she was allowed, Evelyn went back to her job making tires on the production line at the Rubber Company.

Donna came home from Foch Junior High and let the daytime babysitter leave. She took care of the baby until her mother got in from work. Nancy was born in the middle of February, and the cold weather dragged on so long, we didn't get a look at the baby until she was around three months old. As soon as the weather was warm enough, Donna put her in her stroller and brought her over to the house. She was a beautiful baby, and all of us were taken with her right from the start, except for Gene. He held the baby in his arms for a moment and stared down at her. Then he handed her to me and left the room, wiping tears from his eyes.

Donna was crazy about that baby, and took her everywhere she went after school, to our place, to her girlfriends', to the corner sweetshop. She was the best behaved baby anyone had ever seen. Donna told me Nancy even sat quietly in her stroller in the school auditorium and watched Donna rehearse her school plays.

The money I made from my two boarders was a Godsend. I felt strong enough to do more, so I rented a large three-story house on the corner of Kercheval and Lycaste that had nine bedrooms on the upper floors and two on the bottom.

Now I was cooking and washing and cleaning for eleven people. For the first time since Betty Sue left home, I had enough money to pay all the family expenses and still put a little aside each month. I even bought a television for the living room and had a telephone installed. It was the first one we ever had, but the only people I called in Detroit were Bessie and Betty Sue. I even called my sister Helen and my friend from Missouri, Clara, but only once or twice a year. I didn't feel I could afford long distance. Besides, I wrote them both from time to time and would often read their letters several times. I liked having the letters. I kept them in bundles, tied with a ribbon in a bottom dresser drawer.

Betty Sue miscarried twice again in one year. She cried and cried and wailed, "I'll never have my baby. Pretty soon, I'll be too old."

Ellis made clumsy tries to console her, but it didn't help much. Her doctor told her the work she was doing at the factory was probably too much for her, so the next time she got pregnant, she took a leave of absence.

I began paying her to help with the lighter household chores and cooking. I was sixty-three years old and the burden was almost more than I could bear, but for the first time since we came to Detroit, I didn't have to worry about money. George made no effort to help with the work around the house. He called it woman's work. He either hung around with the neighbor's, joking and laughing the way he'd always done, watching the television in the living room while he sipped on a beer, or napping in the basement.

Evelyn's father died not long after Nancy was born. I know how she and Donna loved him, and I felt bad for their grief. Gene and I went to the funeral, but we sat in the back. We wanted to pay our respects but didn't want to stand out. Gene could hardly stand seeing Evelyn with Junior, so we left right after the service.

Chapter 62

When Donna was fifteen and going to Southeastern High in the tenth grade, she came to my house one afternoon carrying a bag of clothes and stayed. Nothing was said about her reason for leaving her mother's place.

I was curious, but she seemed unharmed, so I didn't press her about it. We were all happier when she was in the house. Donna spent her whole life going back and forth, so it didn't seem strange to any of us that a girl so young had always come and gone as she pleased and no one asked why, where she was going, or when she would be back.

Shortly after that, Evelyn left Junior, filed for divorce, and moved into an apartment a few blocks east of our home. I wondered if Donna leaving was connected to Evelyn's divorce. Donna didn't talk about it, and I didn't ask.

An old friend of the Mayse family took over babysitting Nancy. With Junior out of the picture, Donna went to see her little sister more often. She brought her to our house, and the Foley's were happy to have Nancy back to visit.

As they had before, Gene's hopes of winning Evelyn back returned, and he began seeing her again.

Chapter 63

In 1956 Betty Sue was pregnant again and safely into her sixth month, farther than she'd ever been able to carry her other babies. She and Ellis were at our house one Saturday for lunch. Donna and the men sat at the table in the kitchen, and Betty Sue and I were cooking dinner, a big pot of pork neck bones, white cornbread that we fried in a cast iron pan, Irish potatoes, and string beans. George took Betty Sue's hand. "How's my girl feeling today? Are you all right?"

Betty Sue put a plate in front of him, then kissed her father's forehead. "I'm fine, Dad. I feel really good."

Ellis picked up his fork and took a bite. "She's going to have to be more careful this time," he said, "or she'll mess it up again."

You could have heard a pin drop. Betty Sue got a

look on her face that reminded me of Grandma Foley and Bessie, and it made my stomach flop over. She whispered, "Ellis?"

He looked up at her. She doubled up her fist and hit him square between the eyes. His chair fell over backward. He lay there in a stupor, his body still sitting in the fallen chair.

Betty Sue landed a kick to his side. She had her leg back to give him another one when I ran over and pulled her away.

George shook his head. "Honeymoon's over."

Ellis staggered to his feet without help, picked up his chair, and sat back down at the table.

When George finished his sandwich, he stood to leave. "You all right, Ellis?"

"I guess so, but I think I'm going to have two black eyes."

"Looks like it. Come on out to the porch. I want to tell you something."

Ellis held onto the back of the chair to steady himself. He got his balance and followed George out the door. Betty Sue sat and ate as if nothing had happened.

When we went to bed that night, Donna asked me about what her grandpa wanted to tell Ellis. I told her about George's mother, Bessie's sometimes hot-tempered behavior, and how Betty Sue acted like them.

Chapter 64

Ellis was able to talk his boss into giving Paul a chance to work with him. Ellis said he could cover for Paul and keep his attention on the job.

He went to work with Ellis Monday morning. I made him a special lunch with his favorite food, a bologna sandwich and chocolate chip cookies. I said an extra prayer as he left that he would be able to stay with the job. When Paul came home that night, I could tell by the look on his face he wasn't happy. I patted him on the back. "How did it go, Paul? Can you do the work?"

He twisted up his face like he smelled a skunk. "I can do it, but it sure isn't easy. All I do, all day long is pick up a car bumper and hold it against a big brush that spins around and polishes it. It makes my arms hurt."

"It's because your muscles aren't used to it. Once you've been there a few weeks you won't even notice. Let me get some of that Absorbine, Jr. that Gene uses and rub it on your arms. It'll make the soreness go away."

He nodded. I got the bottle and rubbed the ointment up and down both his arms from the shoulder to the wrist. It was the most I had touched him since he was a child.

I woke him the next morning and made his lunch, holding my breath to see if he would go to work the second day. I breathed a sigh of relief when he came downstairs dressed, ate his breakfast, and ran to catch Ellis so they could walk together.

For the rest of the week, I rubbed the ointment on his arms every night. Every morning, I didn't relax until he went to work.

On Friday afternoon of the second week, he drew his first pay. He didn't come home at the regular time. At first, I didn't worry. I figured he stopped with Ellis at Betty Sue's house for a while and would be home for dinner.

Betty Sue was due in four more weeks and she'd put on a lot of weight and waddled more than walked. She still felt like working as much as she could, and she was with me, cooking the evening meal for the boarders. When they finished eating, she helped clean up and wash the dishes. By that time, it was almost seven o'clock. Every evening she worked with me, Betty Sue made up two dinner plates to carry home for her and her husband.

At nine o'clock, Betty Sue was back at my house, worried sick. "Did Paul come home yet?" she asked.

"No. I figured he was at your house."

"Neither one of them is there, Mom. Do you think something happened?"

George sat on the sofa, watching *Gunsmoke*. He didn't take his eyes off the screen and said, "They probably stopped for a beer. It's payday, the first one for Paul. They're just celebrating. They'll be home when they've had enough. Let them have a little fun."

My heart sank as I realized the truth of what he said. It might not be a big deal to George, but our daughter was almost ready to deliver and shouldn't be worried over anything. The last thing I wanted was for Paul to start acting like his older brother, Bud, who'd gotten drunk at every opportunity. Why couldn't my other boys be more like Gene?

When Paul went to work every day for two weeks in a row I thought maybe there was hope for him. Now, that hope was draining out of me.

I put my arm around Betty Sue's shoulder and walked her to the door. "You just go home and rest. Don't worry about them, they're grown men. They can take care of themselves." I walked with Betty Sue down the block to her house, and saw to it that she made it safely inside.

With so many boarders coming and going, my front door was left unlocked. It was shortly after midnight when there came a knock at my bedroom door. I kept it locked when I went to bed, so I got up and asked who was there.

"It's me, Mom," said Betty Sue. I could tell she was crying. I unlocked the door, and Betty Sue came in and sat on the edge of the bed, "He's still not home, Mom. I can't stand it. What if he's hurt somewhere?"

I sat next to her and put her head on my shoulder. "What will I do if he's dead? What will happen to me and the baby?"

"He's all right. I'll go get your father and make him go find Ellis and bring him home."

I went to the basement to George's corner. He had a little bedroom set up there, with a chest of drawers, a table with a checkerboard, and a bed. He was sound asleep, snoring. I shook his shoulder. "Wake up, George. I want you to go find Ellis for Betty Sue. She's all upset, and she shouldn't be worried. What if something happened to this baby? It would kill her."

"What's the matter with the two of you? He's fine. He'll be home when he's through drinking. Just leave him alone."

"I said, get up and go find him."

Awake now, George looked at me. "And I said no! Now, leave me alone!" He rolled over and put his back to me.

I wanted to smack him, but I knew it wouldn't do any good. I went back to my room, where Betty Sue sat on the edge of the bed.

"He won't get up. Why don't you sleep here with me? Ellis will be home in the morning."

Betty Sue set her jaw in a way I knew to mean she was determined. "If Dad won't go look for him, I'll go myself. There's only two or three bars between here and the plant. He's probably in one of them." She turned to leave.

"Wait," I said, "I'll go with you. I won't have you out by yourself at this time of night." I put on a housedress and a sweater and slipped on my shoes. As the two of us left, I put my arm on Betty Sue's, not just to keep her close, but to slow her down. I didn't want her to tire herself any more than I could help.

We walked the long city block to Jefferson Avenue and stopped in the first bar we came to. It was the first time in my life I'd been inside a bar, and as far as I knew, the first time for my daughter. The light was dim. Most of the men sitting at the bar looked like they'd come from work and wore jeans. There were only a few women, and each sat with a man in the booths that lined the wall. I hated the smell of beer and it was almost overpowering. I felt uneasy, knowing I was in a place where I didn't belong. I said a silent prayer asking God to get us out of there.

Betty Sue took her wallet out of her purse and held up a picture of Ellis. "Has he been in here tonight? He might be with a tall, dark-haired man."

The bartender looked quickly at the picture and nodded. "Sure, they were here. They got loud, so I threw them out about two hours ago."

"Did you notice which way they went?"

He shrugged. "Try down the street at Smitty's place. Maybe they're in there."

Betty Sue and I went down the street to Smitty's. The bartender told her Paul and Ellis had been there and gone.

We crossed Jefferson and went up St. Jean, to the last bar in the neighborhood. Looking in through the window, we could see Ellis and Paul sitting on the end of the bar next to the front door, laughing and drinking big mugs of beer.

We opened the door and went inside. Paul caught sight of me and was so surprised, he had to grab the bar to keep from falling off his chair. Betty Sue walked up to Ellis and punched him right on the nose. There was a loud cracking noise, his head jerked back, and blood spurted out. He grabbed his nose with both hands and shouted, "Lord Almighty, woman! What's wrong with you? You broke my nose!"

"I've been worried sick that you were hurt or something, and the whole time you've been drinking."

She pulled back her arm and landed another punch on the same spot. This time, Ellis fell off the barstool and rolled around on the floor. Blood ran between his fingers.

"Stop it!" Paul hollered. As far as I knew, he'd never had a single bottle of beer in his life. When he jumped up, everything he drank that day must have gone right to his head. He passed out in a heap on the floor.

I looked down at the two of them, Paul out like a stone, Ellis howling, holding his nose, and bleeding while he rocked back and forth. "Lord, help," I said aloud.

Betty Sue wasn't finished. She kicked Ellis hard in the stomach. He rolled up in a tight ball.

"Get home, right now," Betty Sue growled at

him. Then she looked at the bartender and shook her finger at him. "You give him one more drink tonight, and you'll have to answer to me."

He held his hands up in front of him. "Lady, he won't get anything else here," he said.

Betty Sue wheeled around, kicked Ellis again, grabbed me by the arm, and barged out of the bar, almost dragging me behind her.

Betty Sue sobbed all the way home. I could feel her tremble and knew it wasn't from sorrow, but from her being so mad and relieved that Ellis was all right.

I held my tongue, knowing that anything I had to say would only make the situation worse. I sat with Betty Sue at her place until Ellis and Paul staggered in. Ellis stood there, blood all over his shirt and pants, weaving back and forth, hanging his head.

"Go on to bed," Betty Sue ordered. The fire in her eyes sparked. Obediently, Ellis made his way down the hall, reeling from one wall to the other, and into the bedroom. I heard a loud creak as he plopped on the bed. Paul leaned against the door frame.

I looked at him in disgust. "You aren't coming in my house drunk. Find yourself somewhere else to sleep."

"Paul can sleep here, on the sofa," Betty Sue said.

She started toward the bedroom, but I was afraid of what she might do to Ellis if I let her go in there. I took hold of her arm. She still shook with anger.

I tugged at her. "Come with me and sleep at home." Betty Sue had told me that sometimes, Ellis had terrible nightmares. "You don't need a drunk rolling around on you with that baby almost ready to be born. I was thinking about the Foley women and was afraid Betty Sue might kill Ellis in his sleep.

Betty Sue took a deep breath and nodded. I could see her make an effort to pull herself together. She went to her room and returned a minute later with her things in a paper bag. Paul was already snoring on the sofa.

By the time we got to bed, it was two o'clock in the morning. I lay there next to her, wide awake. I hadn't been worrying about the baby when I asked Betty Sue to come home with me for the night. In all the years we'd been married, George had never laid a hand on me in anger, had never even spanked one of his children. He'd seldom even raised his voice. It was a curious thing, the streak of violence that ran through the women in this family. I wondered about George's father and his disappearing like he did. Had he come home drunk one too many times?

Paul didn't come back from Betty Sue's until after noon the next day. His eyes were red and swollen, and I could tell he was hung over. We were eating when he came in, and Gene just looked at him and shook his head.

I asked, "Did you get your paycheck cashed?"

He mumbled something and looked at the floor.

"Well?" I asked.

"I got it cashed at the bar."

"How much did you make?"

"I made fifty-five dollars, take-home."

Gene piped up. "You ought to give Mom twenty

dollars to pay your room and board. That's fair."

Paul looked at him like that made him mad. "I don't have it."

"What do you mean, you don't have it?"

"I spent it last night."

Gene stood. "You mean you spent your whole paycheck? You worked a five days in a row for the first time in your life, and you spent it all in a bar?"

Paul stuck out his chin. "It was my money. I can spend it on anything I want."

Gene's face turned red, and I saw him doubling up his fist. I stepped between them, "Paul will have another check coming. Now that he's got a regular job he can pay his way. He won't go drinking every week. Will you, Paul?"

Paul gave Gene an ugly look. "No."

The next week he came home with his check. I walked down to the grocery store with him where he cashed it and handed me twenty dollars. Monday, he quit his job.

Chapter 65

Betty Sue had a healthy little boy, pretty and blond like Ellis. The delivery was fast. The cab barely made it to the hospital on time. I was so grateful they were both safe. I thanked God and hoped that things would be all right for Betty Sue from then on.

No baby was ever more loved by his mother than little Tommy. As we always seemed to do with children, all of the Foleys, including Donna, adored him. I thought that maybe, now that he had a baby to think about, Ellis would stop going to bars, and for a while, he did.

Eleven months later, Betty Sue had another perfect little boy and named him Terry. A year after that, she had a little girl named Patricia, and a few years later, another girl she named Linda. She asked the doctor how to turn off the machinery that had taken so long to get started. He gave her a thing called a diaphragm.

Betty Sue finally had the family she always wanted. She had a nice apartment, and her husband had a good job. She should have been happy, but she wasn't. She'd gained weight with each pregnancy, and didn't like that now her body was like mine, what they call matronly in ladies' dress shops.

She also didn't like that Ellis had taken to going on drinking jags every few months. He always sobered up in time to go back to work on Monday and never lost his job over it.

He would take Paul with him from time to time. Paul wasn't working, so I thought George must have given him money for beer. God knows, he would never get it from me. I never gave him a cent.

Paul knew better than to come home drunk, so he would sleep it off on Betty Sue's sofa. When Ellis stayed out late, Betty Sue would wait until midnight and then go looking for him. I stayed with the children while she was out.

We were hanging out the laundry one morning when I asked Betty Sue, "Do you hit Ellis every time he goes drinking?"

She blushed. "Not so much. I try not to hit him at all, Mom, I really do, but sometimes it just comes over me. I get so mad at him when he stays out late, I just can't seem to stop myself."

I tried to sound unconcerned when I asked the question I really wanted to have an answer to. "I've never seen him hit you back. Does he?"

"No, and I'm glad of it. He's so big, he could probably hurt me if he wanted. He just holds me away from him until I get over it. He says he's safe as long as his reach is longer than mine. He's glad I don't use a bat or something."

I finished pinning up the shirt I was holding and put my hand on Betty Sue's arm. "I want you to stop that, Betty Sue. It isn't Christian, and it isn't good for the children to see. You won't change him. The only harm you'll do is to them."

I know Betty Sue could tell I was giving her a message from my heart.

She looked hard in my eyes. "It's going to be hard not to, Mom. When I get mad, I almost don't know what I'm doing. That ugly feeling comes over me, and it's like I could almost kill him."

"You have children to think of now. What if you did hurt him bad someday and got sent to prison? What would happen to them? I'm getting too old to be able to raise three babies."

Her eyes got big. "I won't hit him anymore, Mom. If I get mad I'll come here and tell you everything I feel, and I won't go home until that feeling passes."

"I pray you can stick to that, baby."

Chapter 66

Bessie and John bought a house in St. Clair Shores, about ten miles away from us. She and I talked on the phone every once in a while, but it wasn't the same as seeing her all the time. The little storefront services we attended in the old neighborhood were too far away from the big house on Lycaste for me to walk to, and it was too expensive to take a cab.

One week I took a bus. The Sunday bus schedule was slow, and it took me over four hours to make the round trip and attend the services. I would have to find somewhere closer to home.

I'd made friends with Stella, the woman who lived around the corner, and asked her where she went to church. She said she wasn't a church-going person and had no idea where I could find a Holiness Assembly. I looked in the big yellow telephone directory the phone company left me but didn't find one.

The next Sunday I decided to go to the little Ebenezer Baptist church a few blocks away. I got dressed and stood in front of the mirror to pin on my hat. I stood there every day to comb my hair, but that day, I looked at myself and was surprised to see how old I'd become.

I kept my hair-chin length ever since that first time I'd cut it on the trip to Detroit from Missouri. When I was young, it was a deep brown. Now, it was a tired looking combination of different shades of gray and a little brown at the back. My waist was thick, my shoulders stooped, and the wrinkles on my face had deepened to crevices. I put on my hat and walked away from my reflection.

Donna went to church with me. Having spent her entire life between Baptist and Holiness, Donna was comfortable in both denominations. On Sunday and Wednesday night, she attended the Baptist Church with her grandmother Mayse.

I couldn't help watching the service with a critical eye. Compared to my own church, the Baptists were so serious. The preacher delivered his message as if it were a school lesson and didn't even raise his voice with any feeling. I was accustomed to a dramatic sermon, with the preacher pacing the floor and pounding on the pulpit.

I missed music that made a joyful noise. The congregation at the Baptist church sang slow and quiet, as if they were afraid they would wake someone up.

No one stood and testified, no one repented hidden sins, and, as far as I could tell, no one enjoyed himself. After the service, only a few people smiled at me and shook my hand as Donna and I walked out. Not one of them made an attempt to talk to me or invite me to come again.

I never went back.

Chapter 67

I prayed day and night about the way things were at home. Paul kept getting jobs and quitting them after a few days, then going out with Ellis for a night on the town with the few dollars he earned. When they weren't back by midnight, Betty Sue went from bar to bar, looking for Ellis until she found him.

George didn't see the problem.

One Friday afternoon in 1957, Ellis showed up at the house. I could tell he hadn't been home yet because he was still carrying his lunch pail. He said. "I'd like to talk to Paul, please."

I went back to the kitchen and sent Paul to the door. Ellis said a few words to Paul, who opened the door and went out, and as the two of them trotted down the steps, Ellis tucked his lunch bucket beside the porch bannister.

They didn't come home by midnight, and Betty Sue came over and asked me to come stay with the children while she looked for Ellis. I knew it was useless to argue with her. I went down to their apartment and fell asleep on the sofa. Betty Sue came home an hour later, pushing Ellis and Paul through the doorway. I didn't say anything, just gave the sofa to my youngest son and went home.

Paul still wasn't home the next day. Betty Sue came over with the children to help me fix dinner.

"Is Paul at your place?" I asked her.

"No. Ellis is off work for re-tooling at the plant and they left around ten this morning. I heard them whispering together. I don't know what they're up to."

She came back later in the day. Ellis hadn't come home and neither had Paul.

Gene went to the basement to play checkers with George. Donna and I settled down to watch the afternoon movie with Bill Kennedy, a Hollywood actor who moved to Detroit and told his audience all about the stars in the movies he showed. Donna, now fifteen years old, loved the movies, and sat by me.

Paul came staggering in the front door around four o'clock. I could see Ellis standing outside on the sidewalk.

"Give me some money!" he demanded. "Me and Ellis want to go have a beer."

I crossed my arms and kept my eyes on the television. "Get out of here. I'm not giving you anything."

Paul held one hand against the wall to steady

himself and went in my bedroom at the end of the hall. He came out carrying my purse and dropped it in my lap. "I only want a couple of dollars."

I clutched the purse. "I said get out of here."

Paul snatched the bag from me and started pawing through it. He had my wallet in his hand. I tried to take it back from him. He shoved me and I fell back in my seat, the wind knocked the out of me.

Donna jumped up from the sofa, grabbed the wallet away from him, and handed it to me. She turned on him. "Paul, you know she'll never give you money to drink. Why don't you and Ellis just go back to his house and sleep it off?"

Paul's face turned red. "I just want a few dollars!"

He knocked one of my pretty figurines off the table. I reached out to catch it but it shattered on the floor. Then he jerked the pillows off the chairs and sofa and threw them around the room. I grabbed his right arm and held it as tight as I could, but he picked up a small metal wastepaper basket that sat next to my chair with his left hand and threw it.

It hit Donna right between the eyes. Stunned, she looked at Paul, then at me. Blood spurted over the three of us. Paul's face went white, and he turned and ran out of the house, slamming the door behind him.

In the basement, Gene and George had heard the shouting. It was something new in a house where no one ever raised their voice. They hurried upstairs to see what the racket was about. Gene was the first one in the room. When he saw the mess and his daughter standing there with her hand over her nose, blood running out between her fingers, he reeled as if someone had punched him.

"What happened?" he shouted.

"Paul came in and wanted money. When I wouldn't give it to him, he had a fit."

Gene's fists clenched. "He hit her?"

"No, he threw the trash can, and it hit her in the face. He didn't mean to do it. It just happened."

Gene ran out of the house. I jumped up and pulled at George's arm. "You better stop him, George. He'll kill Paul."

For an old man, George moved faster than he had in years with me hurrying right after him. Halfway down the block, Gene caught up with Paul and Ellis. He grabbed Paul's shoulder, spun him around, and landed a punch on his jaw. Paul staggered back against a telephone pole.

Ellis tried to pull Gene away and Gene hit Ellis hard, knocking him backward onto a patch of grass. He had the good sense not to get up.

Gene turned back to his brother, hitting him again and again, holding him up with his left hand as he punched him with his right.

George reached them and caught Gene's arm. It took all of his strength to hold it back. He hollered into Gene's ear, *"Gene, stop it! It won't do anyone any good if you kill him."*

Gene quieted down, but George still held onto him.

"Ellis, you better get Paul out of here." George said. "And don't let him come home for a few days."

Ellis stood, keeping his eyes on Gene, and pulled a bleeding Paul away from the telephone pole. He had to wrap one arm around Paul to keep him from falling down. As they walked away toward his apartment, Ellis glanced back over his shoulder several times to make sure Gene wasn't coming after them.

Gene and George stood for a minute, with Gene glaring after Paul and Ellis. His breathing finally slowed, and his face returned to its natural color. George pulled him toward the house. "We better go see how bad Donna got hit. She may need to see a doctor."

The statement shocked Gene. He ran back to the house, leaving his father to follow with us right behind him. He charged into the living room.

I gave Donna a cold towel to hold against her face and tried to clean up the room.

Gene wrapped his arms around her. "Let's take a look and see how bad that is."

Donna lowered the towel and blood started running out of a cut on the bridge of her nose. Gene took her hand and pressed the towel back up to her face. "Call a cab, Mom, I'm going to take her to the hospital."

I made the call, and while we waited, I helped Donna get out of her bloody clothes and into clean ones. Then I pulled a fresh dress on myself. The taxi was there in about twenty minutes. Before we left, I told George to stay at the house. "If Paul shows up here tell him to get out. I mean it. I don't want him here. There's no telling what Gene will do if he sees him."

We went to the emergency room and signed in.

The receptionist told us to take a seat and wait until we were called.

We sat there, Gene and I, with Donna, still pressing the towel against her face We sat there for over three hours. There was no one else waiting.

Gene got up several times and went to the desk, asking how much longer it would be before Donna could see a doctor. The receptionist told him that the first doctor who became available would see her.

By midnight, Donna was getting bored. We went to the ladies' room and stood in front of the mirror. She took the towel away and looked at herself. The bleeding had stopped, and the cut seemed to have closed itself. Both of her eyes were black and purple. Her left eye was almost swollen shut.

She stood there for a few minutes, but the bleeding didn't start again. We went back out to the reception area and she told Gene, "I'm tired of this place. Let's just go home."

Gene asked again at the desk if the doctor was coming. The receptionist smirked. "I have no way of knowing when he can get here. You'll just have to wait."

"Never mind," Gene said.

We walked outside and hailed a cab. Totally exhausted, the three of us returned home.

Chapter 68

The morning after Paul threw the wastepaper basket and hit her in the face Donna gathered up her things and took them to her grandmother Mayse's house. After that, she visited us often, but it was years before she spent another night in our home, and she never brought her baby sister with her again.

Afraid to come home, Paul spent several nights sleeping on the sofa at Betty Sue's house. She finally told me, "I've got to get Paul out of my home. We don't have enough room for him, and I don't want him. When Ellis comes home from work all they do is sit around like two children, watching television and seeing who can fart the loudest. They think it's funny."

George chimed in, "Let him come home, Maude. He's not her responsibility."

I bristled. "Why is he mine? I'm not the one who

let him stay home from school or let him quit every job he ever got. He's a grown man. It's time for him to get a life and his own place to live."

George rubbed his chin. "Maybe he could join the Army. They might make something out of him."

I reflected that they hadn't been able to do much with Bud, but if the Army would take him, at least he'd be out of my house. "All right, you go down to Betty Sue's and talk to him about it. If he joins the Army, he can stay here until it's time to leave."

So Paul came home. When it was time for Gene to come in from work Paul went to his room and stayed out of sight.

The next Monday, he and George went down to the recruiting station. I felt as if a burden were being lifted from me. They came home with bad news. He was 4-F.

Ellis told George the Coast Guard might have easier requirements, and George took Paul to see about it. He didn't make the grade there, either. Then he tried the National Guard. Another rejection.

I felt trapped. It looked as if I was going to be taking care of Paul for the rest of my life.

I was doing laundry three times a week now, trying to keep up with the family and the bedding of my boarders. I was in my seventies, and even with Betty Sue's help, it was getting more and more tiring for me.

I was hanging out the sheets one afternoon, and Stella came over to chat. She picked up a sheet from the basket and began pinning it to the line that ran next to the one I was using.

"Did Paul have any luck getting into the service?" she asked.

I shook my head. "No, none of them want him. He can't pass the tests."

"He tried all of them?"

"He tried the Army and the National Guard. We knew he wouldn't get into the Navy or the Air Force, so there wasn't any use in him even going down there."

"I wonder if he could get a job in the Merchant Marine."

I paused, one arm still holding up the end of the sheet I'd begun to pin on the line. "I never thought of that. Do you think they would be easier on him?"

"I've heard that they're always looking for help. They work with the Navy, but they're a separate organization. They carry the supplies and cargo so the Navy can do its job. My nephew joined up a few years ago, and he's not the sharpest tack on the board."

"I don't even know where to send him to apply."

"I'll ask my sister."

I talked to Paul and George about it, and Paul agreed to give it a try. I felt encouraged that this would be his chance to finally grow up. Away from home, and away from his father, I hoped he would find some direction for his life.

The next morning, Stella came over and handed me a piece of paper with an address on it, "Have him go here. They can tell him right off if he has the job."

George went with Paul. They took a bus to the

downtown Detroit address. They were gone all afternoon, and I prayed they would come home with good news.

Betty Sue and I cooked and took turns going from the kitchen to the front door to look for them. It was almost five o'clock before they got back. When I saw them coming up the street I went out to the front porch to meet them. The look on George's face told me I wasn't going to hear anything I liked.

"What did they say?"

Paul stood on the step behind his father. George tilted his head and held his hands out. "Well, it didn't seem like the right job for him."

"So, they said no?"

George shuffled his feet. "Not exactly."

I felt my face turn red, and my heart began racing. I know my blood pressure must have shot up. "What does that mean? Not exactly?"

"It's pretty hard work, and he could be gone from home six months at a time. They go all over the world."

I looked past George's shoulder to Paul. "So you turned them down?"

Paul jutted out his chin. "Dad said I didn't have to go if I didn't want to."

I was so angry I thought I would faint. When I was younger, I would have accepted it without saying anything and carried on, doing the best I could. I was older now and had enough disappointment in my life.

I turned back to George with a look that made him wince. "So, you're telling me they offered him the job, and you told him he didn't have to take it? What's going to happen to him when I die? Who's going to take care of him?"

"He'll be fine. Gene wouldn't let him go hungry."

The remark angered me even more. "You're keeping him at home like one of those dogs you had back in Missouri. Why would you saddle Gene with him? Gene deserves a life of his own. He doesn't need to be worrying about taking care of a grown man who's too lazy to hold down a job."

George stepped in front of Paul. "Don't talk about him like that right in front of his face. He can't help it if he can't find the right job. It's not his fault."

I glared at him. "No, it isn't his fault, George, it's *your* fault."

"My fault?"

"You wouldn't let me make him go to school. He could have had a half-way decent education. From the time he was in first grade, you coddled him and let him stay home. Now he's a grown man, and he can hardly read and write. He quit every job he ever got because he's following your example."

"What example?"

"You sit out on the porch or down in the basement all day, playing checkers or gossiping with the neighbors over the fence. He doesn't see you doing any work, and he doesn't see why he should do any either."

George hung his head. He didn't have an answer to my charges. The two men walked past me and into the house. I felt light-headed and had to sit down on the porch swing for a bit. Deep inside, I'd finally given up on Paul. I accepted that he would never amount to anything.

I would have liked to rest for a while longer, but it was time to put dinner on the table. Thirteen boarders would be coming home soon, and all of them would be hungry. When my heart stopped pounding, I got up and went back to my work.

After the meal was served, the dishes washed, and the kitchen clean, I went to my room and closed the door. I had a terrible headache, so I put on my nightgown and lay on the bed. Prayers didn't come to me that night. I was too eaten up by my failures. I counted them back to myself in the dark.

I thought about my marriage to George. I'd been so happy with James and craved the same connection, but after all these years and four children, there was no more of a bond between me and George now than the day we met. I'd taken a vow to love him, but I didn't. I never had. So I failed as a wife.

Secondly, I hoped for years to achieve the state of grace so many of my fellow church members seemed to have reached, where I didn't sin any more. I asked God to forgive me for the harmful feelings I had for Evelyn, for Ellis, for Paul, and for George. I wanted to change for the better, but I resented each one of them more every day. I asked God to make me a kinder person.

I believed that God had forgiven me, but I couldn't forgive myself, and now I didn't even go to church anymore. So I failed as a Christian.

I failed as a mother to Bud, and now Paul. He was hopeless, and as much as I wanted to blame George, I had to share the responsibility.

If I'd fought harder to get Paul an education, George might have given in. I should have put my foot down, but I hadn't known how.

At least I had Gene and Betty Sue, both of them loving, caring people, doing the best they could to make their way in the world. They were my justification. They were my testament.

Except for her temper outbursts, Betty Sue was a wonderful woman, cheerful and happy, and a wonderful mother. Her children were happy and well cared for, her home was always clean, and she did her best to support her husband, sinful as he was. She genuinely loved him. Too much, I sometimes thought.

Gene was a good man. He worked hard, loved his daughter with all his heart, treated everyone with respect, and had always been a man I could be proud of. I hoped that someday he would give up his dream of winning Evelyn back and find another partner to share his life.

Then, there was Donna. She was a strange, independent child, coming and going as she wanted, living where she chose, but I loved her and was proud of her, too.

So I counted my failures and counted my blessings. It wasn't a regular prayer, but I finally was able to sleep so I could face the next day.

Chapter 69

George spent more and more time in the back yard, talking to Stella over the fence. I didn't pay that much attention to it. In his late seventies, he didn't ask me for relations anymore, and that was a relief to me.

One Tuesday in 1958 I came out of the basement door carrying a basket of laundry. When I opened the door, George was in Stella's yard, his hands cupped around her face, kissing her on the cheek. Stella was leaning into him, with an easy familiarity. I froze. They didn't see me watching them.

When I saw George do that, a loneliness I can't describe came over me.

One morning, two weeks later, there was a knock at the front door. Through the screen, I saw a man in a suit. "May I speak to George Foley?" he asked.

I opened the door and waved him in. "Just a

minute, I'll get him," I said. I walked through the kitchen and called down the steps, "George, there's a man here to see you."

He came upstairs with a puzzled look. No one had come to the house to see him since he retired.

The man asked him, "Are you George William Foley?"

"Yes, I am," answered George.

"These are for you," the man said, handing George an envelope. Then he nodded to me and said, "Thank you, Ma'am," and left.

George stood there holding the envelope, still wearing the puzzled expression. He tore it open and unfolded the papers inside. After he read them, he shuffled them and read them again. I went to the kitchen and began stirring a big pot of boiling potatoes and humming a tune.

He walked up behind me. "You can't do this, Maude."

"Yes, I can. I've already done it. My mind is made up."

"We've been married over forty years. What's gotten into you?"

I turned around. "I'll tell you what's gotten into me. I saw you in the yard with Stella. In ten seconds you showed her more affection than you've shown me since the day we were married. There were times my heart ached, wishing you would just hold my hand or put your arm around me, but you never did, never."

His mouth fell open. "How was I supposed to know you wanted me to do that?"

"Why should I have to ask for it? I never turned you down in bed. I had your children. I cooked your meals and cleaned your house. I was a good wife to you."

His face turned red. "Did it ever occur to you that I might need the same thing?"

I was stunned. Tears sprang from my eyes. "No, George, it didn't. You always seemed so far away from me that it didn't look like you needed me at all."

"I'm sorry, Maude. Let's just forget this. I won't even speak to Stella again if you don't want me to. I never went to bed with her. It was never anything like that."

"It's not whether you did or didn't go to bed with her. If you slept with her, it would have been easier for me to take. It's that you gave her something you never gave to me. It was the last straw, George."

"The last straw? What do you mean by that?"

"It's one last thing piled up on top of all the other things."

"What other things?"

"Way back, it's the way you let your mother treat me. Do you remember that she tried to kill me once? You just let it go. I had to live in your house in fear of my life."

"I wouldn't have let her hurt you."

"You were in town all day pretending to be a sheriff. How could you have stopped her?"

"I didn't think she would really do anything bad to you."

"You refused to even talk to her about it. You

were so afraid of her, you would have let her kill me and worried about it later."

I took a deep breath and went on. "It's not only that. It's the way you ruined Bud and Paul, letting them drink and run around like they did. It's you being too lazy to do any more work than you had to do to get by, letting me do man's work on the house in Kennett, losing your job there."

"That was because of the Depression."

"What about now? You quit work as soon as you could get your Social Security and you spend all your money on beer and cigarettes. I work fourteen hours a day in this house, sometimes more, cooking and cleaning, but you probably don't even know that. You just come upstairs to eat and watch television. When will I get to retire, when I die?"

He hung his head. "What do you want me to do, Maude?"

"I want you to pack up your things and Paul's. Move out of here and take him with you. I'm not taking care of you two anymore. You can both go live with Stella. We'll see how much she likes you then."

"That's ridiculous. I barely know her."

"It looked to me like you know her well enough."

"We'll see what Gene has to say about this when he gets home."

"I'm not going to change my mind, George. It's made up. I'm through with you."

At three-thirty, George came upstairs from the basement again, the papers in his hand, and waited on the front porch for Gene to come home from work. I saw him sitting there but said nothing.

When he saw Gene coming down the sidewalk George got up and went to meet him. The two of them stopped while Gene read the papers.

George waited on the porch while Gene came charging into the kitchen, waving the papers in his hand. "Mom, what in the world has gotten into you? You can't do this."

"I've already done it, and I'm not going back. I want him and Paul both out of here."

"What will he do? His pension isn't enough for them to live on."

"He should have thought of that before he went messing around with Stella."

"What?" Gene shouted. He took a step backwards, staggering as if he had been struck.

"Ask him about it," was all I said.

Gene stormed out of the room to the front porch. Through the open window, I could hear them talking, Gene's voice loud and excited, George's soft and ashamed.

After a while Gene came inside and went up to his room. George walked by me without saying anything and went back down to the basement.

Chapter 70

Betty Sue came to help me with dinner, and the two of us carried on with our usual mealtime routine. I said nothing to her about the divorce.

Gene left without eating and was gone until almost dark. When he came back, dinner was over. I'd made him up a plate and kept it warm in the oven. Gene waited until Betty Sue was finished helping with the clean-up and left for home before he talked to me.

I was putting away the dishes. He sat at the kitchen table and I put his dinner in front of him. He stared down at the plate but made no move to eat.

"I got an apartment for me and Dad. Unless you change your mind, we'll move out tomorrow."

I didn't answer him right away. I wasn't surprised. I'd half expected that this was what he would do. He was my boy and had been from the beginning, but he loved his father as well.

I asked him, "What are you going to do about Paul?"

"I don't care what happens to him. He's not going with me."

A tear fell on my cheek. I was stuck with Paul. "I hate to see you move out, Gene, but I know you love your Dad. I won't try to talk you out of it."

Gene shoved his plate away. His voice was so low, I could barely hear him. "Mom, he's seventy-six years old, can't you just forget it? He said he'd never go back over there again."

"If that was all there was to it, I would forget it, but there's other things, things you don't even know about."

"What things?"

"Things that are between a husband and a wife, things that aren't any of your business. I'm not going to change my mind, no matter what you say."

Gene went downstairs for a few minutes to talk to George and then back up to his room. The next morning, he and George carried out their clothes and moved to a small upstairs apartment a few blocks away.

I wept from time to time over losing Gene. He was still angry with me and didn't even come to visit for a while. I never wept for George. I didn't miss him at all and seldom even thought about him.

One afternoon, Donna came to see me, and we talked about the state of the family. When Gene called to tell her about his new address and the divorce, she'd accepted it matter-of-factly.

Divorce was nothing new in her life, Evelyn was single again. After that, Donna went to Gene's apartment to see him and her grandfather one time, to my house the next.

After several months of going back and forth, she told me about stopping in at her father's one afternoon. She played a few games of checkers with George, and Gene made their dinner in the tiny kitchen, canned tamales and Spanish rice. While they were eating, Donna said, "Grandma misses you, Daddy. I want you to go over there with me and see her tomorrow."

Gene looked at George, who nodded his head.

"All right," he said.

The next day, she stopped by her father's and the two of them walked to my house. Instead of just walking in, Donna stood behind Gene, and he knocked on the door. When I saw him standing there, I stopped in my tracks. Neither one of us moved until Donna stepped past him and pulled open the screen door, holding it for him until he came in.

He wrapped his arms around me, and we held one another for a long time. We talked for several hours, and after that Gene came by once or twice a week.

Chapter 71

Gene renewed his courtship of Evelyn. He hoped the fact that he'd moved out of my house would help win her over, but his hope didn't last very long. She married again, this time to someone named Gene Fredette, who'd served in the Marines and fought in Korea. He was a bartender at the corner bar she sometimes went to with her friends, and that was where she met him.

A few months after that, my Gene began seeing a pretty neighbor named Helen. She was divorced and had a small son. I hoped he'd finally given up on his dream of winning Evelyn back, and found someone who would treat him right.

Chapter 72

One afternoon in August of 1962, Gene came to see me with bad news. He'd been at Receiving Hospital with his father all night.

It seems that George decided to go to the corner store from his and Gene's upstairs apartment while Gene was at work. Misjudging the first step of the long flight of stairs, he fell all the way to the bottom. He couldn't get up, and he lay there for two hours before Gene came home from work and found him. Gene didn't own a car, so he called the ambulance. The first time he called, it was around four o'clock in the afternoon, and they said they would be there as soon as possible.

He walked to the corner and called them again every half-hour. He was told each time that they would be there as soon as they could so he didn't call a cab.

It was after eight that night before they showed up. George was taken to Detroit Receiving Hospital. He had shattered a hip. A few days later, he developed pneumonia.

What was left of the family, Gene, Paul, Donna, and myself, gathered in the hospital. Totally unaware of what was happening, George thrashed around the bed, throwing off the blankets and pulling out his IV. They finally put restraints on him to keep him quiet.

Betty Sue was so upset she was like a crazy person. She kept telling the nurses to take better care of her father and complaining about everything from the scratchy sheets to the bags on the IV pole not getting changed before they went empty.

I finally told her she was doing more harm than good because the nurses were avoiding George so they wouldn't have to listen to her. That calmed her down for a day, but on the next visit, she was at it again, shouting at the nurses, waving her arms, and complaining. She left the children with a neighbor and sat by George's bed for hours, holding his hand.

I was just about ready to go to bed when Betty Sue came to see me late that Saturday night.

"Ellis has been gone almost two days," she cried. "Paul came home without him hours ago. Come with me, Mom. I have to go look for him!"

"No, you don't. He'll come home when he runs out of money."

"He might be sick."

"You think that every time he up and runs off."

"I know, but I have to go find him. Please come

with me."

"Who's with the children?"

"Paul. He doesn't know where Ellis went after he left him."

I sighed and shook my head. "All right, just a minute."

I picked up my purse, and joined my daughter. We made the usual rounds, asking first at the bars Ellis frequented most often. He and Paul had been to some of them the night before, but no one had seen Ellis. One bartender told her he'd left without Paul shortly before midnight the night before.

At the next place one waitress knew Betty Sue. I waited while Betty Sue spoke with her.

She smiled. "Hi, Louise. I'm looking for Ellis. Has he been here?"

"Yeah, he was here last night. The bartender ran him out at closing time. He was pretty plastered."

"He didn't come home. Where do you think he might have gone? Was he with anyone, maybe a woman?"

"He was alone. Why don't you go on home? He'll show up sooner or later."

"I'm worried about him. What if he's sick?"

Louise put her tray on the bar and leaned toward Betty Sue. "If you don't find him in one of the bars by two a.m., you could check an after-hours place in an upstairs apartment on Hillger Street. Number 1912. Don't let them know you got it from me."

"Thanks Louise."

We left the bar and headed down Jefferson. On

the corner of St. Jean, we waited with a crowd of people for the light.

It was long past my bedtime. I pulled on Betty Sue's arm and said, "We aren't going to find him tonight. Let's go home. I have to get up in the morning, and you'll want to go to the hospital to see your father."

She jerked away from me and spun around. "No! I have to find him. I need him."

She started crying. "Dad's dying in that place. Everything they do just makes him worse. Ellis ought to be home with me, not out drinking."

She threw her arms up as if she were appealing to heaven. "I have to find him."

I tried to reason with her. "It's not going to do us any good to go up and down looking for him."

The more I talked, the more emotional she became. She ranted, "Dad's going to die, maybe tomorrow. Probably tomorrow. I have to find Ellis. I have to!"

Several people, including Betty Sue and myself, stepped off the curb, expecting the light to change in a few seconds. It finally turned green, and Betty Sue stepped out. She was a foot or so in front of me to my left…and then she wasn't.

The convertible that ran the light was going so fast it was only a blur. It grazed me and another woman, knocking us off our feet.

It took me a minute to realize what had happened. I pulled myself to a sitting position. A man leaned over me and helped me to my feet. "Are you all right, lady?"

I brushed the dirt off my dress. "I think so."

I looked myself over. My left arm and leg had scrapes from where I'd fallen onto the concrete, but other than that, I seemed all right.

The group of people spoke angrily about the car. One man said, "I'm going to get the police."
I looked around for Betty Sue, but couldn't find her. I circled the growing crowd of people several times, calling her name, but she wasn't there.

I looked down the street and saw the convertible coming back. There she was, sitting up in the back seat. Then, when the car stopped at the curb on the other side of the street, the young man in the passenger seat jumped out of the car. He ran toward us and started yelling, "I told him to stop! I told him! It isn't my fault."

He went from one man in the crowd to another, grabbing them by their forearms and yelling how he didn't do anything wrong. The driver just sat without moving.

I limped over toward the car to see if Betty Sue was hurt and maybe needed an ambulance. She sat there, staring straight ahead. Before I could get to her, she fell over in the seat. A bunch of people crowded between us and gathered around the car. Then I heard a man say, "This lady's dead!"

I reeled to my left and a man caught me. "No!" I cried. "No!"

The man holding me up had to put his arm around my waist and hold tight to keep me from falling. I tried to get to her, but I couldn't even put one foot in front of the other.

I thought they must be wrong. Betty Sue was knocked out, was all. I was sure she'd be all right in a minute. All those people should get away from her and let her have some air.

I cried, "Get out of my way! Get out of my way! I'm her mother! I have to help her!"

Someone held me back and half-dragged me to a bench on the sidewalk. A police car came and then an ambulance. The medics worked on her for a minute, then lifted her out of the car and put her on a gurney.

It wasn't until they pulled a sheet over her head that I realized the man was right. My daughter was dead. My head started swimming, and I fell over. The man who'd taken me to the bench yelled out, "Hey, doc, over here."

I remember someone putting a bottle of smelling salts to my nose. I didn't pass out, but I stayed in a daze through the whole thing. The medic wanted to take me to the hospital, but I told him I wouldn't go.

The police station was right across the street. They asked me what happened, and I told them what I could. More squad cars came, and other police talked to the people in the crowd. I saw them take the two young men from the convertible away in handcuffs.

I didn't try to get up. I knew I wouldn't be able to stand. Different people kept trying to help me. Someone brought me a glass of water and I took a few sips.

Gene and Betty Sue and those grandbabies were

the only things in this world that mattered to me, and now Betty Sue was gone.

I didn't understand how God could allow this to happen.

Chapter 73

A squad car brought me home. The police officers kept saying they should take me to the hospital, but I didn't want to go. I knew there wasn't anything a hospital or doctors could do to help me. I sent one of my boarders who was home to go to Betty Sue's place and tell Paul to bring the children here if Ellis still wasn't home.

Paul came in and said Ellis had just walked in the door, and he wasn't even drunk. "Go back and get him," I said. "Betty Sue is dead."

Paul ran out and came back with Ellis and the children a few minutes later. If I had been able to stand, I would have gone to the kitchen and got the biggest knife in there and stabbed Ellis to death. I didn't have the strength.

I told Paul to go to Gene's apartment to tell him what happened. I closed the blinds and lay down in my room to let myself cry. My head was hurting so bad I thought it might blow up.

Gene arrived at my door only a few minutes later. He called the doctor, who came right away and gave me a shot of some kind. I slept most of the next few days.

George was seventy-seven and his injuries and the pneumonia were too much for him to survive. He died the next day, never knowing our precious daughter had gone first.

Gene was devastated. Donna grieved. Paul wailed for his father. He sounded like a lost child.

My heart was broken over Betty Sue. As far as George was concerned, I mourned for what should have been, but wasn't.

Paul lost what little spark of life he had and retreated into himself. He had no one to lean on now. I had no sympathy for him. His father and his brother Bud and now his sister were gone. Gene had erased him from his life.

Donna had long ago forgiven him the fight that ended with her trip to the hospital, but she was off living her own life.

Even though we had a TV, Paul spent hours each day sitting in a kitchen chair pulled up to the front window looking out at the traffic.

Gene had to make arrangements for both funerals.

Ellis was in a stupor of some kind. He kept saying, "It's my fault, it's my fault," until I couldn't stand it anymore, and I answered, "You're right. It's your fault. You killed her." That finally shut him up.

Betty Sue's body was shown for one day at the funeral home, and she was buried at Forest Lawn, a short distance from where we buried Bud.

The next day, there was a big article in both *The Detroit News* and *The Free Press*. The car that hit Betty Sue had sped away down Jefferson. Although his friend tried to persuade him, the young man driving it didn't intend to stop. He was afraid he'd have to go to jail.

When his passenger turned his head to look back, he saw Betty Sue sitting upright in the back seat.

The passenger screamed then and insisted the driver stop and he pulled over. At first they thought she was alive and offered to take her to a hospital. When they realized she was dead, they turned the car around and took her back to the scene of the accident. They got there a minute or so after the police arrived

Chapter 74

I hadn't so much as said hello to Stella since the divorce from George, but I remember her coming over every day to cook and take care of things. People from the church and other neighbors brought food, and that helped a lot.

After a week, I tried to get myself back to some kind of routine. There were boarders to be fed and a big house to be cleaned, so the next Monday, I got up early and went back to work. I was nearing eighty, and by the end of the week realized that without Betty Sue to help me, there was no way I could continue to care for a house filled with thirteen boarders and Paul.

I hired a girl to help, but after only five days of shopping for groceries, cooking, and doing laundry, the girl quit. So did the next two. I finally had to admit it wasn't going to work.

I talked to my two favorite boarders, a Mr. Crider, who was my own age and a widower, and a nice young man from Kentucky named Doug. I felt a kinship with them because they had both been raised Holiness, even though they didn't go to meetings anymore. They agreed they would move with us to a smaller house. I found a four bedroom place on Mack Avenue, next to St. Bernard's Catholic Church. With my income cut quite a bit, I was barely able to make ends meet. Gene gave me a little money each week to help out.

Mr. Crider had a car. I told him how I missed going to my own kind of church. From that time on, he drove me and Doug to the services every week.

Ellis remarried only a few months after Betty Sue died and didn't have time for Paul. Without a drinking buddy to pay for his beer, Paul remained sober.

Chapter 75

Donna graduated from Southeastern High School and began working at Michigan Bell as a long-distance operator. Gene and I were so proud of her. Now seventeen, she still lived with her grandmother Mayse and paid room and board. She was making her own way in the world.

Shortly after her eighteenth birthday, Gene received a letter from the Friend of the Court. Evelyn was suing him for back child support. It seemed that when Donna was living with us during vacations and through some of her teen years, Gene had assumed it was all right for him to stop sending money.

Donna took a day off work, and she and I went to court with him on the appointed morning. I told the judge how Gene had kept Donna during school vacations, and that she had lived in his home full time for two years.

Donna told the judge that he'd been the one who took her to the dentist and the doctor, who bought her glasses and books, and gave her spending money and whatever money she needed for school. He'd been the one who bought her every stitch of clothing she'd ever worn.

In spite of this, the judge decided that, since Gene hadn't saved receipts, he was in default and ordered him to pay the contested amount. It took a big chunk out of his savings.

There was one good outcome of the hearing. When we stopped for a meal on the way home from court, he picked at his food, shoving it around his plate. "I guess you were right about her all these years, Mom. I finally saw Evelyn through your eyes. I always hoped I could make her love me, but I know now that she never did, not one single day."

Gene had finally stopped loving the woman he'd cherished and pursued for almost twenty years. He could now think about finding a woman who would love him for himself. I breathed a sigh of relief and thought, "Let Evelyn enjoy the money. We're finally rid of her."

When she was nineteen, Donna married Lonnie Mabry, a young man who'd courted her off and on throughout their teens. Gene never liked him, but he never liked any of the boys Donna knew. Lonnie was in the Army, just out of basic training. They had a small wedding at the Baptist church, and he left for his advanced training class. Donna went on living with her

455

grandmother Mayse.

In the middle of her first year of marriage, Donna was overjoyed to tell me she was expecting her first child. We'd always loved children, and all of us, even Paul, looked forward to the baby coming.

Chapter 76

Gene came to see me every afternoon for the first few weeks after George and Betty Sue died. I knew he was grieving, and being with me seemed to comfort him.

One afternoon he drove up in a 1958 cream and tan Pontiac Bonneville. I went out to admire it. Gene was proud of the car. It was the first one he ever owned. He drove me around the block, and when we got back to my house, he parked it out front and told me, "If I'd had a car the day dad fell, I could have picked him up and driven him to the hospital myself instead of waiting all that time for the ambulance. I don't ever want to be in that position again."

I understood. "I know, but don't go punishing yourself. Your dad was in pretty bad shape from the fall. I don't think he would have made it anyway."

"Still, I have one now."

"That's good, Gene."

We went inside, and he sat at the kitchen table. I made him something to eat and mentioned the subject I'd been thinking about ever since the funeral.

I brought it up carefully. "Do you ever think about moving back in with us, now that your dad's gone?"

Gene took a deep breath. I think he'd been expecting me to ask exactly this. "No, Mom. That wouldn't be a good idea."

"I just thought I'd ask."

"You know how I feel about Paul. I don't think I could live under the same roof with him. You don't have enough rooms here anyway. You would have to ask Doug or Mr. Crider to move, and I know how good they've been to you and how much you like them."

"I could always find a bigger place."

"Well, the truth is, I've been seeing someone pretty regular. Her name is Loretta. I like her a lot, Mom. I want to maybe have a life with her."

He'd said that he *liked* this Loretta, not that he loved her. Maybe that was all for the better. He'd loved Evelyn so much that she'd made his life miserable for a long time.

I sat next to him and put my hand on his. "You deserve to be happy. I hope it works out for you."

Evelyn gave birth to another little girl and named her Linda. Donna was delighted with the baby and brought pictures of her to show to me. Linda was a pretty little thing, with tight blonde curls. She was one more thing that widened the permanent gulf between

Evelyn and Gene, and that was fine with me.

In September of 1962, Donna still worked at the telephone company. She would have to quit soon because the company policy was that she couldn't work past her sixth month. She visited me about once a week.

She would be leaving soon for Fort Riley, Kansas. Lonnie had found an apartment in Manhattan, a town a few miles from the Army base. Gene and I hated to see her go, but at the same time, we were proud of her and the life she lived.

Loretta called to tell me that Gene was having trouble with his kidneys and was in the Harper Hospital for treatment. I called Donna to let her know. She had her own car, so she stopped by and picked me up, and the two of us went to see him together.

Gene's face lit up when Donna came in the room. She'd had morning sickness for a long time but had finally been able to keep down enough food that she'd put on some weight. In her sixth month, her being in a family way was finally beginning to show.

Gene gave her a big smile. "I'm fine. I'm only in here for some tests. Don't let it worry you. You go ahead out to Kansas. I'll be out of the hospital in a few days and back to work on Monday."

I was cheered a little by his behavior and the pink on his cheeks.

Lonnie came home on leave, and after a final visit to the hospital, he and Donna left on their trip to Kansas.

Donna wrote home to me right away with her

address and phone number, and we wrote letters to one another about every two weeks.

Donna's daughter Melanie was born at Erwin Army Hospital at Fort Riley in November of 1962. Donna called to say it was a quick and easy delivery.

Gene and I treasured the pictures of the pretty little girl Donna sent home with her next letter.

Chapter 77

I'd lost one son and both my daughters. George died, and Donna lived half way across the country. Soon, my life changed even more, and for the worse. Mr. Crider, who was one of my last two boarders, became ill and went to live with his son and daughter-in-law. The other boarder, Doug, married and moved away. I was left alone in the house with Paul, who still hadn't found a job to his liking.

I was often tempted to turn him out, but my weakness kept me from doing it. He passed his days sleeping late, sitting in front of the window, watching television, and going back to bed.

I kept my house clean, as always. I lived for the few minutes Gene spent with me when he came to visit. He stopped by twice a week and drove me to the market. Most other days if I needed something I had to buy it at the corner store, which was more expensive. I couldn't carry home more than one bag, and Paul wouldn't go with me to help.

When Gene offered to give me money, I usually refused it, saying I was making out all right...but I wasn't telling him the truth. The truth was my lifetime savings were getting used up fast, and what I drew from Social Security wasn't enough to support one person, much less two.

Gene brought his girlfriend Loretta to meet me. When they pulled up in front of the house, I noticed she was driving his car and it struck me as odd. I worried about the way he looked. His skin had a greenish color to it that worried me, and he walked slower than he normally did. I wondered if she drove because he wasn't well enough.

We were polite to one another, but I didn't care for her, and I thought it must be some flaw in my own character. Maybe I would never like a woman my son picked, but I would do my best to make Loretta feel comfortable for Gene's sake.

He'd given up his apartment and moved in with Loretta, but they hadn't married. That didn't sit well with me. Gene still wasn't well enough to go to work. He told me that as soon as he was back on his feet, they would have a wedding. As much as I didn't want him living with a woman who wasn't his wife, I didn't care for the idea of Gene marrying Loretta.

Gene was in and out of the hospital for months. His kidneys, injured in the fall from a roof all those years before, were shutting down on him.

Loretta worked day shift, so on weekdays I walked over to their apartment and made lunch for him. I was surprised at what she kept in the refrigerator. I'd seen the list of foods Gene's doctor recommended, and there was too much in there that wasn't on the list.

He was still able to get up and eat at the table. I set his plate in front of him. One particular day, I'd carried over some homemade chicken soup. It had always been one of his favorites. I stewed a big hen, added wide noodles, carrots, celery, and onions, the way he always loved.

I bought salt substitute especially for the things I made him because his doctor had put him on a salt-free diet. What I made for myself and Paul had regular salt and black pepper.

He ate a good amount. I sat next to him. "I saw cucumbers in the refrigerator. Are you supposed to be eating things like that?"

"I guess it's all right. The doctor gave Loretta a list of what I could have."

"What about the other things...radishes, olives?"

Gene smiled at me. "I'm fine, Mom, don't worry so much."

I did worry. He looked worse every day. I didn't know if Loretta was helping him or hurting him.

Chapter 78

I think now God gives each one of us a measure of happiness for our lives, and some are allowed more than others. It's like the ration stamps that were handed out during the war, so much butter, so much sugar, and then no more. I also think that sometimes the good stretches are so good that it must count for double time, like the two years when I was married to James.

The rest of my own happiness was strung out through my life in dribs and drabs, and most of that revolved around Betty Sue and Gene. It tapered off as I lost the ones I loved, first my mother and father, then James, Lulu, then Betty Sue. Now, I was sure I was facing the loss of Gene. It would seem I'd used up my share of happiness.

Every time I left him, my head ached for hours, sometimes the pain was so sharp I had to take aspirins and lie down in the dark all afternoon before it went away.

One morning in April of 1963, Loretta called the house to tell me that Gene had been taken to the Harper Hospital in an ambulance. Riding the bus downtown and transferring, it took me two hours to reach the hospital. The whole time, I had to keep myself from running to the front and pounding on the driver so he would drive faster.

When I got there he was in intensive care. The sight of him scared me half to death. He was lying totally still, with no color in his face. There were two IV tubes in his arms and wires from different monitors attached to him. I held his hand and tried to talk to him. He opened his eyes and managed a weak smile, then closed them again.

I sat in the chair next to the bed. After several hours, his doctor came in and examined him. When he finished, he took my hand and led me out into the hallway.

"I'm sorry Mrs. Foley. There isn't a lot we can do for kidney failure of this sort. I'm going to try transfusing him again. Sometimes it does help quite a lot."

"Should I call his daughter? She's in Kansas. Her husband is in the Army."

He hesitated. "Yes, I think you'd better call her."

Donna got a flight home with Melanie, and Mr. Crider's son met them at the airport. They came to my house and picked me up, then drove directly to the hospital. Donna brought the baby into Gene's hospital room. It was the day after a transfusion, and Gene was better. He was so excited. He sat up on the edge of the bed and held his granddaughter, rocking her in his arms.

"She's so beautiful," he said. "She's like a big doll, isn't she?"

He looked at me. "She looks just like Donna, doesn't she, Mom?"

He held Melanie's face up to his cheek and closed his eyes while he rocked her back and forth for several minutes. We stayed as long as the nursing staff would let us and came back the next day and the day after, staying as long as we could.

The doctor was amazed at Gene's improvement, and said that he could probably go home in a few days. He was sitting up, even walking a few steps.

Donna left Michigan, but I knew she felt uneasy about it.
A month later, Gene was back in the hospital, this time worse than ever. He slipped in and out of consciousness. I was desperate. I felt so alone, felt as if the whole world were falling in on me. I called Donna again.

There wasn't enough money for an airplane, so Donna took the train. It was a long trip, and she had to change trains in Chicago with a layover of three hours. She got home too late. Gene passed away during the night.

Donna stayed with me while she was in Detroit. We pulled out a drawer from the dresser and put in a pillow to make a bed for Melanie. Donna shared my bed again, the way she had as a young girl.

I had given birth to five children, and I lost four. It was terrible for me when Lulu died, but there were Bud and Gene to be cared for, and it eased the grief. When Bud died, I had others to look after. Then I lost Betty Sue, and it broke my heart. Now, I'd lost Gene, and it was a thousand times beyond a broken heart. What did I have left to live for?

Chapter 79

Gene left a ten-thousand-dollar insurance policy naming me as beneficiary. The funeral home took the promise of part of it to pay for the funeral that cost five thousand dollars.

Gene took after me in that he had a lifetime habit of saving money. When Donna and I went to the bank where he'd always had his account, they told us the money had already been taken out and the account closed. Donna and I talked late into the night the way we used to, and I told her about Gene's last days. One of the last things he said to me was that I should give half the money to her. I promised I would send it when I got the check.

Loretta didn't come to the funeral, and when we went to her apartment, it was empty. We never found out what happened to Gene's car. I never heard from

Loretta again. I was right not to trust her.

Donna and Melanie returned to Kansas. I was much more than alone. I was alone with Paul.

Chapter 80

Mr. Crider was no longer able to drive, but his son came each Sunday, picked me up, and took me to church. I lived for those few hours each week when I could feel part of a church family again.

I was broke, my savings gone. I waited for the money to come from the insurance company. It would have to last me as long as I lived. All I had coming in now was my Social Security.

I prayed the check would come soon. I had to pay rent, the electric, gas, and water. I had to buy groceries for myself and Paul. I made corn meal mush and oatmeal for breakfast, we ate bologna sandwiches for lunch, and mostly collard greens or beans for dinner. I bought just enough meat for seasoning the beans.

Paul wouldn't even look for work.

Two months passed since Gene died, and the check from the insurance company hadn't come yet. I put in for welfare, but was told it took time to qualify. I gave up the telephone, and it hurt me when I had to tell the paperboy I couldn't take the *Free Press* anymore. I'd read the paper every day since before I voted that first time, but I had to cut back wherever I could.

I'd been looking for the mailman every day, and the check finally arrived. He handed me the envelope that morning and I got my purse, walked the quarter mile to the bank, and deposited it right away.

When I got home, I was worn out and only wanted to rest. I walked in the house and Paul met me at the door. "I need some money for cigarettes," he said.

I hate to tell you that it's possible for a mother to hate her own child, but sometimes, even if just for a second, it is.

I shook my head. "You haven't smoked since your father moved out. You're going to have to do without or get some sort of a job if you want cigarettes. I can't afford to buy them for you."

He jerked my purse out of my hand and rifled through it. I had about three singles in paper money and some change. He took one of the bills, threw my purse on the table, and strode out of the house.

Paul came back from the store, pulled his chair up to the front window, and sat, staring out and smoking.

I thought about calling the police and having them put him out of the house, but didn't know if they would even come. If they did, would they simply laugh at me? I wanted to force him to get out, to make him leave, but I wasn't a young woman any more. What if something happened to me and I was all alone? How long would I lie there before someone found me? It was something I feared, so if he needed me, maybe in a way, I needed him.

There was no love from Paul toward me either-- not that I could see, not ever. Maybe that was my own fault.

Paul treated me as if I hadn't lost anything, hadn't lost James, and Lulu, and Betty Sue, and now Gene. I'd carried and birthed and nursed five children, and this was the only one I had left in my old age. The best thing I could say about him was that it was better to have him in the house than to face dying alone.

I looked back over my life, all the way back to the day my parents died. If I hadn't been at my sister's house, maybe I could have warned them, but I might also have died in the fire with them.

If I had refused to marry James until after I finished school, would he have waited for me? What would Helen and Tommy have done if I'd said no? They couldn't have thrown me out of the house.

If I'd somehow kept James from playing baseball that day, would he still be alive, or would he have hated me for robbing him of his big chance?

If I'd refused to marry George to keep people from gossiping about me, would I have ever found someone else, or would I have lived out my life as a widow and never had Betty Sue and Gene in my life?

If I hadn't nursed Clara and Mom Foley through the flu, would Lulu have been spared the infection? I often wondered if I were the one who brought the thing that killed her into the house.

If I'd been firmer with Bud and Paul and not let George coddle them, would their lives have turned out better?

My head pounded with knife-sharp pains. I went to my room and pulled the window shade all the way down. I lay on the bed in the dark afternoon and closed my eyes.

I've heard people say they had no regrets in their lives. I wish I could have said that, but there were so many regrets, so many mistakes.

Epilogue
from
Donna

The morning after the funeral, someone (one of my maternal aunts, I think) drove me back to my grandmother's house on the way to the airport. There were three things I wanted from her personal belongings. Holding Melanie, my aunt waited in the car while I went in the house. My uncle Paul was waiting at the door, his face torn up. "They came yesterday and took all her things," he told me.

"Who?" I asked.

"Ellis and his wife."

Betty Sue's husband had more nerve than I realized.

I looked around the living room. The furniture was there, but all the knick-knacks, the doilies, everything that could be carried away in a car, were missing.

I went to my grandmother's bedroom. The big

family Bible, the thing I wanted most, was gone from the dresser. Except for a few wire hangers, the closet was empty. The navy blue, mirrored tray that sat on the dresser and held her *Evening in Paris* cologne was gone. I opened the dresser drawers one at a time, from top to bottom. They were all empty.

I almost asked Paul why he didn't stop them, call the police, do something, but I remembered the power Ellis had always had over him. He would have been as helpless as a child.

He gave me Ellis's address. It was just around the corner. I rang the bell, and Ellis's new wife answered with Betty Sue's little girl perched on her hip. Tommy and Terry clung to her skirt. The boys shied away when I went to hug them. They didn't remember me.

"There are only three things of my grandmother's I want," I told her.

"What are you talking about? I don't have anything of your grandmother's."

"Paul told me you came last night and took her clothes and all her other things. I don't care about most of that, but I want the Bible, the photo albums, and the nightgown that was wrapped in tissue in the bottom drawer."

"I don't have any of that."

"Where are they, then?"

"I don't know, ask Ellis."

"Where is he?"

"He's gone drinking. Maybe you can find him in one of the bars on Jefferson."

I knew it was useless to ask her to let me come in

and look for what I wanted. I didn't have time to go from bar to bar, looking for Ellis the way my Aunt Betty Sue had done so many times.

"I can't. I have to catch a plane. Tell him I'll pay him for them if he'll send them to me."

I took a piece of paper from my purse, scribbled my address and telephone number on it, and handed it to her. I returned to the car, knowing I would probably never hear from Ellis again, and I didn't.

Melanie sat on my lap and sang and watched the trees and buildings as we rode to the airport. I didn't want to upset her, so I held back my tears.

The money my grandmother deposited into her account became part of her estate. It was divided four ways. Paul received one thousand dollars, Ellis' children split another thousand, and I was given one thousand. I don't know what happened to the rest of it.

Paul called me about a month later. His money was gone, and he wanted to come live with my family in Kansas. I told him that wasn't possible. I heard a few years later that he'd been murdered on the streets of Detroit.

I could have asked my Aunt Fredia who my real father was, and she would have told me the truth. I didn't care. I already had the best daddy in the world.

Although my father kept a Kodak Brownie handy and loved snapping pictures, I don't have many of my childhood or my father's family. There are no mementoes, nothing that would be considered a keepsake.

I didn't realize until I started writing this story

476

that my grandmother, Nola Maude Clayborn Connor Foley, had already given me the most important thing of all. Those long ago nights we shared her bed, she gave me her incredible life.

THE END

Grandma Maude and Donna

Gene 1962

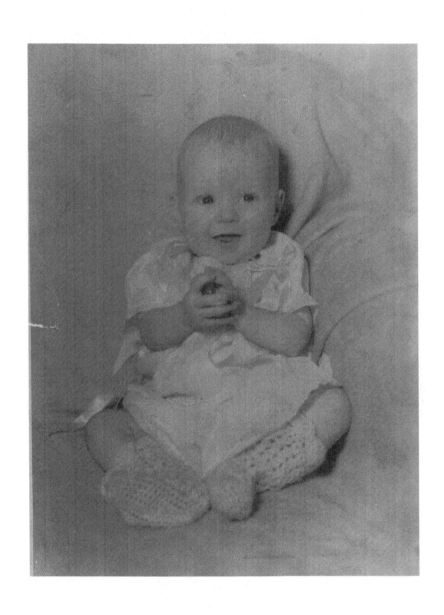

Baby Donna 1943

Evelyn 1940

The Detroit

Monday, August 06, 1962

DEAD ON ARRIVAL

A young Detroit motorist struck a woman pedestrian whose body was catapulted into the rear seat of his top-down convertible, then carried the woman around for 20 minutes before surrendering, police charged today. Held in Police Headquarters jail is Gary D. Paves, 21, of 2170 Lakewood. He is charged with leaving the scene of the fatal accident late last night.

Mrs. Betty Sue Marshall, 39, of 2651 Lycaste, the mother of four, was dead on arrival at Receiving Hospital at midnight.

Ordered to report to Accident Prevention Bureau officers today for further questioning was a passenger in Paves' car, Wilbur D. Moughler, 22, of 1101 Lakeview, who told police the accident was unavoidable, and that he persuaded Paves to return to the scene and surrender. The accident occurred at 11:30 P.M. at the northwest corner of Jefferson east and St. Jean, across the street from the Jefferson police precinct station.

GIVES CHASE A witness, Joseph Booker, 1545 Defer, told officers he heard the impact of the car striking

Ren
foll
imp

The
that
rela
the
beh
of a
exp
in li
its
beh
con
or v

It m
tote
thir
dec
mo

The Detroit News, August 6, 1962
A young Detroit motorist struck a woman pedestrian whose body was catapulted into the rear seat of his top-down convertible, then carried the woman around for 20 minutes before surrendering,

police charged today.

Held in Police Headquarters jail is Gary D. Paves, 21, of 2170 Lakewood. He is charged with leaving the scene of the fatal accident late last night.

DEAD ON ARRIVAL

Mrs. Betty Sue Marshall, 39, of 2651 Lycaste, the mother of four, was dead on arrival at Receiving Hospital at midnight.

Ordered to report to Accident Prevention Bureau officers today for further questioning was a passenger in Paves' car, Wilbur D. Moughler, 22, of 1101 Lakeview, who told police the accident was unavoidable, and that he persuaded Paves to return to the scene and surrender.

The accident occurred at 11:30 P.M. at the northwest corner of Jefferson east and St. Jean, across the street from the Jefferson police precinct station.

GIVES CHASE

A witness, Joseph Booker, 1545 Defer, told officers he heard the impact of the car striking Mrs. Marshall and saw the car speed away. "I jumped into my own car and gave chase," he said, "but I lost them in traffic."

Police said no officers saw the accident because the precinct station was changing shifts at the time.

They said Moughler told them that Paves drove for three or four miles, changing direction frequently, before he returned to the scene and surrendered at Jefferson Station. "As soon as we hit her I screamed at Paves to stop," Moughler told police, "but he kept on, and it took me some time to argue him into going back."

Jefferson Station officers rushed Mrs. Marshall to Receiving Hospital in an ambulance to no avail. An autopsy was scheduled today.

Police said other witnesses told them Mrs. Marshall was staggering in the middle of the street and waving her arms and was narrowly missed by several other automobiles before Paves' car struck her.

Police said that Paves, a gas station mechanic who is unmarried, was incoherent when first questioned. All he would say, according to detectives, was that he did not see Mrs. Marshall and did not know he hit her or that her body was in his car until he was a mile or two from the police station.

Later, police said, Paves insisted that he only drove around the corner, where his car stalled, and that he did not know Mrs. Marshall's body was in his car until it stalled. Then, officers said Paves told them, he returned to the scene.

Paves also told police that he and Moughler had dropped off two girlfriends just prior to the accident after drinking a beer apiece in a tavern.

Mrs. Marshall's husband, Ellis T., 37, said earlier yesterday she had visited her father, George Foley, 79, who is seriously ill in Receiving Hospital.

Afterward, her husband said, she visited a tavern near the accident scene to chat with a friend who works as a waitress there.

"It is a terrible tragedy," said Marshall, who works at the Fleetwood plant of General Motors' Fisher Body Division.

"I haven't told our children yet. I know I will have to tell them sometime today, but I just can't think how to do it."

The children are Thomas, 7; Terry, 5; Patricia, 4, and Linda, 1.

Other Books by Donna Mabry

The Alexandra Merritt Mysteries:
The Last Two Aces in Las Vegas
The Las Vegas Desert Flower
The Las Vegas Special
Rough Ride in Vegas
M.I.A. Las Vegas
Lost Luggage

Thrillers:
The Right Society
The Other Hand
Deadly Ambition

The Manhattan Stories:
Jessica
Pillsbury Crossing
The Cabin
Kimimela
The Russell House (soon to be published)

Comedy:
Conversations with Skip

www.donnafoleymabry.com

Made in the USA
Charleston, SC
25 August 2015